# History

## for the IB Diploma

# The Great Depression and the Americas 1929–39

## Nick Fellows and Mike Wells
### Series editor: Allan Todd

Cambridge University Press's mission is to advance learning, knowledge and research worldwide.

Our IB Diploma resources aim to:
- encourage learners to explore concepts, ideas and topics that have local and global significance
- help students develop a positive attitude to learning in preparation for higher education
- assist students in approaching complex questions, applying critical-thinking skills

CAMBRIDGE
UNIVERSITY PRESS

CAMBRIDGE UNIVERSITY PRESS
Cambridge, New York, Melbourne, Madrid, Cape Town,
Singapore, São Paulo, Delhi, Mexico City

Cambridge University Press
The Edinburgh Building, Cambridge CB2 8RU, UK

www.cambridge.org
Information on this title: www.cambridge.org/9781107656420

First published 2013

Printed and bound in the United Kingdom by the MPG Books Group

A catalogue record for this publication is available from the British Library

ISBN 978-1-107-65642-0 Paperback

Cambridge University Press has no responsibility for the persistence or
accuracy of URLs for external or third-party internet websites referred to in
this publication, and does not guarantee that any content on such websites is,
or will remain, accurate or appropriate.

This material has been developed independently by the publisher and the
content is in no way connected with nor endorsed by the International
Baccalaureate Organization.

# Contents

# 1 Introduction

This book is designed to prepare students for the Paper 3, Section 7 topic, *The Great Depression and the Americas 1929–39* (in HL Option 3, Aspects of the History of the Americas) in the IB History examination. It will introduce the economic developments of the period, and will look at the growth of the world economy from the late 19th century to the 1920s. It will also deal with some key economic terms and concepts. There will be an explanation of:

- the causes of the Great Depression in the USA, looking at both long- and short-term factors and reflecting on debates among economic historians about causes
- the causes of the Depression in Canada and Latin America
- the reaction of different states to the most severe global economic downturn ever seen (worse than the one that began in 2008)
- attempts to relieve economic distress and restore the economy
- attempts in Latin American countries to introduce economic diversification (to avoid dependence on a narrow range of exports)
- the social impact of the Depression, particularly in relation to key groups such as African-Americans and women.

There will also be analysis of the effect of the Great Depression on the arts and cultural life in the USA.

## Activity

What features make up an economic 'depression' (what we would now call a 'recession')? Carry out research using the internet to help you answer this question. Find *five* ways an economic depression changes life for people living in the affected country.

# Themes

To help you prepare for your IB History exams, this book will cover the main themes and aspects relating to *The Great Depression and the Americas 1929–39* as set out in the IB *History Guide*. In particular, it will consider the major areas described below:

- the political and economic causes of the Great Depression in the Americas and whether there were regional differences
- the policies followed by US president Herbert Hoover and how successful they were
- US President Franklin D. Roosevelt's 'New Deal' – what it was, its aims and whether it was a success; why and how the New Deal was criticised and how valid the criticisms were
- how Canadian governments responded to the Great Depression – the policies followed by prime ministers Mackenzie King and R. B. Bennett, and whether there was a Canadian 'New Deal'; how successful the policies were, and why and how they were criticised
- Latin American responses to the Great Depression:
  - the effect on Brazil; the response of Brazilian president Getúlio Vargas and the policy of import substitution industrialisation (ISI); how successful Brazilian responses to the Great Depression were
  - the nature of ISI and its successes in Latin America
  - the impact of the Great Depression on Mexico
- the impact of the Great Depression on different groups in society: women, African-Americans and other ethnic minorities
- the impact of the Great Depression on the arts – the increase in federal government support for the arts, especially photography, painting and theatre; the significance of art produced during the period; why movies and radio developed so much during the Great Depression; the extent to which the economic and political climate explains the development in the arts during the 1930s.

# Theory of knowledge

In addition to the broad key themes, the chapter contains Theory of Knowledge (ToK) links, to get you thinking about aspects that relate to history, which is a Group 3 subject in the IB Diploma. *The Great Depression and the Americas 1929–39* topic has several clear links to ideas about knowledge and history.

Economists continue to debate the causes of the Great Depression and there remains controversy about governments' reactions to it. At times, the deeply political nature of this topic has affected historians' accounts of the leaders involved, and the policies and actions taken. Clearly, questions relating to the selection of sources, and the way historians interpret these sources, have strong links to the IB Theory of Knowledge course.

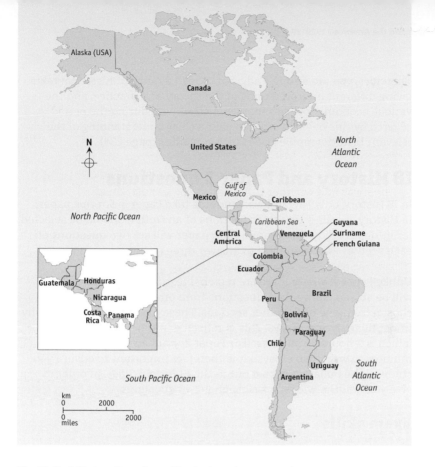

*The United States, Canada and Latin American countries*

For example, when trying to explain aspects of particular policies, political leaders' motives, and their success or failure, historians must decide which evidence to select and use to make their case and which evidence to leave out. But to what extent do the historians' personal political views influence them when selecting what they consider to be the most relevant sources, and when they make judgements about the value and limitations of specific sources or sets of sources? Is there such a thing as objective 'historical truth'? Or is there just a range of subjective historical opinions and interpretations about the past, which vary according to the political interests of individual historians?

There is a great deal of historical controversy about the role of leaders, such as US presidents Roosevelt and Hoover. Once thought of as being inhumane and incompetent, Hoover has received more sympathetic treatment by some recent writers. Roosevelt, formerly considered the greatest reforming president of the 20th century, has been the subject of some revisionism and criticism. Economic history is particularly prone to intense debate, as contemporary commentators tend to refer to the past in ways that justify their views on what current economic policy should be.

Therefore, you are strongly advised to read a range of historical texts giving different interpretations of the theory and practice, and the various economic policies that were attempted during the period covered by this book, in order to gain a clear understanding of the relevant historiographies (see Further reading, page 234).

# IB History and Paper 3 questions

In IB History, only Higher-level students take Paper 3. For this paper, IB History specifies that three sections of an Option should be selected for in-depth study. The examination paper will set two questions on each section – and you have to answer three questions in total.

Unlike Paper 2, where there are regional restrictions, in Paper 3 you will be able to answer *both* questions from one section, with a third chosen from one of the other sections. These questions are essentially in-depth analytical essays. This is reflected in the time available, which is 2 hours 30 minutes. (For Paper 2, you had only 1 hour 30 minutes to write two essays.) It is therefore important to ensure you study *all* the bullet points set out in the IB *History Guide*, in order to give yourself the widest possible choice of questions.

## Exam skills

Throughout the main chapters of this book, there are activities and questions to help you develop the understanding and the exam skills necessary for success in Paper 3. Your exam answers should demonstrate:

- factual knowledge and understanding
- awareness and understanding of historical interpretations
- structured, analytical and *balanced* argument.

Before attempting the specific exam practice questions that come at the end of each main chapter, you might find it useful to refer *first* to Chapter 8, the final exam practice chapter. This suggestion is based on the idea that, if you know where you are supposed to be going (in this instance, gaining a good grade), and how to get there, you stand a better chance of reaching your destination!

## Questions and markschemes

To ensure that you develop the necessary skills and understanding, each chapter contains comprehension questions and examination tips. For success in Paper 3, you need to produce essays that combine a number of features. In many ways, these require the same skills as the essays in Paper 2.

However, for the Higher-level Paper 3, examiners will be looking for greater evidence of *sustained* analysis and argument, linked closely to the demands of the question. They will also be seeking more depth and precision with regard to supporting knowledge. Finally, they will be expecting a clear and well-organised answer, so it is vital to do a rough plan *before* you start to answer a question. Your plan will show straight away whether or not you know enough about the topic to answer the question. It will also provide a good structure for your answer.

It is particularly important to start by focusing *closely* on the wording of the question, so that you can identify its demands. If you simply assume that a question is *generally about this period/leader*, you will probably produce an answer that is essentially a narrative or story, with only vague links to the question. Even if your knowledge is detailed and accurate, it will only be broadly relevant. If you do this, you will get half-marks at most.

Another important point is to present a *well-structured* and *analytical argument* that is clearly linked to *all the demands of the question*. Each aspect of your argument/analysis/explanation then needs to be supported by carefully selected, precise and relevant own knowledge.

In addition, showing awareness and understanding of relevant historical debates and interpretations will help you to access the highest bands and marks. This does not mean simply repeating, in your own words, what different historians have said. Instead, try to critically evaluate particular interpretations. For example, are there any weaknesses in the arguments put forward by some historians? What strengths does a particular interpretation have?

## Examiner's tips

To help you develop these skills, most chapters contain sample questions, with examiners' tips about what to do (and what *not* to do) in order to achieve high marks. These chapters will focus on a specific skill, as follows:

- Skill 1 (Chapter 2) – understanding the wording of a question
- Skill 2 (Chapter 2) – planning an essay
- Skill 3 (Chapter 3) – writing an introductory paragraph
- Skill 4 (Chapter 4) – avoiding irrelevance
- Skill 5 (Chapter 5) – avoiding a narrative-based answer
- Skill 6 (Chapter 6) – using your own knowledge analytically and combining it with awareness of historical debate
- Skill 7 (Chapter 7) – writing a conclusion to your essay.

Some of these tips will contain parts of a student's answer to a particular question, with examiner's comments, to give you an understanding of what examiners are looking for.

This guidance is developed further in Chapter 8, the exam practice chapter, where examiner's tips and comments will enable you to focus on the important aspects of questions and their answers. These examples will also help you avoid simple mistakes and oversights that, every year, result in some otherwise good students failing to gain the highest marks.

For additional help, a simplified Paper 3 markscheme is provided on page 219. This should make it easier to understand what examiners are looking for in your answers. The actual Paper 3 IB History markscheme can be found on the IB website.

This book will provide you with the historical knowledge and understanding to help you answer all the specific content bullet points set out in the IB *History Guide*. Also, by the time you have worked through the various exercises, you should have the skills necessary to construct relevant, clear, well-argued and well-supported essays.

# Background to the period

## The industrial revolution

Starting in Britain in the 18th century, an industrial revolution began to transform society. It was accompanied by significant population growth and rapid advances in technology.

- The growth of cities and new transport links, including canals, better roads and railways, transformed many areas.
- Improvements in agricultural productivity meant that a growing population could be fed. For instance, the population of Britain increased from around 5 million in the mid 18th century to approximately 30 million by the mid 19th century.
- Factories produced a range of goods that were previously unknown.
- Lifestyles were revolutionised, as were working conditions in industrial countries. Men, women and children now laboured in factories and workshops rather than on the land.

The world did not industrialise equally. Britain was the first industrial nation; Western Europe industrialised rapidly after 1815, as did parts of the northern USA. After 1860, Germany's industrial development began to rival that of Britain and the USA. Italy and Russia expanded their industries rapidly after 1880. Outside Europe, modern industry remained limited. To ensure markets and raw materials for their factories, Western powers colonised many areas. Other areas, such as China, were not taken over but were dominated by Western trade.

# The global economy of the late 19th century

Several developments transformed the global economy during the 19th century:

* steam ships with refrigeration facilities carried food products from all over the world to Europe and the USA
* advances in agricultural machinery and the expansion of railways meant that more food and agricultural products were available; cotton, rubber, wheat, meat, tropical foods, silk, tea, coffee and sugar – became increasingly popular in industrial countries
* cheap and plentiful industrial products were sold in return, making it unprofitable for many countries to develop their own industries.

Even if European powers with large overseas empires did not formally take over (colonise) countries outside Europe, they dominated them economically. Such countries depended increasingly on exporting key crops to the United States, Canada and the European powers. A classic example is the sugar that Cuba exported to the USA: Cuba's reliance on the US market for this cash crop gave the USA considerable control over the country, even after Cuba's independence in 1902 (the USA intervened militarily in Cuba four times from 1902–21).

The range of global goods available in Europe and the USA by the early 20th century would have amazed people a century earlier. Furthermore, the United States and Europe had a huge influence on other countries. For example, Japan's whole society was transformed after 1853 by the introduction of Western railways, clothes, buildings, political ideas, weapons and culture. This world trade depended on a stable means of payment.

## The Gold Standard

The huge expansion of international trade was possible because of a highly developed financial system based on the Gold Standard.

Starting with Britain in 1844, most developed countries based the issue of paper money firmly on gold reserves in their national banks. Thus, on British banknotes, the Bank of England promised 'to pay the bearer the sum of five pounds'. This meant the holder of the banknote could exchange the piece of paper, worthless in itself, for five gold coins. The Bank of England's gold reserves were almost equivalent to the paper money in circulation, although there was an element of 'faith': the bank was allowed to print more money than it had in gold on the assumption that not everyone would demand to have their banknotes exchanged at the same time. The excess sum of printed money over and above the gold reserve was regulated by the terms of the Bank's Charter.

The Gold Standard meant that international trade could be conducted in pounds sterling with complete safety. It also prevented fluctuations in value between major currencies and prevented inflation. The money supply would only go up when gold reserves went up as economic activity increased. Because prices generally rise when the amount of money in circulation goes up, the Gold Standard kept prices stable.

An elaborate network of international trade and payments emerged by the late 19th century:

- large numbers of trading ships crossed the world
- banks handled huge numbers of transactions
- insurance companies protected ships and cargoes
- more and more companies formed to produce goods for the international market
- additional capital (money invested in business) supported this rapid growth in economic activity
- a greater number of shares in companies were created, bought and sold in stock exchanges.

Investment in countries, enterprises and governments became common in developed countries. The major investment centre before 1914 was the City of London – the square mile of the old city that housed the main banks and stock dealers, borrowers, lenders, insurance companies and shipping firms. There were also major stock markets in Paris, Berlin and New York.

## Capitalism

The development of capitalism, as **Karl Marx** called it in his book *Das Kapital* (1867), was one of the most significant changes brought about by economic growth in the 19th century. It provided money for new inventions, including developments in global transport. It also fuelled the growth in trade, and provided funds for governments who needed to borrow.

**Karl Marx (1818–83)** Marx was an economist, philosopher and historian. Born in the Rhineland, he spent much of his life in exile from his native Germany. He argued that attempts at revolution were historically inevitable because of the inherent contradictions of the capitalist system. *Das Kapital* (1867) is Marx's most famous work. His ideas inspired Lenin to lead the Bolsheviks in the Russian Revolution of 1917.

However, capitalism could also bring instability when investments got out of control. Sometimes as share prices went up, people invested money in a company without enough consideration of its real value; if confidence in the company was subsequently lost, the share price fell rapidly, resulting in a 'crash'. This was a fall in the value of the company's shares, which meant they were now worth a fraction of what investors previously paid for them. Investors could lose huge sums of money during such a crash.

Stock market crashes were not unusual in the 19th century. One of the most severe was in 1873. By this time, the crash did not merely affect one country but the whole world. If economic activity slowed down in the advanced countries, then other countries around the world who relied on selling them agricultural products (the so-called 'primary producers') were also hit hard. This in turn prevented them from buying Western products, which made the economic downturn worse.

Some saw the new global economy as disastrous – Marx predicted that the capitalist system would ultimately self-destruct, and the possibility of revolution would follow.

Supporters of the capitalist system believed it was self-regulating. They argued that once prices had fallen, trade and investment would pick up again and there would be recovery; left alone, capitalism would overcome its crises. Their view was that if some firms went bankrupt, then others would simply use their resources – their skilled workforce, their technology, their experience.

Even before 1914 it was clear that periodic economic slumps had severe effects worldwide. If too many goods were produced and prices fell, then millions of people suffered. With more and more people working in factories, living in cities and dependent on trade, there was a risk that unemployment (a term only used widely from the 1880s) would lead to widespread poverty and political unrest.

## The First World War 1914–18

The 'Great War' of 1914–18 had a considerable effect on the world economy. There were winners and losers. The war itself led to increased opportunities for some in the short term, but the aftermath of war had some damaging long-term results. Countries needed to pay for armaments, so they printed more money and left the Gold Standard (see pages 11–12 and 15–16); as a result, prices rose. Huge loans were made by the United States (which did not enter the war until April 1917) to France and Britain, and these had the effect of disrupting the whole financial system.

The First World War also changed the nature of international trade. It created a huge market for world produce, and encouraged primary producers in many countries to grow and sell more to meet the demands of a world at war.

By 1918, the effect of the war on world trade had been devastating:

- Germany was ruined by the war and did not resume trade on any significant scale until the mid 1920s
- Russia dropped out of global commerce following the Bolshevik Revolution of 1917 and the subsequent Russian Civil War, which lasted until 1921
- the Austrian and Turkish empires collapsed, disrupting the whole trade of Eastern Europe
- Great Britain lost its economic primacy; this was the result of war debts, loss of markets and the rise of competitors, and a decline in sales of the products of its traditional industries.

However, not all nations suffered. Japan used the disruption of trade in Asia to increase its own industries and supply of goods and raw materials. The Americas benefited from supplying vast amounts of goods and raw materials to Europe. The USA emerged from the First World War as the greatest economic power in the world and enjoyed a post-war 'boom'. This prosperity was not shared by the whole of the United States, however: while cities, industries, transport and communications experienced growth, agriculture did not.

## Post-war economic problems

In the years following the First World War, agricultural prices fell globally. Many countries sought to protect their farmers and industries through customs duties (additional costs on imports that made imported goods more expensive to sell than goods produced at home). The introduction of customs duties marked the end of free trade between nations based on the Gold Standard.

The world's major financial centre was now Wall Street in New York, home to the New York Stock Exchange. However, the US stock market proved very unstable in the late 1920s. Although share prices seemed to be going up, many businesses and shareholders were irresponsible in their financial practices.

In October 1929, there was the most devastating stock market crash since the mid 19th century. The Wall Street Crash was followed by the Great Depression – the longest and most severe worldwide economic depression of the 20th century, affecting all industrialised nations until the late 1930s or early 1940s.

After the Wall Street Crash, unemployment rose and business and trade declined. To counter these effects, many countries in the Americas introduced greater state control and rejected traditional political groups. In the case of the USA, this was done through normal constitutional means, by electing the reforming Democratic leader Roosevelt. In parts of South America, the Depression produced revolutionary change or political leaders installed by military coups. There were some remarkable economic innovations in the 1930s to meet the challenges of the Great Depression, although few actually delivered the radical and complete reform of economic life that they promised.

> **Discussion point**
>
> Before you begin to work your way through this book, try to find out a bit more about the United States in the 1920s. Why was it so different from the pre-war period? What signs of prosperity were there in the so-called 'Jazz Age'? What pictures and images can you find of a 'wild' or 'modern' USA?
>
> After your research, discuss whether you think the United States was really prosperous or fundamentally weak beneath its glamour and apparent prosperity.

# Terminology and definitions

The history of the Great Depression can be complicated. In part, this complexity reflects the range of economic terms involved in studying and understanding the various arguments and developments of the period. You will need to be familiar with a few basic terms.

## Primary producers

Primary produce is material taken from the land or sea. Primary producers are the people who grow, harvest or extract food and raw materials, including agricultural products, fish, trees and minerals such as coal. Primary production is distinct from what economists refer to as secondary production – manufacturing and processing.

## Gold Standard

A country is said to be on the Gold Standard when its central bank is committed to giving gold in exchange for any of its currency. The Gold Standard was thought to promote stability. It also kept exchange rates (the rates at which currencies of different countries are bought and sold) constant. This in turn encouraged trade.

- If a country exports more than it imports, gold flows into the central bank's reserves, thus allowing the supply of currency to be expanded. This raises prices and therefore reduces the demand for exports.
- If a country imports more than it exports, the amount of gold in the central bank's reserves falls, so less currency is issued. This reduces prices and makes exports cheaper, thereby increasing demand for exports.

The Gold Standard was suspended during the First World War, as Britain was its major regulator and needed to print money to fight the war. The Gold Standard was restored in 1926 and ended in 1931.

## Free trade and tariffs

Britain's economy was the strongest in the world in the 19th century. Britain pursued a policy of free trade and did not charge any tariffs – taxes on goods imported from other countries. Most other powers imposed such taxes to protect their industries against foreign competition. After the First World War, tariffs or import duties rose considerably, especially as a result of US financial policy. After 1932, most countries had import duties. These taxes on trade have been blamed for the worldwide economic depression of the 1930s.

## Stocks and shares

In order to raise money, companies sell part-ownership to the public. These 'shares' in the company can then be bought and sold through the stock markets of different countries. For example, the US stock market is called Wall Street; the French stock market is La Bourse; in Britain, there is the London Stock Exchange.

The prices of shares can rise and fall according to the confidence that investors have in individual companies and the economic situation generally. If there is a great demand for shares, share prices rise; if there is little demand, share prices fall.

After the First World War, there was a significant increase in share ownership, particularly in the USA. This in part reflected the huge confidence people had in the economy. However, a crisis of confidence in the economy as a whole and in investments caused a rapid decline in the prices of shares in October 1929, in what has become known as the 'Wall Street Crash' or 'Great Crash'.

## Inflation and deflation

Inflation is when prices rise. There was considerable inflation during and after the First World War as demand grew for primary products.

Deflation is when prices fall. Primary producers faced falling prices in the 1920s and 1930s, and after 1929 there was a general trend for all prices to fall.

## Demand

This is the term given to the willingness or ability of buyers to pay for goods and services offered by suppliers. After 1929, the Great Depression restricted the demand for goods and services worldwide because buyers lacked the money to pay for them. Governments in the Americas reacted in various ways. Some measures aimed to avoid overproduction, either by encouraging production of fewer goods or a greater range of goods. Other policies encouraged demand by creating more jobs and greater income through public works or state subsidies.

The management of demand was one of the major developments brought about by the Great Depression.

# Summary

By the time you have worked through this book, you should be able to:

* understand how the Great Depression resulted from long-term developments in the world economy
* describe the greater role of the United States in world and regional economies after 1918
* distinguish the weaknesses of the US economy in the 1920s and explain how the instability of the US stock market led to a major financial crash in 1929
* understand why the Wall Street Crash led to an economic depression in the USA that also affected the economies of Canada and Latin American countries
* explain US policies to help the economy recover and the impact of these on economic, social, political and cultural life in the United States
* outline how governments in Canada responded to the economic crisis and describe the impact of their policies
* understand Latin American strategies for economic diversification in response to reduced demand for basic products
* describe some of the political and social effects of the Great Depression on Latin American countries by focusing on Brazil and Mexico
* make judgements about the extent and effects of the Great Depression in the period 1929–39 in the Americas, and the efforts that were made to deal with its consequences.

# 2 Political and economic causes of the Great Depression in the USA

## Key questions

- What were the causes of the Great Depression?
- What was the Wall Street Crash and why was it so important?
- Who was most to blame for the Great Depression?

This chapter deals with the long- and short-term causes of the Great Depression in the United States. It makes a distinction between the collapse of the US stock market in October 1929 and the Great Depression, which had its roots in longer-term economic factors. The economic importance of the USA grew after the First World War. Debate about whether the US government and the regulatory bodies were to blame centres on different views of the role of the state in economic matters.

# Overview

- The development of the US economy in the 19th century and the growth of world markets led to greater prosperity for many Americans in the initial years of the 20th century.
- By the 1920s, some areas of the US economy and country grew rapidly, while others did not. The agricultural sector experienced low prices and the industrial sector was in danger of producing too much. There was also considerable inequality in incomes.
- Although the Republican governments of the 1920s believed in economic freedom ('laissez-faire'), the US Congress passed a law increasing tariffs (customs duties) on imported goods. There has been considerable criticism of US government policies for helping to bring about financial crisis and then failing to deal with it.
- There was considerable growth in investments in the 1920s. Many made their fortune; yet the financial regulation was insufficient to prevent the problems that led to the 1929 stock market crash.
- The collapse of the US stock market in 1929 triggered a worldwide economic depression that had longer-term causes. The regional dominance of the USA meant it hit the Americas particularly hard.

*The United States of America, which is made up of 50 individual states*

# What were the causes of the Great Depression?

## The boom years of the 1920s

After 1921, the USA experienced high levels of economic growth characterised by:

- the rapid expansion of the automobile industry and industries that supplied parts for cars
- a growth in housing, which included the development of suburbs
- a range of new consumer goods and electrical items
- an increase in services and the financial sector.

The signs of prosperity were obvious. Statistics show one of the most impressive increases in production. Gross national product (GNP) growth during the 1920s was relatively rapid, at 4.2 per cent a year from 1920 to 1929 (*Historical Statistics of the United States*, or *HSUS*, 1976). GNP per capita grew 2.7 per cent per year between 1920 and 1929. The problem was that because of the weakening of trade union influence and companies' focus on making a profit, the real wages of most workers did not increase in line with the rise in economic activity. There was more money to be made from land speculation than farming or mining, and there was increased speculation on the stock market.

### SOURCE A

Real average weekly or daily earnings for selected occupations, 1920 to 1930

| Year | (1) Weekly: skilled and semi-skilled male production workers (workers in 25 manufacturing industries) | (2) Weekly: unskilled male production workers (workers in 25 manufacturing industries) | (3) Weekly: female production workers (workers in 25 manufacturing industries) | (4) Weekly: bituminous coal-lignite mining | (5) Daily: farm workers |
|------|------|------|------|------|------|
| 1920 | 29.16 | 22.28 | 15.14 | — | 2.82 |
| 1921 | 26.19 | 19.41 | 14.96 | — | 1.96 |
| 1922 | 28.73 | 20.74 | 16.19 | — | 2.04 |
| 1923 | 30.93 | 22.37 | 17.31 | 25.51 | 2.36 |
| 1924 | 30.61 | 22.45 | 16.78 | 23.47 | 2.40 |
| 1925 | 30.57 | 22.41 | 16.78 | 25.64 | 2.30 |
| 1926 | 30.60 | 22.47 | 16.72 | 27.51 | 2.32 |
| 1927 | 31.09 | 23.22 | 17.14 | 23.85 | 2.32 |
| 1928 | 31.94 | 23.89 | 17.15 | 24.46 | 2.30 |
| 1929 | 32.60 | 24.40 | 17.61 | 25.11 | 2.30 |
| 1930 | 29.93 | 22.47 | 16.40 | 22.61 | 2.21 |

U.S. Department of Commerce, Bureau of the Census. 1976. Historical Statistics of the United States: Colonial Times to 1970. Washington D.C., USA. USGPO.

## How important was the stock market crash of 1929?

After a period of great speculation (buying, holding or selling stocks) on the US stock market, in which millions of dollars were invested in shares, there was a sudden loss of confidence. In October 1929, investors started selling, not buying, and the value of shares fell dramatically. Millions of dollars were lost in this 'Great Crash'. After the crash – and some say because of it – there was a long period of economic depression in the USA. Millions were unemployed, businesses collapsed and many banks were unable to give depositors their money. The Depression also affected Canada and Latin American countries, making the 1930s a time of considerable hardship and change. The Great Depression was experienced as the world's worst economic disaster and has kept that reputation.

*Still from John Ford's 1940 film of* The Grapes of Wrath, *based on John Steinbeck's novel. The film follows a family of 'Oakies' – Oklahoma farmers hit by the dry weather that created a dust bowl and forced to leave their homes. The actor Henry Fonda (below right) became a symbol of decent Americans hit by the Great Depression.*

### Activity

Look again at key economic terms in Chapter 1, pages 15–17. Then write out a definition of the following terms *in your own words*:

- inflation
- Gold Standard
- exchange rate
- primary producer.

# Explanations of the Great Depression

In 1929, the US capitalist system was close to collapse. To many, this economic system was essential to progress and civilisation. The collapse of the US economy was experienced as such a major upheaval that commentators continue to analyse and discuss the causes of the Depression today.

By and large, the causes of the Depression fall into several broad categories, as described below.

## The role of the global economy

The expansion of the global economy in the later 19th century, with developments in transport, technology and credit (see pages 11–12), meant that the world was more united by economic activity. This left individual nations more vulnerable to international events beyond their control. For example, the First World War had a devastating long-term impact on international trade and payments – as president Herbert Hoover was quick to point out when defending the USA's role in the financial crisis.

## The role of US Republican governments

In the United States in the 1920s, there was minimal government interference in economic activity, since it was believed this would enable individuals to prosper. This laissez-faire approach (literally 'leave alone') was based on the belief in the self-regulating nature of markets (see page 13) and a deep opposition to government interference in key sectors (especially finance). In addition, there was also a commitment to tariff policies that limited trade.

The Republican presidents of the 1920s (Warren G. Harding, Calvin Coolidge and Herbert Hoover), as well as their ministers and financial experts, were widely blamed for the Great Depression at the time. They continue to receive a great deal of criticism today.

## The role of US investors

The actions of US investors are also seen as a major factor in bringing about the Great Depression. The 'boom years' of the 1920s encouraged investors to be greedy and seek 'quick' profits through irresponsible investment. Too often, investment was not in reputable companies but was carried out as a sort of 'stock market game'.

It can be argued that these unsafe investment practices caused the stock market crash and contributed to the Depression. At the time, cautious rural Americans often blamed reckless urban dwellers for the economic disaster, even if it could be argued that US governments were ultimately responsible for regulating the financial system.

## The nature of the capitalist system

To some extent, the nature of the capitalist system – with its cycle of growth ('boom') followed by loss and stagnation ('bust') – was to blame. The countries that shared in this economic system were dependent on each other for their successes. This meant that the primary producers (the countries selling agricultural products to the USA), particularly Latin American countries, were drawn into the economic disaster when the Depression began in the USA. In turn, as the Latin American demand for US goods dried up, the economic decline became worse.

The alternatives to the capitalist system were socialist or communist systems, which are both based on a critique of capitalism by Karl Marx (see pages 12–13). Marx envisaged workers sharing in the profits of industry, which would be owned and run by the community, according to their needs. Socialists believed in public ownership, not the dictatorship established in the USSR by Stalin, which was unaffected by the Great Depression. After the Bolshevik revolution in Russia in 1917, communists established control over the economy in the name of the working classes and ended the parliamentary democracy briefly established by the February/March Revolution. Both socialist and communist systems won more support worldwide after 1929.

# The long-term causes of the Depression

## Overproduction

A common view was that modern agricultural methods since the 19th century had led to agricultural overproduction in the USA:

### SOURCE B

We still pray to be given each day our daily bread. Yet there is too much bread, too much wheat and corn, meat and oil and almost every other commodity required by man for his subsistence and material happiness. We are not able to purchase the abundance that modern methods of agriculture, mining and manufacturing make available in such bountiful quantities.

*From an article in the US magazine* Current History, 1932.

The 'modern methods' referred to in the article go back well into the previous century. The crisis of overproduction is viewed, in the long term, as having been caused by the opening of the prairies in the USA and the greater exploitation of natural resources worldwide. Other commentators made a similar point about overproduction of all sorts of goods, both industrial and agricultural.

*Farmers introduce the latest farming machinery to work their land in Texas;*
*advances in agricultural methods in the 1920s resulted in overproduction*
*on an enormous scale*

## Globalisation

The growth of globalisation was one of the major developments of
the late 19th century. World trade grew substantially – in 1870, it
accounted for 9.2 per cent of total trade; by 1914, the figure was
13.5 per cent, an increase of almost 50 per cent.

The growth in the USA's involvement in world trade from the late
19th century was significant. Central to this increase were changes
in transport infrastructure. Internal railways allowed goods to be
transported to ports faster and cheaper. There were also faster
and more regular steamships, new refrigeration methods and
improved ports. Together, these developments made domestic and
international transportation quicker and cheaper. Shipping costs as
a percentage of the total cost of exports fell – it was 50 per cent less
expensive to ship wheat from New York to Liverpool in 1914 than
in 1870 (4.7 per cent of transport costs as a factor in the total price,
down from 11.6 per cent). This reduced the gaps between prices in
different regions, and standard world prices began to emerge.

The increase in trade also reflected stable exchange rates, as most
countries operated the Gold Standard (see pages 15–16) and there were
not rapid fluctuations in the relative value of currencies. This allowed
traders to predict prices, and investors to commit money overseas
with a sense of security.

From the mid 19th century, the USA experienced considerable economic growth, and by the 1920s was a major world economy. The USA developed new railways and new ships; it expanded its agricultural production by the use of technology such as the combine harvester and, by the early 20th century, the tractor. In common with other agricultural sectors in the world, US farmers used new fertilisers from a growing chemical industry. The opening of the American prairies for agricultural land was a major world development, as it meant more food could be carried quicker and cheaper to urban centres in the USA and Europe. The huge rise in US industrial production and city populations after 1870, boosted by population growth and increased demand, changed the nature of the United States.

## SOURCE C

Percentage growth in US industrial production, 1850–1914 (1850 = 100)

| 1850 | 100 |
|------|--------|
| 1867 | 210.0 |
| 1885 | 490.7 |
| 1901 | 1277.1 |
| 1914 | 1774.1 |

US Bureau of Statistics.

The official statistics from the US Bureau of Statistics (Source C) show the percentage growth of US industrial production. The notional ('baseline') figure for 1850 is 100, so production by the 1860s had more than doubled, and by 1914 production was 17 times greater than in 1850. Note that production doubled between the 1860s and 1880s, and more than trebled again by 1914.

It can be argued that the seeds of the Great Depression were sown in this national and international economic transformation between 1870 and the First World War.

## The First World War and its impact on the Depression

The First World War (1914–18) marked the end of the exchange rate stability associated with the Gold Standard. This disrupted international trade, as did Russia's withdrawal from the international economic system after the Russian Revolution of 1917 and the break-up of the Austrian and Ottoman Empires. After 1914, Germany was no longer a great economic or colonial power; Britain was heavily in debt to the USA; France had endured heavy losses and damage to some important industrial areas.

The First World War also affected pre-war trends in industry.

- Heavy industry, textiles, shipbuilding and engineering – the main industries of the industrial revolution – were in decline in the late 19th century. However, the First World War increased military demand for these products and so trade in them slowed down.
- The prices of primary products fell before the war, but after 1914 they were again in demand as imports fell and food and raw materials were used to support the war effort. To profit most from the high prices, farmers borrowed money to cultivate 'marginal' lands (i.e. lands previously considered unsuitable for farming).

When the war ended in 1918, there was a drop in demand for raw materials, food and heavy industrial products. This coincided with less world trade, more instability in exchange rates (which made trade more difficult), a reduction in money for investment, and a fall in demand for traditional products.

Some sectors of the world's economy that developed before 1914, such as financial services and luxury goods, were less affected by the war because they tended not to overproduce, so there was always a stable market for these products. However, a decline in the traditional areas of industry and agriculture led to a fall in prices for farmers worldwide. This in turn meant fewer people buying the industrial goods. The more advanced industrial countries depended on farmers buying their goods from the income they gained through the sale of primary produce.

After 1918, the tendency among governments was to limit and protect trade, and tariff barriers were more common. The US Congress was keen to protect US producers, and in September 1922 President Warren Harding signed the Fordney–McCumber Tariff Bill (named after Joseph Fordney, chair of the House Ways and Means Committee, and Porter McCumber, chair of the Senate Finance Committee). The Fordney–McCumber Tariff raised the duty on imported goods to an average of 38.5 per cent on their value. It led to other countries retaliating and therefore restricting US trade.

After the First World War, the world economy was less open to trade. Yet population growth meant that more people in all countries depended on world economic growth, and suffered when it fell away. The post-war peace treaties further restricted European economic development by demanding reparations (compensation) from conquered nations.

## Discussion point

What was the most important long-term cause of the Depression? Discuss this question as a class. (There is no 'right answer'.)

## Activity

Working in a group of three, each group member should choose a development in the world economy between 1850 and 1920 – globalisation, overproduction or the impact of the First World War. Each person explains how their chosen development contributed to the Depression in a group presentation to the class. Finally, discuss as a class which development was the most important.

## The impact of the First World War on the USA

Although the United States faced a different, much less favourable global economic environment after 1918, it was in a strong position.

- During the First World War, the USA changed from a net borrower to a net lender.
- The major financial centre of the world was no longer the City of London but Wall Street in New York.
- What economists called the 'tertiary sector' – the provision of services and 'invisible' exports, such as insurance, financial services and entertainment (as opposed to 'visible' exports, i.e. actual manufactured goods, such as cars) – now centred on the United States.
- The US economy was able to diversify (branch out) due to high levels of technological progress. The provision of new domestic products and motor vehicles was a major growth sector, while traditional industrial products such as textiles or heavy engineering declined. This trend was fuelled by modern financial practices such as credit agreements (to spread the cost of goods over regular payments) and more accessible loans.

The 'Tin Lizzie' Ford motor car, produced between 1908 and 1927; in the 1920s, car ownership in the USA was 60 per cent (a figure not matched again until the early 1950s)

Construction was another growth area. This modernisation depended on a large domestic market that experienced economic prosperity in some sectors in the 1920s. The growth in construction at home compensated for the difficulties that traditional US products faced in a shrinking and restricted international market.

### Activity

In groups, draw up *two* posters summarising the main changes that occurred in the US economy between 1870 and the mid 1920s.

* One poster should celebrate the progress the USA has made.
* The other poster should be a warning to the people of the USA of the dangers of these economic changes.

Put the posters up on the wall and discuss which would have been more convincing to Americans in the mid 1920s.

## Structural weaknesses in the US economy

While several sectors of the US economy experienced growth in the 1920s, there were long-term structural weaknesses.

After the First World War (1914–18), many sectors of the US economy enjoyed years of prosperity. However, agriculture did not – although it remained a very significant part of American life. After 1896, farmers in the United States enjoyed ample profits due to increased demand from a growing population. The First World War also produced a surge in profits, with farmers borrowing to increase production and take advantage of high prices brought about by wartime demand. Farmers' incomes increased quite dramatically during the war, and farmers grew visibly wealthier, with high expectations of future growth.

From 1920, however, there was a period of falling prices and decreasing demand. The basic problem was overproduction: mechanisation had increased productivity and reduced the need for animal feed. This made land available for more cereal growing, but demand for cereal-based products was in a long-term decline. Changes in society meant a more varied diet of fruit, vegetables and meat, and less consumption of bread, maize and corn. As a result, European imports fell. Combined with the expansion of farming, this meant that production outstripped demand after the First World War, not just in the USA but globally.

Farmers' demands for protection from falling prices made matters worse. The 1922 Fordney–McCumber Tariff placed higher duties on imported agricultural goods, which protected domestic producers (whose goods would be cheaper), and was partly in response to demands from farming associations. Farmers also wanted – and nearly obtained – a bill that would have subsidised (artificially raised) prices to maintain the standard of living at 1914 levels.

Legislation reduced interest payments on loans and gave farmers access to cheaper credit. However, these measures only encouraged production to continue at unnecessarily high levels. (Agricultural supporters in Congress voted for the bill for subsidies between 1924 and 1926, and it was expected to pass; however, President **Calvin Coolidge**, supported by Secretary for Commerce **Herbert Hoover**, rejected the bill.)

**Calvin Coolidge (1872–1933)** Coolidge was the son of a storekeeper from Vermont. He was Republican vice-president between 1920 and 1923, then president from 1923 to 1929. He opposed the USA's involvement in international affairs and discouraged government intervention in the US economy unless absolutely necessary.

**Herbert Hoover (1874–1964)** Hoover was from a Quaker family and became a mining engineer. He was food commissioner in 1917 and helped organise relief for starving refugees in Europe in 1920. He was a major influence on US economic policy in the 1920s, before becoming president in 1928. He believed in 'rugged individualism' (that individuals should rely on themselves rather than the government for support), yet government aid to the poor and unemployed actually increased after 1929. Hoover was heavily criticised for not doing enough to alleviate the effects of the Depression, although some historians praise his policies.

The underlying problem – of too much production of the wrong crops for a declining and changing market – was not addressed. Higher machinery costs also reduced profits, real income and spending power. A large section of the US economy provided a shrinking market for manufactured goods and limited capital for investment. The decline in agriculture came before the slowdown in industry, and then made it worse.

The other problem was the diversification (branching out) of US industry in response to market needs. Older industries such as coal, railway building, heavy engineering and textiles were in decline, and these were large-scale employers. Newer consumer industries made considerable profits – especially construction industries and those producing motor vehicles, electric power, consumer durables and artificial fibres. Advertising helped to generate demand for these modern products, and during the 1920s advertising developed on a tremendous scale. Great claims were made for advertising as an economic and social force for good.

However, because of the restrictive trade policies after 1922 and the reduction in overseas markets due to European economic recovery, these industries depended heavily on the home market. This dependence was dangerous for a number of reasons.

- First, there was less disposable income in the agricultural sector, due to falling prices and lower demand. This meant that there were no longer the funds to pay for, or replace, cars, clothes and consumer goods.
- Second, despite the various payment deals available, such as payments spread over an extended period and readily available credit, the demand for new products was not continuous. Consumer goods tended to be hardwearing: once a family bought a product, it did not easily wear out and people used it for a long time. 'Built-in obsolescence' (deliberately making products that wear out so that consumers buy more), was not a feature of 1920s American life but was introduced from 1945.
- Third, despite cheaper food prices, real wages did not increase much in the 1920s. Trade unions lacked influence over powerful industries to ensure wage rises. While workers were generally better off than farmers, their wages lagged behind productivity. Therefore, although there were faster assembly lines and new machinery, workers did not have additional money to spend on the new goods.

Sales, therefore, depended more and more on the wealthier sections of urban society, rather than being evenly spread though the agricultural and blue-collar (manufacturing) sectors.

By 1928–29, even growth industries such as the car and construction industries were starting to enter a downturn. Investors now experienced a crisis in confidence in the underlying strength of the US economy. The shortfalls in demand could not be made up for by foreign sales for various reasons, including the restrictive tariff policies. Neither farmers nor workers could afford to buy enough to sustain the level of economic activity that developed during the boom years. Also, the majority of major consumers among the wealthier sections of US society were investors in the stock market, which had undergone a major expansion since 1926. With the loss of confidence in the value of US industries, consumption fell among wealthier Americans. Because the wealthier sections of urban society were such important buyers of goods, this left the US economy in crisis in terms of demand (see page 17).

The heavy concentration of economic power by large-scale industries was a feature of the USA's boom years, yet it had damaging consequences. The persistent decline of rural America was another threat to prosperity during the 1920s. Both of these dangers were masked by the spectacular growth of big cities and the appearance of prosperity and modernisation.

**Discussion point**

'The United States' prosperity of the 1920s was built on insecure foundations.'

In pairs, look through the previous and following sections and find *eight* points that might support this view. Discuss which point is the most important, then try and put the eight points you have selected in some order of importance. If you disagree on the order, try to work out why.

# What was the Wall Street Crash and why was it so important?

## The role of government bonds

Before 1914, private shareholding (individuals holding shares in a company) was relatively limited. Between 1917 and 1919, the US government sold $27 billion worth of bonds, called Liberty Bonds and Victory Bonds, to 22 million Americans.

Bonds were a way for governments to raise funds. By purchasing a bond for $100, the buyer was effectively lending this money to the government. The government agreed to repay the buyer with interest over the term of the bond, for example $1 interest per year for 30 years, and the original capital (of $100) at the end of the loan. The government guaranteed this income. The investor could also sell the bond, in which case the new owner would receive the annual interest.

Americans were in the habit of bond buying, so it was a small jump to buying shares. Shares worked on the same principle, but the interest paid (the so-called 'dividend') was not guaranteed, as it was in the case of government bonds. If the company did badly there would be less income, and if the company collapsed then all the investment would be lost. Because this made the investment riskier, the dividend paid was higher on a share than the interest paid on a government bond.

## Stock market practices

Both government bonds and shares in individual companies could be bought and sold by traders in the stock market.

The number of shares listed on the Stock Exchange rose from 500,000 in 1925 to 101,127,000 by 1929, by which time there were two million investors in US corporations. Cuts in income tax (tax on earnings) and capital gains taxes (the tax paid on the profit made when shares or bonds were sold) made more money available for investment.

A typical investment might be, for example, that an investor buys $100 of shares in an engineering business. The money is used for buying new premises. The business does well and the investor gets an annual return (the dividend). Eventually, the shareholder decides to sell. If the company has done well and has good prospects, then the share value will have risen, as other people want to share in the profits.

It was easy to establish companies and 'float' them on the stock exchange – that is, to offer the general public ownership in the company for a return of any profits. There were also easy loans made available by share dealers (stockbrokers) to those who wanted to invest. These practices created a big problem: investors by the late 1920s were not buying shares in the hopes of future dividends, but simply to make a quick profit.

For example, an investor buys $100 shares in an engineering business – he has put $10 of his own money towards the cost of the shares; the broker lends the other $90. Because the price of shares is rising every day, in a week or two the shares are worth $200. The investor sells, pays the broker back with interest and keeps the remainder as profit to reinvest. This practice is called buying 'on the margin'. The company may not even be properly trading – it may exist simply to acquire share capital.

With buying 'on the margin', investors, brokers and businesses all gain until confidence breaks down. For example, if $100 profit is reinvested in a company but there are fears that the shares are worthless, no one wants to buy them. Everybody suddenly wants to sell their shares in the company, and so the price of the shares falls dramatically. Investors have to pay back the brokers, yet they cannot do this out of profits (they have actually made losses), so they have to withdraw funds from their bank accounts.

By 1929, there were not enough people left to buy the shares that had risen to inflated levels. There were about 1.5 million substantial investors, and by October 1929 they had stopped buying. The share value of many companies fell sharply. Thousands of investors lost money and needed to withdraw money from their bank accounts. However, because the banks invested depositors' money on the stock market, they did not have sufficient funds to pay all the depositors their money. This caused the depositors to panic and withdraw all of their funds, causing the banks to fail. The failure of the banks meant that firms were unable to pay wages or dividends, and eventually went out of business.

The start of this downturn was 24 October 1929, known as 'Black Thursday'.

*The continental edition of the London* Daily Mail *reports 'Black Thursday',*
*Friday 25 October 1929*

# 'Black Thursday'

The stock market collapse was a major crisis. On 23 October, 6 million
shares were sold. On 24 October – 'Black Thursday' – 12.9 million
shares were sold, with a total loss in share price value of $14 billion,
equivalent to an 11 per cent market loss. From Black Thursday to 29
October, US stocks lost over $26 billion of value as over 30 million
shares were traded. Thereafter, prices continued to fall, wiping out an
estimated $30 billion in stock values by mid November 1929.

Black Thursday marked the start of a steep drop in share prices.
Millions of small investors and people who had invested in unit trusts
and pension funds lost money. The effects were far-reaching:

- the Crash revealed the inherent problems of the US economy
- those who lost money were unable to buy goods at a time when
  fewer motor cars, homes and domestic products were being sold
- borrowers were unable to repay loans to brokers and banks
- banks were anxious about making new loans
- companies were uneasy about maintaining production levels when
  there was no guarantee that people could afford to buy their goods.

Black Thursday was not the first time there had been a major stock market collapse – and sadly it was not the last. One example is the Florida 'land boom' of the early 1920s, when there was tremendous investment in housing. Investments peaked in 1924 and began to fall away in 1925. Investors ignored warnings about the risks involved; even respected businessmen were prepared to put forward money for loans. Almost a century later, the US subprime mortgage crisis of 2008 occurred because of the willingness of US banks and financial institutions to loan money to people on low incomes so they could buy homes they could not possibly afford.

## Activity

Find out about the stock market crash of 2008 and compare it with that of 1929. Why was buying 'on the margin' criticised in both years?

## Discussion point

Consider the views below. How convincing do you find each one? Select either view A or view B, then discuss your chosen viewpoint with a class member.

**View A:**
*The 1920s saw the increasing greed of millions of investors, the irresponsibility of lenders and the lack of wisdom of regulators. These problems, encouraged by a belief held from the very top of US society and government downwards that the system was safe, can be blamed for the stock market crash and the subsequent Depression. It could be argued that buying more and more consumer goods had become fashionable. There was little sign of any concern about quick profits among the general population.*

**View B:**
*Modern economies need investment, and the growth of share ownership in itself was not especially harmful or greedy. Regulators tried to establish control when the market became unmanageable, but events moved too quickly and the crisis itself might have been brought about by warnings. Consumer spending and home demand countered the effects of a long-term decline in heavy industry. Placing blame with a whole society is always difficult, and perhaps not the task of a historian.*

# Who was most to blame for the Great Depression?

The analysis in the previous sections does not focus on the role of US governments and Congress in bringing about the Depression. In this section, you will consider their role more closely.

# US tariff policy and its impact

The introduction of protective tariffs (import duties) can either be seen as a continuation of isolationist trends in US history or as a result of the First World War. Pre-war policy was to reduce import duties, but post-1918 the USA increased them.

Tariffs were a major source of disagreement in US political life in the 19th century. The Democrats had reduced them before the First World War, but in 1920 the Republican Party had a majority in Congress and there was a Republican president, **Warren Harding**. Also, the USA's post-war prosperity was in decline and there were fears of foreign competition.

**Warren Harding (1865–1923)** Harding was from Ohio. He became a publisher and then a Republican politician. He opposed the international and liberal policies of the Democrats, and supported free enterprise and business. Harding won a large majority in 1920, and was president from 1921–23. His administration suffered various financial scandals, and he died in office.

In September 1922, Harding signed a law that raised the average import duty on goods coming into the USA to 38.5 per cent from the 25 per cent rate set in 1913 by the Underwood Tariff. The Fordney–McCumber Tariff was named after Joseph Fordney, the chairman of the House of Representative's Ways and Means Committee, and Porter McCumber, chairman of the Senate Finance Committee.

## The Fordney–McCumber Tariff

The trading partners of the USA were outraged by the Fordney–McCumber Tariff and responded by increasing their import duties. This restricted world trade at a time when it would have supported economic recovery. The Fordney–McCumber Tariff was heavily criticised by exporters, and by some economists and politicians, as giving in to isolationists and special interests in the USA. **Henry Ford**'s opposition to the tariff shows that business interests did not dictate US economic policy.

**Henry Ford (1896–1947)** Ford was from a farming background in Michigan. He became interested in cars after reading about German engineers, and built his first car in a backyard shed. He raised money to build his Model A automobiles in 1903, and then moved to mass production by 1916. Ford supported free-market policies, used violence against trade unionists, and opposed the New Deal reforms of the 1930s. He was one of the USA's most successful businessmen of the 20th century.

Farmers' associations had called for a tariff to stop imports reducing their prices, but the Fordney–McCumber Tariff actually reduced foreign markets for US agricultural exports. This resulted in a rise in consumption at home, machinery, raw materials for agricultural processing and a range of domestic products became more expensive, and overall this caused farmers' real incomes to fall. The tariff also reduced farmers' ability to buy other goods. Indeed, it could be argued that the increased costs of agricultural equipment reduced the real incomes of farmers considerably.

The overall effect of the Fordney–McCumber Tariff was to cause the USA to look inwards and follow a form of economic isolationism. This was in direct contrast to previous post-war policies, which aimed at free trade so that US producers could take advantage of foreign markets and reduce their dependence on domestic demand. The trend was confirmed in 1929 when, faced with a downturn that was to become the Great Depression, Congress introduced another tariff.

### The Hawley–Smoot Tariff

The Hawley–Smoot Tariff became law on 17 June 1930. Named after Willis Hawley, chairman of the House of Representative's Ways and Means Committee, and Reed Smoot, chairman of the Senate Finance Committee, it raised import duties on 3200 products to 66 per cent, making it one of the largest import taxes in US history. The tariff has become infamous in world economic history for its severity. President Hoover was forced to sign the law in 1930 but passionately opposed it. The USA's trading partners, especially Canada, responded angrily and raised tariffs on US exports. This slowed down trade at a time when it was in the interests of the United States to promote it.

## The role of government

The question of how far the US government was responsible for the Great Depression is an interesting but controversial topic. The answer to this question depends on current views of society and the economy.

### Criticisms of the Republican presidents

In 1930, pressure from Congress led to tariff policies that were not introduced by the federal government but were accepted politically. The Republican presidents – Warren Harding, Calvin Coolidge and Herbert Hoover – and the federal institutions they were supposed to manage, have received significant criticism from left and right, both at the time and subsequently. Coolidge is criticised for having little understanding of foreign policy or finance and economics in the modern world. The unquestioning support of all three Republican presidents for 'laissez-faire' capitalism is viewed as limited; certainly Hoover's phrase 'rugged individualism' came to haunt him when unemployment and poverty reached unacceptable levels.

Academics and historians who were influenced by the new economic ideas of **John Maynard Keynes** offered bitter criticisms of the Republican leaders prior to 1932.

**John Maynard Keynes (1883–1946)** Keynes was a Cambridge academic and government adviser. In 1936, he wrote *The General Theory of Employment, Interest and Money*, which has greatly influenced modern economics. Keynes' followers urged governments to borrow and spend to avoid economic depression and unemployment.

More recently, followers of economists such as **Milton Friedman** have blamed the federal government for failing to regulate the money supply as a major cause of long-term economic depression.

**Milton Friedman (1912–2006)** Friedman was a highly influential economist who opposed the theories of the British economist Maynard Keynes. He argued that governments could not control unemployment by spending, since this would cause inflation by increasing the money supply and making unemployment worse. Friedman viewed the money supply as the major cause of depressions, so argued that it ought to be the first concern of governments.

 # Theory of knowledge

### History and economics
How important is economic knowledge for understanding history? There is little agreement among economic theorists about the nature of economic phenomena. Does this make authoritative historical judgements about economic events impossible?

During the Depression, the reforming Democrats played up the inadequacies of the Republican presidents and governments. In 1933, the incoming Democratic president, **Franklin D. Roosevelt**, made a devastating attack on the quality of business and political leadership.

**Franklin Delano Roosevelt (1882–1945)** Roosevelt came from a wealthy family. He was assistant secretary for the navy and governor of New York, and he fought against physical disability caused by polio in 1921 to become US president in 1933. He introduced radical social and economic reforms in his New Deal policies (see pages 63–89). Roosevelt led the United States in the Second World War (1939–45) but died in April 1945, shortly before victory.

### Activity
In what ways do Sources D and E on page 38 give different views of the economic situation?

## SOURCE D

Plenty is at our doorstep, but a generous use of it languishes in the very sight of the supply. Primarily, this is because the rulers of the exchange of mankind's goods have failed, through their own stubbornness and their own incompetence... True, they have tried. But their efforts have been cast in the pattern of an outworn tradition. Faced by failure of credit, they have proposed only the lending of more money... They only know the rules of a generation of self-seekers. They have no vision, and when there is no vision the people perish. There must be an end to a conduct in banking and in business, which too often has given to a sacred trust the likeness of callous and selfish wrongdoing. This Nation is asking for action, and action now.

*President Franklin D. Roosevelt's inauguration speech, 4 March 1933.*

## SOURCE E

The USA has come nearer to the abolition of poverty and the abolition of a fear of want than humanity has ever come before. The slogan of progress is changing from the full dinner plate to the full garage. We are nearer today to the ideal of the abolition of poverty and fear from the lives of the people than ever before in our history.

*Extract from an election speech by Herbert Hoover, 1928.*

*Herbert Hoover and President Franklin D. Roosevelt (right) en route to Roosevelt's inauguration on 4 March 1933*

### SOURCE F

Harding believed that business development would lead to prosperity for all and that it was the government's role to encourage enterprise. That did not mean that he was viciously anti-labour or insensitive to the plight of the farmers. He was sometimes unsure of himself on complicated matters such as international debt. He was well aware of the desirability of highway, aviation and water development, radio regulation, further government welfare work and conservation products.

The majority of voters wanted the prosperity and tranquillity that the Republicans promised. As far as most citizens were concerned, internationalism and liberalism had gone far enough. [In 1924] Coolidge seemed the only choice for most Americans.

What Coolidge did or accepted or presided over was popular with most Americans [from 1924 to 1928]. Prosperity was the keynote, and during the Coolidge presidency prosperity seemed to depend upon tranquillity and low taxes. The majority of Republicans and Democrats approved in general of his policy of encouraging business. Certainly there was insufficient support for federal action in other economic sectors. Positive [controlling] legislation usually ran against the wishes of a majority of Americans. He told Congress on December 4 1928: 'The country can regard the present with satisfaction and anticipate the future with optimism'.

*Adapted from McCoy, D. 1972. Coming of Age. London, UK. Penguin Books. pp. 84 and 114–15.*

### Activity

How does Source F defend Republican policy? Is this argument convincing?

## Historical interpretations

While few historians defend the actions of Coolidge and Harding, Hoover has received more favourable historical treatment.

- Hugh Brogan (*The Longman History of the United States of America*, 1985) entitled his chapter on the Republicans 'Irresponsibility 1921–33'.
- Esmond Wright (*The American Dream*, Blackwell, 1996) stated that most historians regard Coolidge as complacent, inactive and lacking in vision.
- David Reynolds (*America, Empire of Liberty*, Allen Lane, 2009) thought Hoover did too little, too late.

- Eugene Lyons' biography (*Our Unknown Ex-President: A Portrait of Herbert Hoover*, Doubleday, 1948) views Hoover as a scapegoat who was unfairly blamed for the Depression.
- More recently, Martin L. Fausold (*The Presidency of Herbert C. Hoover*, University Press of Kansas, 1988) describes Hoover as coping well with the economic problems of the 1920s.

> How far were the Republican governments of the 1920s responsible for the Great Depression?

## The case against Harding, Coolidge and Hoover

The main criticisms of the Republican presidents of the 1920s are summarised below.

- They failed to use their powers to prevent the growing gap between rich and poor and to protect weaker sections of the economy and society. By this failure they created an unstable financial situation that left the USA vulnerable to depression.
- They put too much faith in business. Harding said that his aim was to put more business in government and less government in business. By trusting business, he allowed big corporations to exploit workers; by trusting bankers and financiers, he enabled domestic debt to build up and investment in poorly regulated stocks and shares. This approach continued under his successors, who failed to see the developing crisis.
- They accepted 'get rich quick' business morals, and this encouraged greater numbers of US citizens to speculate on the stock market. It also encouraged dishonest businessmen to set up false companies and engage in dubious financial schemes.
- Lack of government regulation led to a major stock market crash in 1929, which was a major cause of the subsequent Depression.
- The Republican governments failed to support weaker sectors of the economy and made business too dependent on a restricted customer-base. They rejected major legislation to help farmers; they weakened the powers of labour unions; they accepted Congress's heavy tariffs, which in turn restricted overseas markets.

The Republican presidents of the 1920s turned against the traditions of regulating businesses, banks and credit; they failed to set an appropriate moral tone against excessive greed; they did not encourage greater responsibility in bank lending, stock market buying and selling, and social welfare. For this, many argue that they are primarily responsible for both the stock market crash of 1929 and the subsequent prolonged period of economic depression and unemployment.

*Life in a 'Hooverville', 1931; these shanty towns in Washington were named after the president who was so confident about prosperity; they were partly responsible for Hoover's falling popularity and subsequent poor historical reputation*

## The alternative view: a defence of Harding and Coolidge

In their criticism of the Republican presidents of the 1920s, the economic reformers of the 1930s and historians such as J. K. Galbraith, writing in his highly influential *The Great Crash 1929* (Harcourt, 1954), failed to recognise that the 1920s political leaders needed to cut taxes and repay a large national debt. Galbraith was a Keynesian economist and adviser to Democratic presidents in the USA from the 1930s to the 1960s. He was convinced by the arguments of Keynes that governments should spend their way out of depressions. In *The Great Crash*, he argued that explanations that focused too much on the structural weaknesses of the US or world economy took away responsibility from the bankers, financiers and speculators who caused the Crash which caused the Depression. Subsequent works, such as Donald McCoy's *Coming of Age* (1972), placed less importance on the Great Crash and more on longer term factors, viewing the Depression as 'a dramatic symptom of more complicated international and national causes'.

The following arguments are used to justify Republican policies:

### Political realities

The priority of US administrations in the 1920s was to reduce the costs of federal government and the heavy burden of debt interest through the growth of income from business. Government regulation and restriction was seen as contrary to this plan. Indeed, the high growth levels in many areas of the economy made restrictions and controls very unpopular, and few except for the old-fashioned Progressive left in 1924 supported this idea. In any case, the legal and constitutional powers of central government to control business, to undertake some sort of redistribution of wealth and to help declining sectors of the economy were limited.

### Unrealistic alternative suggestions

Various groups who found themselves in economic difficulties asked the government for help. However, it is unlikely that this would have solved their problems.

- If the government had met the demands to subsidise (artificially raise) farm prices, this would have meant putting federal money into producing more food and raw materials that could not be sold.
- Subsidies to industries or wage rises would not have solved the problem of production outstripping demand in key areas.
- The introduction of taxes to pay for higher wages for producers of unsaleable products would have helped to distribute purchasing power. While this approach would be perhaps more justifiable, it would be unlikely to make a great difference. This was because the key problem was overproduction – not only in the USA, but in most industrial nations in the 1920s.

### The influence of public opinion

If the Republican administrations of the 1920s had sought greater equality of income and imposed stricter regulations on business and finance, it is doubtful whether these measures would have had much popular support. Even organised labour unions basically wanted a greater share of business profits rather than the regulation of business.

As governor of New York in the 1920s, Franklin D. Roosevelt never proposed financial regulation or spoke out against corporate immorality and greed. This is because public opinion was favourable to free-market economic policy that seemed to be delivering wealth.

## The Wall Street Crash and the Great Depression

The major event that is considered to have brought about the Depression was the collapse of the US stock market in 1929. This is not necessarily the case. If the economy had been healthier, then the Wall Street Crash might simply have been another financial crisis, such as that of 1873. However, the Crash did impact on the Depression. For this, the stock market regulator – the Federal Reserve – was held partly responsible.

There is no doubt that the rapid expansion of stock market activity since 1926 worried the Federal Reserve. The Wall Street Stock Exchange did not regulate its activities well, and certain areas could have been addressed – especially that companies had to provide only minimal details about their nature and activities before seeking investment. There were also various dishonest practices that could have been curbed. Yet it is not true that the Federal Reserve did nothing. It raised discount rates – the rates it charged to the banks – from 3.5 per cent in 1928 to a high 6 per cent in 1929 in order to reduce borrowing and control a boom that the governor of the Federal Reserve, Roy Strong, publically condemned.

A more technical argument that the federal authorities were to blame comes from the ideas of the conservative economist Milton Friedman.

In the 1960s, Friedman and Anna Schwartz, in A *Monetary History of the United States* (Princeton University Press, 1963), challenged the accepted view that stock market speculation led to the Great Crash. They demonstrated the inherent weaknesses of unregulated capitalism and the foolishness of the laissez-faire policies of the 1920s. In Friedman and Schwartz's view, more government intervention was necessary to manage spending, boost demand and control capitalism – something brought about by Roosevelt's New Deal (see Chapter 3). Friedman argued that the Wall Street Crash resulted in serious bank failures from 1930–33, as investors panicked and withdrew their funds from banks, which in turn brought on the Depression.

*Milton Friedman, the idol of conservative economic thinkers*

When a depositor puts, for example, $10 in a bank deposit, the money does not sit in the vaults, but most of it is used for investment by the bank. Investing the money increases the bank's profits. The bank keeps a fund in case the depositor wants their money back, but not all of it – as is it unlikely that, in normal times, all depositors will want their deposits at the same time. However, after the Crash of October 1929, bank customers did want their money back and there was a 'run on the banks'. This means that ordinary users of banks lost confidence and took their money out, which threatened the very existence of banks and caused many to collapse. This 'run on the banks' was partially stopped by Roosevelt's decision to close the banks for a week in 1933 in an attempt to restore confidence. However, the bank failures and the withdrawal of deposits cut money supply for investment and running businesses, and this created an economic depression.

The Federal Reserve Bank of New York had been created in 1914 precisely to prevent this situation. If it had lent money to stop banks from failing, then there would have been no economic depression, just a bump in investment affecting all of the people who actually held stocks and shares. However, instead of releasing funds to the banks, the Federal Reserve allowed the banks to fail. This inaction, not an inherent fault in capitalism, caused the Crash to become the Depression. It led to claims that a massive government intervention was necessary, when in fact appropriate and quite limited action by the Federal Reserve would have saved the situation. This explanation rejects the view that there was a crisis of capitalism that could only be solved by governments worldwide borrowing and spending their way out of a financial crisis.

These arguments focus on how the 1929 crisis was managed. They play down the role of excessive and irresponsible speculation, even though it brought about a crisis. They do not address the long-term problems of agriculture. They also fail to account for the rising unemployment in basic industries as a result of long-term decline, and falling sales in newer industries before 1929.

## Activity

Hold a class debate about how far the US governments of the 1920s are responsible for the Great Depression. One group will argue in defence of the US governments; the other group will prepare criticisms of them. Each group should use cards with clear debating points on one side and supporting evidence on the other.

## Discussion point

How valid or useful is it for historians to consider whether the Wall Street Crash and Great Depression could have been avoided if different policies had been followed?

## Activity

Create a table like this. Look back over the chapter to fill in as many factors as you can.

| Possible cause of the Great Depression | How it contributed to the Depression | Evidence against this view | Links to other factors |
|---|---|---|---|
| The rise of a global economy in the 19th century | Farm production increased to meet global demand; increased production and transport. Long-term fall in prices and overproduction. | US agriculture expanded 1896–1920. Lower prices increased urban real wages and demand. In many countries, farming adapted. Urban population grew. Agriculture diversified. | Has to be seen in context of First World War, which accelerated production, increasing farming debts and overproduction. Also has to be seen alongside failure of governments to deal with economic problems. |
| The effects of the First World War | | | |

- **Conclusions:** decide what is the most convincing reason or combination of reasons and attempt some synthesis. This means bringing together different elements in an analysis. (You may want to change your mind when you look at this chapter again.)

- **Reflection:** do current political, social or economic issues influence your views? What is the key evidence that has led you to your latest conclusion about the causes of the Depression?

- **Reaching a view:** it is important to establish a view and make sure that it is logical and supported by knowledge (even if you come to revise your view later).

# End of chapter activities
## Paper 3 exam practice
### Question 1
Analyse the causes of the Great Depression in the USA.
[20 marks]

### Skill focus
Understanding the wording of a question

### Examiner's tips
Though it seems almost too obvious to need stating, the first step in producing a high-scoring essay is to look **closely** at the wording of the question. Every year, students throw away marks by not paying sufficient attention to the demands of the question.

It is therefore important to start by identifying the **key or 'command' words** in the question. In the question above, the key words are as follows:

- analyse
- causes.

Key words are intended to give you clear instructions about what you need to cover in your essay – hence they are sometimes called 'command' words. If you ignore them, you will not score high marks, no matter how precise and accurate your knowledge of the period. For this question, you will need to cover the following aspects:

- **Analyse** – you should be able to *explain* the causes of the Depression, not just describe what happened. This is a common mistake – the two are linked but are not the same. Analysis involves a sense of judgement about what is most important.
- **Causes** – you could discuss the causes of weaknesses in the US economy, and you will need to decide whether these are short-term or long-term causes.

For this question, you will need to cover the following aspects:

- government policies or failures
- the impact of the US financial crisis.

## Common mistakes

Under exam pressure, two types of mistakes are particularly common.

One mistake – touched on above – is to begin by giving some pre-1929 context but then to continue giving a detailed account of the stock market crisis or even US life in the 1920s. You need to provide an analysis of a range of explanations of causes and offer a balance between long- and short-term factors.

The other, more common, mistake is to focus too much on one cause. Do not give a long description of the growth of stock market speculation or the problems of US farmers in the 1920s. The question asks you to focus on causes, so to obtain a high grade you will need to discuss a range of causes.

## Activity

In this section, the focus is on understanding the question and producing a brief essay plan. So, look again at the question, the tips and the simplified markscheme on page 219. Now, using the information from this chapter, and any other sources of information available to you, draw up an essay plan (perhaps in the form of a spider diagram), which has all the necessary headings for a well-focused and clearly structured response to the question.

## Paper 3 practice questions

1   Assess the economic effects of the First World War on the USA.

2   How far do you agree that the Great Crash in 1929 was the most important cause of the economic depression in the USA?

3   How far were economic policies in the USA to blame for the Great Depression?

4   Why was the economic depression so severe in the USA?

5   Were long-term economic weaknesses the most important element in bringing about the Great Depression in the USA?

# Question 2

Compare and contrast the causes of the Great Depression in two countries of the region.
[20 marks]

> Read Chapters 4 and 5, which look at the causes of the Great Depression in Canada and Latin American countries, before answering this question.

# Skill focus

Planning an essay

# Examiner's tips

As discussed on page 45, the first stage of planning an answer to a question is to think carefully about the wording of the question so that you know what is required and what you need to focus on. Once you have done this, you can move on to the other important considerations:

- Decide your **main argument/theme/approach** *before* you start to write. This will help you identify the key points you want to make. For example, this question clearly invites you to compare and contrast the causes of the Depression. This involves looking at common causes and those that are different. You will have to decide whether it is better to look at your chosen countries separately, for instance dealing with the USA first and then Canada, or whether you are going to deal with similarities between the two and then differences.
- Plan **the structure of your argument** – i.e. the introduction, the main body of the essay (in which you present precise evidence to support your arguments) and your concluding paragraph.

For this question, whatever overall view you have about the differences and similarities, you need to decide what the common elements are and what makes for regional differences. It would help to have an overall view – were the similarities more significant than the differences, for example?

Focusing on the common elements between the causes of the Depression in the two countries is a better approach than merely thinking about what happened, as the focus will then be on explanations of similarity and difference.

Try to **link** the points you make in your paragraphs, so there is a clear thread that follows through to your conclusion. A possible structure for the essay is to group the similarities and then the differences. This will help to ensure that your essay is not just a series of unconnected paragraphs, and the reader will be able to follow your explanations and to assess how well they are supported.

You may find that drawing up a brief 'table' helps you with your essay planning; for example:

| Introduction: | |
|---|---|
| Similarities: | |
| Differences: | |
| Conclusion: | |

You have to be careful not to write two mini-essays, though – one on the USA and the other on Canada. So, after this groundwork, expand the plan to focus on comparison and don't just explain the causes or describe what happened.

When writing your essay, include **linking phrases** to ensure that each 'factor' paragraph is linked to the question. For example:

- The most important cause that affected both the USA and Canada was...
- However, there are clear differences between the causes of the Depression in the two countries. The main difference is...
- The changes in agriculture were a long-term development that brought about economic depression in both the USA and Canada. The main element was...
- However, this was a long-term development; in the short term the collapse of the US stock market had a major effect...

There are clearly many factors to consider, which will be difficult under the time constraints of the exam. Producing a plan with brief details (e.g. dates, main events/ features) under each heading will help you cover the main issues in the time available. It will also give you something to use if you run out of time and can only jot down the main points of your last paragraph(s). The examiner will be able to give you some credit for this.

## Common mistake

Once the exam time has started, one common mistake is for candidates to begin writing **straight away**, without being sure whether they know enough about the questions they have selected. Once they have written several paragraphs, they run out of things to say – and then panic because of the time they have wasted.

Producing plans for **each of the three questions** you have to write in Paper 3 at the **start** of the exam, **before** you start to write your first essay, will help you decide if you know enough about the questions to tackle them successfully. If you don't, then you need to choose different questions!

> Remember to refer to the simplified Paper 3 markscheme on page 219.

## Activity

In this section, the focus is on planning answers. So, using the information from this chapter and any other sources of information available to you, produce essay plans – using spider diagrams or mind maps – with all the necessary headings (and brief details) for well-focused and clearly structured responses to **at least two** of the following Paper 3 practice questions.

> You will need to read Chapters 4 and 5, which focus on the Great Depression in Canada and Latin American countries, before answering these questions.

## Paper 3 practice questions

1   How important was government policy in bringing about economic depression after 1929 in any *two* regions of the Americas?

2   How important were long-term causes of economic depression after 1929 in any *two* regions of the Americas?

3   What made Latin American countries so vulnerable to the economic crisis of 1929?

4   Compare the strengths and weaknesses of the economies of Canada and the USA in the 1920s.

5   Assess the economic effects of the First World War on any *two* states in the region.

# 3 The USA and the New Deal

## Key questions

- What was the impact of the Great Depression on the United States?
- How effectively did Hoover deal with the problems caused by the Depression?
- How effective was the first New Deal in solving the problems caused by the Depression?
- Why was there criticism of the New Deal?
- How successful were the Second and Third New Deals?

This chapter assesses the severity of the Great Depression in America. It considers Hoover's response to the Depression and whether he did enough to solve the nation's problems. It also reviews the response of Roosevelt's administrations and asks whether the administrations were effective in dealing with the difficulties or whether it was the outbreak of the Second World War in 1939 that brought about US economic recovery.

The chapter also examines the opposition to the New Deal and considers whether the criticisms of it were justified.

# Overview

- The Great Depression had a serious impact on the United States, both in terms of the numbers who became unemployed and economic decline. It also challenged traditional American values, such as self-help and voluntarism.
- The Hoover administration introduced a limited range of measures to deal with the crisis. However, these were not seen to go far enough and Herbert Hoover lost the 1932 presidential election to Franklin D. Roosevelt.
- Roosevelt introduced a wide range of measures, called the 'New Deal', during his first two terms as president. The measures tackled unemployment, farming, industry, housing, trade union rights and regional problems.
- Some critics of the New Deal argued that Roosevelt's policies destroyed the American belief in freedom; others argued they did not go far enough to tackle the problems. How far the measures helped recovery is debatable, as the USA slipped back into recession in 1937 and the US economy recovered only with the outbreak of the Second World War in 1939.

# What was the impact of the Great Depression on the United States?

## The economic impact of the Depression

Source A on page 52 provides a useful overview of the economic impact of the Depression, but it does not tell the whole story. Official government sources indicate that by 1933, 12.8 million Americans were unemployed. The Labour Research Association put the figure closer to 17 million. However, these figures ignore US part-time workers or those who were underemployed, suggesting that the extent of unemployment was even greater.

SOURCE A

US unemployment, GNP and growth rate, 1929–32

| Year | Unemployment | Gross national product (GNP) | Growth rate |
|------|--------------|------------------------------|-------------|
| 1929 | 3.2% | $203.6 billion | 6.7% |
| 1930 | 8.9% | $183.5 billion | -9.6% |
| 1931 | 16.3% | $169.5 billion | -7.6% |
| 1932 | 24.1% | $144.2 billion | -14.7% |

The distribution of unemployment was also uneven, and some areas were particularly badly hit. One-third of the US workforce was unemployed, but in Cleveland, Ohio, unemployment reached 50 per cent and in Toledo it was 80 per cent. Certain industries were also badly affected: car production fell by 80 per cent. The journalist Beulah Amidon described the effect of the Depression on the car industry:

SOURCE B

When I was taken through some of the eighty-seven buildings that make up the plant I was reminded of the old desert towns left in the wake of the mining rush. There was the same sense of suspended life, as I moved among silent, untended machines or walked through departments where hundreds of half-finished automobile bodies gathered dust.

*Beulah Amidon writing in 'Toledo: A City the Auto Ran Over', Survey, 1 March 1930.*

Towns that had military bases, government buildings or state universities often escaped the worst effects of the downturn. The same was true for towns that had specialist industries such as cigarette manufacture or oil, for example Richmond, Virginia, or Kilgore in Texas.

As unemployment rose, there were fewer people in productive work, and the economic growth rate declined 6.7 per cent in 1929 (it dropped to minus 14.7 per cent by 1932). These figures were also reflected in the fortunes of individual industries. The workforce in the coal industry declined by 300,000, and iron and steel production fell by 59 per cent. The industrial decline was severe, yet the agricultural market virtually collapsed. Farm income fell from $13.9 billion in 1929 to $7.1 billion by 1933, and farm wages per day fell from $2.30 in 1929 to $1.15 by 1933.

At the same time, the availability of credit virtually vanished. Bank closures soared from 5,000 in the period from 1921 to 1929 to over 10,000 between 1929 and 1933. The total amount of lost deposits rose from $200 million in 1929 to $1700 million by 1931.

Bank closures largely occurred when depositors lost confidence and withdrew their money, causing a 'run on the banks'; the banks could then not meet demand and were forced to close. Other bank closures were the result of farmers failing to meet mortgage repayments, and depositors withdrawing their money when they lost their jobs. Furthermore, many Americans who had borrowed money could no longer meet the repayment schedules, leaving banks without sufficient funds to repay depositors and adding to the loss of confidence.

The banks' problems meant they did not have money to lend to investors and were also unwilling to take risks, resulting in a lack of economic investment.

## The social impact of the Depression

Americans were unprepared to deal with unemployment on this scale. It created enormous strains in family life, reflected in:

- a decline in the number of marriages from 1.23 million in 1929 to 982,000 in 1932
- a falling birth rate from 21.2 per thousand in 1929 to 19.5 per thousand in 1932
- an increase in suicides from 14 per thousand in 1929 to 17.4 per thousand in 1932.

However, perhaps the most obvious sign of the scale of unemployment in the United States was the growing number of homeless, as noted in the evidence given to a committee of Congress in 1931:

SOURCE C

Thousands of working-class families have been thrown out of their homes because they can no longer pay their rent. In the streets of every large city, workers are dropping, dying and dead from starvation and exposure. Every newspaper reports suicides of these workers, driven to desperation by unemployment and starvation.

*Evidence given by William Foster, leader of the American Communist Party, to a Congress committee, 1931.*

On the edges of many American towns, shanty towns grew up. These were also known as 'Hoovervilles' because president Hoover appeared to be doing so little to help. These are perhaps most famously described in John Steinbeck's novel, *The Grapes of Wrath*:

## SOURCE D

There was a Hooverville on the edge of every town … the houses were tents, and weed-thatched enclosures, paper houses, a great junk pile. The man drove his family in and became a citizen of Hooverville – always they were called Hooverville … If he had no tent, he went to the city dump and brought back cartons and built a house of corrugated paper. And when the rains came the house melted and washed away.

Steinbeck, J. 1939. The Grapes of Wrath. *New York, USA. The Viking Press.*

*This Hooverville, photographed in 1937, was built on the edge of Seattle; about 1000 families lived there*

Some men, known as 'hobos', travelled from place to place on railway wagons looking for work; there were estimated to be about two million of them by the early 1930s. The Southern Pacific Railroad claimed to have thrown 68,300 hobos off its trains in 1932, a figure that indicates the scale of the problem.

*Hobos hitching a ride on a train, circa 1931*

There was no federal unemployment benefit and most Americans believed strongly in the work ethic, arguing that if you were able-bodied and unemployed it was your own fault. This attitude meant that help was very limited. Some towns organised programmes that offered temporary homes, jobs and clothes, but due to the scale of the problem they failed to meet demand. As the number of unemployed grew, income from taxes fell and therefore the amount of government aid available also declined. Private charities, such as the Salvation Army, provided soup kitchens and meal centres; however, they were able to supply only 6 per cent of the necessary aid, and state governments and federal government agencies could not fill the gap.

The human costs of the Depression were appalling. A survey found that 20 per cent of New York's children were undernourished. As the crisis deepened in 1931 and 1932, many states reduced their relief spending for the very poorest; for example, in Michigan, relief payments fell from $2 million in 1931 to $832,000 in 1932.

Some innovative schemes were set up. In Seattle, the unemployed were allowed to pick unmarketable fruit and vegetables. However, for many the stark reality was selling their possessions, using up their savings and then receiving relief. To discourage claimants from doing this, at least ten states imposed penalties for those on relief, or removed claimants' right to vote.

The situation was no better in the countryside. As people struggled to buy basic goods and even food, prices fell and farmers could no longer afford to harvest their crops. When this happened, crops simply rotted in the fields. Many farmers were also unable to afford food for their livestock and so the animals were killed. With income falling, farmers struggled to meet their mortgage repayments; by 1936, 42 farms in every thousand were repossessed.

Source E describes some of these effects of the Depression on American agriculture.

### SOURCE E

I talked to one man in a restaurant in Chicago. He said that he had killed 3000 sheep this fall and thrown them down the canyon because it cost $1.10 to ship a sheep and then he would get less than a dollar for it. He said he could not afford to feed the sheep and he would not let them starve so he just cut their throats and threw them down the canyon.

The farmers are being pauperised by the poverty of industrial populations and the industrial populations are being pauperised by the poverty of the famers. Neither has the money to buy the product of the other; hence we have overproduction and under-consumption at the same time.

*Evidence given by Oscar Ameringer to a sub-committee of the House of Representatives, 1932.*

### Discussion point

In groups, decide what were the most serious problems facing urban dwellers and farmers, and explain your choice.

Were the consequences of the Depression greater for those living in the towns and cities or the countryside?

# How effectively did Hoover deal with the problems caused by the Depression?

Herbert Hoover is often seen as a 'do nothing' president, but this view is simplistic and ignores the significant number of measures that he introduced. Despite the common view that Hoover was uncaring, he worked long hours to tackle the problems caused by the Depression. However, the optimism he displayed in public caused many to believe that he was out of touch. This lost him credibility and was played upon by the Democrats in their 1932 presidential election campaign poster.

*1932 Democrat campaign poster*

The Wall Street Crash of 1929 and subsequent economic depression dominated Hoover's presidency (the Crash happened nine months into his presidency). Before the Crash, Hoover had introduced measures to deal with the agricultural problems, summoning a special session of Congress in April 1929. However, Hoover's response was limited, as was that of the Republican Party, since they believed in self-help and voluntary co-operation. Hoover's outlook is summed up in the State of the Union Address he gave in 1930 (Source F):

### SOURCE F

Economic depression cannot be cured by legislative action or executive pronouncement. Economic wounds must be healed by the action of the cells of the economic body – the producers and consumers themselves.

*President Herbert Hoover, speaking in the 1930 State of the Union Address, 2 December 1930.*

Hoover did not ignore the USA's economic problems, but many of the measures he introduced failed to meet the needs of the time.

## Hoover's agricultural policies

The Agricultural Marketing Act of June 1929 attempted to tackle one of the major problems faced by farmers during the 1920s – falling prices. The Act set up a Federal Farm Board, which was given funds of $500 million to create marketing co-operatives in an attempt to stabilise prices. However, the biggest problem was overproduction, and the Board was not given the power to reduce production.

The Act also established the Grain Stabilization Corporation. In 1931, this bought grain at 80 cents a bushel, but world prices were only 40 cents a bushel. Therefore, the Act was criticised by taxpayers, who saw their money go to waste, and it also contributed to the problem of overproduction, as farmers could get a higher price through the Board. In response, Congress proposed a Bill to get farmers to reduce production, but Hoover threatened to veto it as it undermined his belief in voluntary action.

President Hoover's agricultural policies failed not only because of overproduction, but because they ignored the foreign situation. There was little point in keeping prices high by subsidies when imports were cheaper. As a result, the Hawley–Smoot Tariff was introduced in 1930. This added an average of 40 per cent on imported agricultural goods. It resulted in other countries putting similar tariffs on US goods and a subsequent decline in exports, which damaged the economy further.

## Voluntarism

Early responses to the Great Depression were based on the idea of 'voluntarism'. By this, Hoover tried to persuade businesses to continue as though there were no economic downturn:

- Business leaders were called into the White House and persuaded to pledge to maintain wage and employment levels.
- Municipal and state governments were encouraged to create public work schemes.
- In October 1930, the Emergency Committee for Employment was established to co-ordinate voluntary relief agencies.
- This was followed in 1931 by the establishment of the National Credit Corporation (NCC). This was designed to help smaller banks make loans to regenerate the economy. The NCC had an initial capital fund of $500 million, provided not by the government but donated by major financial institutions.

Despite these measures, banks continued to fail, and by the end of 1931 the NCC had spent only $10 million, as bankers were unwilling to change their outlook or invest in failing concerns. Initially, there were tax reductions to try to stimulate the economy by giving people more money to spend. Finally, in 1931, Hoover increased government spending to $2.2 billion.

These policies were not enough, as the problems were too great to be solved by voluntarism and local responses. But to expect the government to have brought in far-reaching measures was unrealistic, as the USA was not accustomed to intervention by the federal government.

The policy of voluntarism collapsed as the impact of the Depression became deeper. By 1931, both General Motors and United States Steel had broken their pledges on wages and public charities had cut relief payments. These failures were reflected in a loss of electoral support for the Republicans; by November 1930, they had lost eight seats in the Senate and control of the House of Representatives. At the same time, the government grew concerned about achieving a balanced budget, and in 1931 sought to decrease federal spending and rejected some relief bills. Moreover, interest rates were raised in 1931; this made borrowing more expensive and reduced the money available for spending.

## The Reconstruction Finance Corporation (RFC)

The failure to resolve the deepening crisis prompted, according to some accounts, a change in policy. Whether this was due to the forthcoming presidential election or a realisation that earlier measures did not go far enough is a matter of debate. Whatever the motives, many now agree that the introduction of the Reconstruction Finance Corporation (RFC) was the most radical of Hoover's measures and can be seen as a forerunner to the New Deal.

The RFC was established in January 1932. It received $2 billion to make loans to rescue ailing banks and insurance, railroad and construction companies. The aim was to restore confidence, but critics have argued that only larger-scale enterprises benefited. There is some validity in this argument: although 90 per cent of the loans went to small and medium sized banks and 70 per cent of the loans went to banks in towns with a population of less than 5000, in terms of amount, 50 per cent of the loans went to just 7 per cent of the borrowers, who were the major banks. Also, of the first $61 million lent, $41 million went to just three institutions, and the biggest loans to railroad and utility companies went to the largest companies. The government argued that if the loans went to the largest employers, they would be helping more people; critics argued that individuals gained little.

## The Emergency Relief and Construction Act

As a result of mounting political pressure, Hoover also agreed to the Emergency Relief and Construction Act. This authorised the Reconstruction Finance Corporation to lend states $1.5 billion to finance public works. However, to receive the money, states had to be bankrupt and use the money to generate revenue to pay off the loans. Even with these severe conditions placed upon lending, critics within the Republican movement argued that the USA was becoming like the Soviet Union in terms of state control.

In February 1932, Hoover also agreed to the Glass–Steagall Act, which provided $750 million of gold reserves for loans to private businesses. However, he blocked the Garner–Wagner Relief Bill, which would have allowed Congress to provide $2.1 billion for jobs, and continued to refuse direct federal aid for unemployment. Instead, Hoover sought a policy of self-help and established the Emergency Committee for Employment. As repossession of homes continued to rise, Hoover also introduced the Federal Home Loan Bank Act in July 1932, but as the maximum loan was only 50 per cent of the property's value, it was simply not enough.

# The 'do nothing' president?

Given the various measures introduced to counter the economic depression during Hoover's presidency, it is unfair to portray Hoover as a 'do nothing' president. His more radical measures may have been 'too little, too late', but the success of his policies also depended upon other factors. He needed state governments to keep spending, farmers to cut production, employers to retain workers, reform of the banking industry, financiers to invest government money in private enterprises and bankers to supply credit. These conditions did not happen and therefore the crisis continued.

However, Hoover's image was completely damaged by the events of the Bonus March of June 1932.

## The Bonus March

In 1924, the government voted to pay war veterans a bonus of $500, but it was not payable until 1945. With many of these former veterans unemployed, in June 1932 about 20,000 marched on Washington to ask for their bonuses to be paid early. By 15 June, they had established a series of peaceful camps in the capital and stated that they would not disperse until the bonus was paid. On the same day, the House of Representatives passed the Bonus Bill, which would have brought forward the date for the veterans to receive their cash bonus. However, the Senate defeated the Bill on 17 June. The marchers waited for Hoover to react. The president refused to meet the protestors and a standoff developed.

On 28 July, Hoover issued an order to remove the protestors. The secretary of war, Patrick Hurley, called in **General Douglas MacArthur**, who was convinced that the protestors were not only a threat to law and order but also communist rebels. MacArthur ignored Hoover's instructions to treat the protestors with respect, and instead sent in troops and police with tear gas and burned the camps, killing two protestors in the panic. Hoover did not criticise MacArthur's actions and even tried to defend them. However, most damaging to Hoover's reputation was his comment, 'Thank goodness we still have a government which knows how to deal with a mob.'

**General Douglas MacArthur (1880–1964)** MacArthur attended West Texas Military Academy and then West Point, where he graduated top of the class. Having fought in the First World War, in 1925 he became the youngest US major general and in the 1930s was US chief of staff. He retired from the army in 1937, but was recalled during the Second World War when he became field marshal of the Philippine army. He then oversaw the occupation of Japan, from 1945 to 1951, and led UN forces in the Korean War (1950–51), until President Truman removed him for making public statements that contradicted the administration's policies.

### Activity

List *five* reasons for the Hoover administration's failure to solve the problems caused by the Depression. Then choose the reason you think is most important and debate your choice with a partner.

## Historical debate

There has been considerable debate among historians about the effectiveness of Hoover's response to the Depression. Writers such as Charles Kindleberger (*The World in Depression 1929–39*, University of California Press, 1986) represent the traditional view that the Depression would have ended sooner and its impact been far less severe if the administration and Federal Reserve Bank had been more willing to lend money to the banks that were struggling. Paul Boyer (*The Enduring Vision*, 1995) argues that the continunation of the Depression was due to Hoover's inability to accept responsibility (see Source G).

## SOURCE G

Hoover blamed the Depression on global forces and argued that only international measures would help. He supported a one-year cancellation on war debts and reparation payments. In 1931, dreading an unbalanced budget, Hoover called for a tax increase, thereby angering voters. The man once portrayed as a masterful manager was now portrayed as incompetent and hard-hearted. Unable to concede error, Hoover told an aide, 'No President must ever admit he has been wrong.'

*Boyer, P. et al. 1995. The Enduring Vision: A History of the American People, Volume 11: Since 1865 (5th edition). Boston, USA. Houghton Mifflin.*

However, if Boyer and Kindleberger thought that Hoover should have done more, Paul Johnson (*A History of the American People*, HarperCollins, 2000) argues that Hoover should have done less, and that the economy would have recovered without intervention through a natural recovery of the trade cycle. Johnson states that Hoover's policies, such as the Hawley–Smoot Tariff, made matters worse because they damaged international trade.

Historians such as James Patterson and Hugh Brogan challenge the traditional, negative view of Hoover. Patterson (*America's Struggle Against Poverty in the Twentieth Century*, Harvard University Press, 2000) argues that Hoover was active in trying to combat the Depression. Most notably, Patterson describes how Hoover called for federal intervention, cancelled war debt payments to the USA, sped up work on the Boulder Dam and approved the creation of the Reconstruction Finance Corporation. In Patterson's view, this demonstrates that Hoover moved away from the belief in 'rugged individualism' that many writers argue characterised his administration. Hugh Brogan (*The Longman History of the United States of America*, 1985) qualifies Patterson's interpretation: he argues that although Hoover introduced measures to tackle the crisis, they were never enough to halt the collapse. Despite the Reconstruction Finance Corporation, Brogan argues that Hoover did nothing for the mass of the population.

## Activity

Make a copy of this table then fill it in to show the arguments for and against the view that Hoover was a 'do nothing' president.

| Evidence that Hoover was a 'do nothing' president | Evidence that Hoover was not a 'do nothing' president |
|---|---|
| | |
| | |

When you have completed the chart, write a paragraph to explain your view of Hoover.

# The 1932 presidential election

The clearest verdict on Hoover's administration was the 1932 presidential election: Franklin D. Roosevelt won 22.8 million votes, with Hoover polling only 15.8 million. More importantly, 42 out of 48 states voted for Roosevelt – yet Hoover won 40 per cent of the popular vote, suggesting that many still supported his policies of voluntarism and rugged individualism.

Instead of offering new policies in the election campaign, Hoover concentrated on claiming that things would be worse if the Democrats gained power. However, Roosevelt's smile and optimism proved far more popular with the electorate than Hoover's grim looks. This difference was important because, in some ways, the two candidates seemed to have similar policies: the programmes of both candidates featured government support for ailing businesses and job-creation schemes. Voters knew Hoover's beliefs and how he had responded to the Depression; although they did not know exactly what Roosevelt would do, they believed he would do something. For this reason, Roosevelt's presidential campaign gave the American people hope when compared with Hoover's campaign. There was even a genuine concern that unless something drastic was done the country might slide towards revolution.

### SOURCE A

Never before in this country has a government fallen to so low a place in its popular estimation or been so universally an object of cynical contempt. Never before has a President given his name so freely to latrines and offal dumps, or had his face banished from the screen to avoid the hoots and jeers of children.

*The views of a political commentator, writing after the 1932 presidential election.*

Although Roosevelt won the election, his inauguration was not for another four months and therefore Hoover continued in office as a 'lame duck' president as the crisis continued.

# How effective was the first New Deal in solving the problems caused by the Depression?

## How did Roosevelt respond to the crisis in the first 100 days?

The months between Roosevelt's election victory and his inauguration in March 1933 saw the American economy slip further into economic depression. Although Hoover tried to involve Roosevelt and ensure there was a smooth transition, the latter was determined not to be associated with an administration that had lost credibility. As a result, it might be argued that Roosevelt wanted the Depression to get worse so that he could blame Hoover but also get the credit for improvements. Hoover also criticised Roosevelt for stealing his policies; there is certainly some truth in this claim, particularly with regards to banking legislation.

The first 100 days of Roosevelt's presidency were characterised by frenzied activity, with the introduction of a huge amount of legislation that was designed to save both the USA and the capitalist system. It has been easy for historians, with the benefit of hindsight, to categorise the legislation and suggest there were three strands to Roosevelt's policies – relief, recovery and reform. However, there is debate as to whether the New Deal was a cohesive set of measures or simply a series of reforms designed to deal with the crisis the government faced.

Roosevelt outlined his ideas behind the New Deal in his inauguration speech of 4 March 1933:

### SOURCE I

This great nation will endure as it has endured, will revive and will prosper. So first of all let me assert my firm belief that the only thing we have to fear is fear itself – nameless, unreasoning, unjustified terror which paralyses needed efforts to convert retreat into advance. In every dark hour of our national life a leadership of frankness and vigour has met with that understanding and support of the people themselves, which is essential to victory.

Our greatest primary task is to put people to work. This is no unsolvable problem if we face it wisely and courageously. It can be accomplished in part by direct recruiting by the government itself, treating the task as we would treat the emergency of a war, but at the same time, through this employment, accomplishing greatly needed projects to stimulate and reorganise the use of our natural resources.

*Extract from President Roosevelt's inauguration speech, 4 March 1933.*

The impact of Roosevelt's speech was far reaching and it began to restore self-confidence in the American people:

### SOURCE J

It was one of the turning points of American history. In a few minutes, Roosevelt did what had so wearingly eluded Hoover for four years: he gave back to his countrymen their hope and their energy. By the end of the week, half a million grateful letters had poured into the White House.

*Brogan, H. 1985. The Longman History of the United States of America. Harlow, UK. Longman.*

The measures brought in during the first 100 days, between 4 March and 16 June 1933, can best be understood by considering them in terms of banking, farming, unemployment, industry, home ownership and regional deprivation.

## The agencies created during the first 100 days

| Date | New Deal agency | Work |
|---|---|---|
| 31 March | Civilian Conservation Corps (CCC) | Camps for young men established; work done included conservation work; paid $1 per day |
| 12 May | Federal Emergency Relief Administration (FERA) | Provided $500 million to hungry and homeless; $1 given to state government for every $3 FERA spent on relief |
| 12 May | Agricultural Adjustment Administration (AAA) | Adjusted the amount of crops grown to try and boost prices |
| 18 May | Tennessee Valley Authority (TVA) | Built a series of dams on the river; controlled flooding; generated electricity; created jobs |
| 16 June | Public Works Administration (PWA) | Created jobs through public works |
| 16 June | National Recovery Administration (NRA) | Persuaded employers to pay fair wages and charge fair prices |

# Banking reforms

The first area that Roosevelt dealt with was the banks. In 1932, banks had been closing at the rate of 40 per day, and between January and March 1933 gold reserves had fallen from $1.3 billion to $400 million, while banks had only $6 billion to meet $41 billion worth of deposits. On the day of Roosevelt's inauguration, all the banks were closed. This was due to growing concerns that if the banks opened, many more would go bust – in the run up to the election, several banks had failed as people no longer trusted them and were withdrawing their money, a demand that many banks could no longer meet.

The Emergency Banking Relief Act was passed on 9 March 1933 and solved the immediate banking crisis (Congress passed the legislation after a 40-minute debate). The Act closed banks for four days while their finances were examined. Where it was discovered that a bank's finances were completely hopeless, it was permanently closed; banks that were in a stronger condition were promised grants to restore public confidence in them. The Reconstruction Finance Corporation was authorised to support banks by buying bank stocks and taking on many of their debts. As a result, 5000 banks reopened and money was available as restart loans for industry.

At the same time, Roosevelt explained the crisis to the nation in a radio broadcast. These broadcasts would become a characteristic of his presidency. He appealed to the people to put money back into banks rather than withdraw it. This approach was successful, and by the start of April 1933, some $1 billion had been returned in deposits and the banking crisis was over.

Roosevelt was concerned about the uncontrolled financial activity that had played a role in the Crash of 1929. In order to control the stock market, the Truth-in-Securities Act was passed in May 1933. The aim of the Act was to give investors confidence that the company was viable and that they were less likely to lose their money. Companies that issued new shares were now required to provide full information about the company. If they failed to do this, directors could be prosecuted.

### Criticisms of Roosevelt's banking reforms

Despite the success of Roosevelt's response to the banking crisis, it met with criticism from various sources.

- Supporters of Hoover argued that these measures could have been passed before Roosevelt's inauguration and that Roosevelt delayed them so that he gained the credit.
- Some commentators claimed that there should have been even more government control of the banking system.
- Others complained that the legislation favoured the large banks as they were given more control over smaller ones; although this was necessary if the system was to be saved from collapse (which was Roosevelt's aim), thereby avoiding the need to build a different banking system.

## Solving the problems of farming

It would be fair to argue that farming was given a greater prominence in these first 100 days, and possibly throughout the New Deal, than industry. There were a number of reasons for this.

- Agriculture employed 30 per cent of the workforce, so if farmers could be given more money they would spend more, which would help industry.
- If agriculture recovered, farmers would be able to make the mortgage repayments and banks would not repossess farms.
- There were also political reasons for Roosevelt's actions: the farmers had supported Roosevelt and he considered it his duty to repay them, but he was also under pressure from the Farmers' Holiday Association, who wanted the pay and conditions of farmers improved.
- Finally, Roosevelt genuinely believed that agriculture was the 'backbone' or mainstay of the US economy – that without a successful agricultural sector, there would be no long-lasting prosperity.

The biggest agricultural problems were low prices and overproduction. The major pieces of legislation that addressed these issues were introduced in May and June 1933. They were the Farm Credit Act, the Emergency Farm Mortgage Act and the Agricultural Adjustment Act.

The Credit Act of June 1933 reorganised all the agencies dealing with agricultural credit into one organisation so that it was easier to co-ordinate. The Emergency Farm Mortgage Act, also introduced in June, made loans available to farmers who were in danger of having their farms repossessed. In June 1934, this legislation was extended when the Frazier–Lemke Farm Bankruptcy Act provided funds for famers who had already had their farms taken so that they could purchase them back.

However, the greatest challenge was overproduction, which helped to keep prices low. Roosevelt was willing to pay farmers for not producing so that prices could start to rise. This was done through the Agricultural Adjustment Act (AAA). The aim was to restore prices to pre-First World War levels. The money for paying farmers not to produce came from a tax levied on food processing companies, who then passed the additional cost onto consumers through higher prices. However, reducing production raised the issue of existing crops being destroyed and animals killed when many people were hungry, so the financial compensation was paid on the basis of acres left uncultivated. The system was voluntary and depended upon farmers meeting together to agree an acreage reduction and supervising each other to ensure that the agreed acreage was kept. This approach was generally successful, as the acreage under cultivation was reduced by over 76 million acres between 1933 and 1935. The AAA allowed the destruction of some exisiting crops – mostly cotton, cattle and piglets. Consequently, the price of cotton rose from 6.5 cents per pound to 10 cents per pound. There was a great outcry over the slaughter of 6 million piglets, although some were used to feed the unemployed.

Roosevelt's agricultural polices appeared to work, as farm income rose from $4.5 billion in 1932 to $6.9 billion by 1935. However, wealthier farmers profited the most, as they decided which lands were taken out of cultivation, and more subsidies went to those with more land. Furthermore, loans made available to farmers were often used to buy more efficient machinery. This, together with the reduction in the amount of acreage under cultivation, meant that the numbers employed on farms actually decreased, as fewer workers were needed.

In Source K on page 68, Roosevelt's labor secretary, **Frances Perkins**, gives her assessment of Roosevelt's response to the Depression.

**Frances Perkins (1882–1965)** Perkins was born in Boston. She became a social worker and then a teacher. In 1910, she took a master's degree at Columbia University. She was appointed secretary of the Consumer's League and this brought her into contact with influential politicians. She joined the Industrial Board in New York in 1919, and in 1924 became its chairman, reducing the hours of working women. As governor of New York, Roosevelt appointed her industrial commissioner. Given her industrial experience, she was appointed labor secretary in 1933 and remained in the post until Roosevelt's death. She was the first female cabinet member.

As Roosevelt described it, the 'New Deal' meant that the forgotten man, the little man, the man nobody knew much about, was going to be dealt better cards to play with. He understood that the suffering of the Depression had fallen with terrific impact upon the people least able to bear it. He knew that the rich had been hit hard too, but at least they had something left. But the little merchant, the small householder and home owner, the farmer, the man who worked for himself – these people were desperate. And Roosevelt saw them as principal citizens of the United States, numerically and in their importance to the maintenance of the ideals of American democracy.

Perkins, F. 1946. *The Roosevelt I Knew. New York, USA. The Viking Press.*

### Activity

Look carefully at the aims Roosevelt set out in his inauguration speech (Source I on page 64). What measures were taken to meet each of the aims? Did he achieve his aims?

## Measures to tackle unemployment

Unemployment was tackled through two major legislative initiatives: the Civilian Conservation Corps (CCC) and the Federal Emergency Relief Agency (FERA).

### The Civilian Conservation Corps (CCC)

Within three weeks of Roosevelt's presidency starting, the Civilian Conservation Corps (CCC) was established, on 31 March 1933. The CCC provided work on environmental projects for young men aged between 18 and 25 years. Initially, men signed on for six months, but many returned when they were unable to find other work. They were paid only $30 a month, or $1 per day, of which $25 had to be sent home. Rules were strict and work was organised on military lines, with workers wearing a uniform; some claimed it was no more than forced labour. The workers were employed in a variety of tasks, including fish farming, fighting forest fires, controlling mosquitoes and creating shelterbelts to stop soil erosion. Although conditions were tough, working for the CCC gave the young unemployed self-respect, and for those from cities, it was a chance to experience the 'great outdoors'. However, those taken on were usually young white males (due to racial discrimination) and there was no guarantee that after their time in the CCC they would not claim relief again.

*Young men, members of the CCC, building a wall, 1933*

## The Federal Emergency Relief Administration (FERA)

The Federal Emergency Relief Administration (FERA) was established by the Federal Emergency Relief Act of May 1933. FERA made grants of federal money to state and local governments, in order to provide emergency, short-term relief to the unemployed. Roosevelt, like Hoover, did not believe in paying 'the dole' (unemployment benefit), and wanted the unemployed to be gainfully employed; however, the crisis was so deep that this was not instantly possible.

FERA provided $500 million, which was divided between states. Half the money was used for relief, while the government used the remaining half to pay $1 to each state for every $3 it spent on relief. The money was intended for soup kitchens, blankets, unemployment schemes and nurseries. However, it brought the government into conflict with several states. The Act required each state to establish a FERA office and organise relief programmes by either borrowing or increasing taxes, but states such as Ohio refused and **Harry Hopkins** (see page 70), in charge of the programme, threatened to deny Ohio any money.

Many states were concerned to balance their budgets and did not want to spend money on relief, believing that poverty was the fault of the victim. The opposition limited the effectiveness of the scheme, but so did the funds available – by 1935, FERA paid about $25 per month to a family on relief, while subsistence (the minimum amount needed to survive) was closer to $100.

**Harry Hopkins (1894–1946)** Hopkins was born in Iowa. He worked in social welfare in New York, where he met Roosevelt. He was an adviser to Roosevelt when the latter was governor of New York State. Hopkins believed the unemployed should be given work not dole, even if it was more expensive to provide relief work. He was in charge of the Civil Works Administation (CWA) and in 1935 became the director of the Works Progress Administration (WPA); he was secretary of commerce from 1938 to 1940. Hopkins was probably Roosevelt's closest aide and was given a room in the White House during the Second World War.

## Reviving industry

The scale of the industrial collapse meant that industrial recovery was a priority. The economy grew by 10 per cent from 1933 to 1936, but unemployment still remained at 14 per cent. Congress proposed to restrict the working week to 30 hours so that the available work was spread more widely, but Roosevelt stopped the plan, as he believed it would not increase income or the demand for goods. Instead, he brought in the National Industrial Recovery Act (NIRA) on 16 June 1933, the last of the first 100 days. One of the main authors of the NIRA was **General Hugh Samuel Johnson**.

**General Hugh Samuel Johnson (1882–1942)** Johnson was born in Kansas in 1882. He graduated from the US Military Academy and fought in Mexico in 1916. By the end of the war, he was a brigadier general. Energetic and enthusiastic, Johnson was appointed to lead the NRA in 1933, but he was a controversial figure and drinking heavily on the job, and Roosevelt eventually dismissed him in 1934.

### The National Recovery Administration (NRA)

The National Industrial Recovery Act set up the National Recovery Administration (NRA). This encouraged industries to agree to a series of codes of practices covering issues such as child labour, long hours, low pay and labour relations. Provided companies agreed to the codes, they were allowed to display the NRA logo – a blue eagle with the slogan 'We do our part' underneath.

The response to the NRA was encouraging: 557 codes were drawn up that covered most industries, and some 23 million workers were employed in companies that had agreed to the codes. The government hoped that consumers would support those firms that had signed up and boycott other firms, which were seen as unpatriotic and selfish.

However, many of the codes were drawn up too quickly and proved unworkable, as firms could not afford the wages or the hours.

Small firms were disadvantaged by the codes, as large firms were able to restrict competition and increase their profits by raising prices and keeping wages low. It may have looked impressive, but it did not bring about a recovery; some large firms, such as Ford, never joined, while others used the codes to indulge in unfair practices.

### SOURCE L

The Blue Eagle was meant to symbolise unity and mutuality, and no doubt it did for a season, but Johnson's ubiquitous 'badge of honour' also clearly signified the poverty of the New Deal imagination and the meagreness of the methods it could bring to bear at this time against the Depression. Reduced to this kind of incantation and exhortation for which they had flayed Hoover, the New Dealers stood revealed in late 1933 as something less than the bold innovators and aggressive workers of government power that legend later portrayed.

*Kennedy, D. M. 1999. Freedom from Fear. New York, USA. Oxford University Press, Inc. p.184.*

### Activity

Look at Source L then answer the following questions:

- What is Kennedy's view of the NRA and the Blue Eagle?
- What is his evidence to support this view?
- Is Kennedy's view justifiable? Explain your answer using the information in this section and gained through further research on the NRA.

## The Public Works Administration (PWA)

The National Industrial Recovery Act also established the Public Works Administration (PWA). The idea behind this was to help the economy to grow by providing government money for public works schemes. The aim was to use unemployed, skilled workers on large-scale public works projects, and under **Harold Ickes** (see page 72), the programme was given $3.3 billion. It was hoped that these large-scale construction projects would stimulate a range of industries, increasing employment and the availability of money for workers to spend, in this way further stimulating the economy. However, the scheme developed slowly, as Ickes was careful to ensure that the money was spent wisely; he was criticised for spending only $110 million in the first six months. Ickes argued that he did not want to waste taxpayers' money and that large-scale schemes needed careful planning. Even though the programme began slowly, between 1933 and 1939 it was responsible for building 13,000 US schools and 50,000 miles of roads.

**Harold Ickes (1874–1952)** Ickes was born in Pennsylvania and educated at Chicago University. He was Secretary of the Interior from 1933 to 1944, and was in charge of the Public Works Administration (PWA) from 1933. He believed that schemes organised by the PWA should have a lasting value and was unwilling to waste public money. Ickes may have hoped to become vice-president. He resigned in 1946, as he was more liberal than many ministers appointed by president Harry Truman.

## Supporting homeowners

During the Depression years, many unemployed homeowners lived with the threat of having their homes repossessed. This situation was tackled by the Home Owners Loan Corporation, which was established by the Home Owners' Loan Act of June 1933. The Corporation provided low-interest loans to allow the adjustment of mortgages to cope with unemployment. This meant that mortgages could be rescheduled for longer periods, removing the threat of eviction for many Americans.

## Tacking regional deprivation

Probably the most famous of the Acts introduced by the Roosevelt administration was the Tennessee Valley Authority Act of May 1933, which established the Tennessee Valley Authority (TVA).

### The Tennessee Valley Authority (TVA)

Even before the Depression, the Tennessee Valley area was deprived, containing seven of the poorest states. Half the population were dependent upon relief, while in 1932 only 2 per cent of famers had electricity.

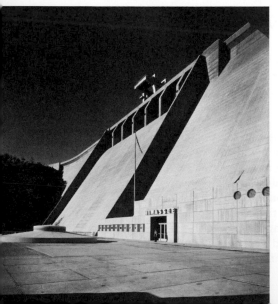

The TVA aimed to make the region more prosperous through regeneration and by encouraging industry and agriculture. The project saw the construction of 33 dams designed to generate electricity through hydroelectric power; they also controlled the flooding that occurred every year, washing away topsoil and ruining farmland. The construction of the dams and a 650-mile waterway also created leisure opportunities and opened up the region for trade, in this way encouraging firms to locate there.

*Nottely Dam, a Tennessee Valley Authority project completed in 1942*

The building of the dams generated work and the creation of the power plants added to the availability of jobs, transforming the region, as this contemporary report (Source M) suggests:

## SOURCE M

A Promised Land, bathed in golden sunlight, is rising out of the grey shadows of want and squalor and wretchedness down here in the Tennessee Valley these days. Ten thousand men are at work, building with timber and steel and concrete the New Deal's most magnificent project, creating an empire with potentialities so tremendous and so dazzling that they make one gasp. Thousands of them are residents of the Valley, working five and half hours a day, five days a week for a really LIVING wage and in their leisure time they are studying – farming trades, the art of preparing themselves for fuller lives they are to lead in the Promised Land.

*Lorena Hickok's report to Harry Hopkins on the success of the Tennessee Valley Authority project in Alabama, 6 June 1934.*

## Activity

Read Source M and then answer these questions:

1 Why do think that Hickok describes the Tennessee Valley as the Promised Land?
2 Why do you think Hickok emphasised the word 'living' (emphasis shown in capital letters in the source text above) when describing the wages?

However, the government had to proceed with caution, as private companies opposed the right of a government agency to manufacture and sell electricity – particularly when it was cheaper; critics accused the government of state planning. Despite this opposition, the project was a success. It was largely responsible for an increase in average income in the region by 200 per cent in the period from 1929 to 1949, and an increase in the supply of electricity to farms from 2 per cent in 1932 to 75 per cent by 1945.

## Discussion point

In which area of activity were the government measures most successful? Why do you think that was the case?

## Why were the first 100 days important?

The action of the government restored confidence. This was aided by the president's broadcast 'fireside chats', in which he explained his policies to the American people. Moreover, his actions demonstrated the energy of the president to the people and they came to trust him. Roosevelt's Democrat administration halted the banking panic and established institutions to restructure the economy. The biggest public works programme started, but at the same time money was put aside to provide emergency relief, with recognition that charities and state governments could not deal with the scale of the problem. At a regional level, the TVA was a unique experiment in regional development. Therefore, despite some shortcomings and failures, the first 100 days were vital in creating a new sense of hope and optimism, even if the administration faced criticism from both sides of the political spectrum.

> What was achieved during the first 100 days? Were the changes far-reaching or long-lasting?

## The First New Deal after the first 100 days

While the great bulk of legislation was introduced during the first 100 days, there were some changes after 16 June 1933. Perhaps the most important of these was the Civil Works Administration (CWA), established in November 1933. Although the CWA was temporary, it was crucial in dealing with the crisis of supporting the unemployed through the winter of 1933–34. Under the direction of Harry Hopkins (see page 70), the organisation was given a budget of $400 million to provide emergency relief. In two months, the CWA found work for some four million people in public works schemes. However, when the schemes ended in March 1934, those four million became unemployed once more, although FERA did agree to fund more public works schemes. Some critics argued that the jobs created by the CWA were worthless 'boondoggles' (meaning a waste of both time and money).

There were two other significant reforms in this period:

- The Federal Housing Administration (FHA) was set up by the National Housing Act of June 1934 with the intention of stabilising the housing market and preventing defaulting on mortgage payments and subsequent repossession. In an attempt to stimulate the housing market, the FHA guaranteed private mortgages, reduced down payments from 30 per cent to 10 per cent and extended repayment times.

- The Securities and Exchange Commission (SEC) was established by the Securities Exchange Act of June 1934 to regulate trading in stocks and bonds. It was designed to prevent a repeat of the events of the 1920s that had led to a surplus of shares and the existence of many dishonest organisations looking to make money from investments in fraudulent enterprises.

## The impact of the First New Deal: an assessment

Taken as a whole, these reforms transformed the activities of government – never before had a United States government been so active in peacetime. Conservative historians, such as John Flynn (*The Roosevelt Myth*, Devin-Adair Co., 1956) and Richard Hofstadter (*The American Political Tradition and the Men Who Made It*, Vintage Books, 1989), have questioned how such a far-reaching series of measures that challenged traditional American values came to be implemented. It does not appear as though Roosevelt had a plan when he came into office; rather the measures were a response to a series of crises that the government faced. The varying nature of the reforms supports the view that Roosevelt took advice from a wide group of advisors, weighed up their suggestions and then made his decisions. Different influences and emphases can be seen in each of the reforms, adding further weight to the argument that the government was simply responding to events rather than implementing a grandiose and pre-planned scheme to save capitalism. By the end of this period, as regulation increased and government took on more responsibilities, the American people became reliant on the government for solutions to their problems.

### Activity

Copy and complete a chart like the one below to summarise the work of the agencies during the First New Deal. When completing the chart you will need to:

- decide whether the agency was concerned with relief, recovery or reform and complete the second column
- in the third column, explain your choice
- in the fourth column, summarise the successes and failures of the agency (you could use one colour for successes and one for failures).

| Agency | Relief, recovery or reform? | Explanation | Successes? Failures? |
|--------|------------------------------|-------------|----------------------|
|        |                              |             |                      |
|        |                              |             |                      |

Then write a paragraph explaining the nature of the First New Deal. What was its main concern – relief, recovery or reform? Why do you think this was its focus?

## Historical debate

In the years after the New Deal, most historians and commentators were positive about its impact. They saw the United States government as taking responsibility for social welfare and bringing about what the historian Carl Degler called a 'third American Revolution' (*Out of Our Past*, Harper & Row, 1957). William Leuchtenberg (*Franklin D. Roosevelt and the New Deal, 1932–40*, 1963) supported this view, claiming, 'It is hard to think of another period in the whole history of the republic that was so fruitful or a crisis that was met with such imagination'.

Historians of the 'New Left', such as Howard Zinn, Paul Conkin and Barton Bernstein, challenged this interpretation in the 1960s. They argued that the solutions offered were limited: Bernstein ('The New Deal: The Conservative Achievements of Liberal Reform' in *Towards a New Past*, Knopf, 1968) wrote that the New Deal 'failed to solve the problem of the Depression, it failed to raise the impoverished and it failed to redistribute income'. Yet this assessment is unfair, as radical change was not the aim of the New Deal.

In the 1970s, historians and economists also criticised the New Deal for setting the USA on the wrong course. Commentators such as Milton Friedman (*Free to Choose: A Personal Statement*, Harcourt, 1980) argued that it encouraged governments to spend, increased inflation and reduced free-market activity.

Donald McCoy (*Coming of Age*, 1972) argued that the New Deal was successful in bringing some relief and reform: 'the relief given to the needy was substantial and reform significant.' However, McCoy acknowledged that efforts to promote recovery were less effective.

Much recent writing has taken a balanced view of the impact of the New Deal. David Kennedy (*Freedom from Fear*, 1999) argues that although the New Deal did not bring about economic recovery, redistribute national income or end capitalism, it recognised organised labour, introduced greater regulation to the economy and provided greater financial security for Americans. This more balanced approach is also expressed in Paul Johnson's *A History of the American People* (HarperCollins, 2000), where Johnson argues that the recovery was slow and that only in 1937 did production levels briefly pass those of 1929.

However, Hugh Brogan (*The Longman History of the United States of America*, 1985) argues that placed in context, the New Deal was a success as it preserved American democracy, the constitution and capitalism (see Source N).

SOURCE N

Thanks to Franklin Roosevelt, in short, six years transformed America from a country which had been laid low by troubles which its own incompetence had brought on it, and which it was quite unable to cope with, to a country, as it proved, superbly equipped to meet the worst shocks that the modern world could hurl at it.

Brogan, H. 1985. *The Longman History of the United States of America.* Harlow, UK. Longman.

 **Theory of knowledge**

History and opinion

Why do historians have different views about events in the past? Does this make history more or less valid as an academic discipline if it can be so much a matter of opinion?

# Why was there criticism of the New Deal?

It is perhaps not surprising that there was some hostility to the New Deal. The opposition took two forms: those who believed that the New Deal interfered too much with the American 'way of life' and those who felt it did not go far enough.

During the Roosevelt administration, the United States government became involved in the economic life of the country in an unprecedented way. Many Americans believed that it was not the business of the government to create jobs, control prices and introduce regulations on work conditions. The policies also required those who were in work to pay higher taxes to fund some of the schemes, which in turn caused resentment.

Some critics of the New Deal argued that the measures undermined the values of American freedom, while others accused Roosevelt of moving the USA towards socialism. Roosevelt was even accused of pursuing similar policies to those of Josef Stalin and his Five-Year Plans in the USSR.

Despite Roosevelt's success in the 1932 and 1936 presidential elections, those who opposed his policies had some impact on the direction of the subsequent New Deals, as the next section will show.

## Republican opposition to the New Deal

It was perhaps not surprising that Republicans disliked the measures. Some felt that Roosevelt simply adopted Hoover's policies; others argued that the measures were too complicated to work, as there were many codes and regulations to follow. Many Republicans thought it was not the government's role to deal with wages and that the market should be left to regulate the economy. They claimed that organisations such as the TVA provided unfair competition and interfered with the role of individual states; they viewed support for the unemployed through taxes as unfair on the wealthy, who worked hard for their money. There were also complaints about the levels of the deficits, and arguments that the schemes did not work, as unemployment levels were not falling.

Republican criticisms may have affected Roosevelt's decision in 1937 to cut back on government programmes and tighten the availability of credit through the Federal Reserve. These measures made borrowing money more expensive and helped to send the USA back into economic depression, as the final section of this chapter will show (see pages 82–89).

*'What We Need Is Another Pump'; this 1933 cartoon mocks Roosevelt for pouring more than $16 billion into the US economy as an emergency measure to 'balance' the budget*

## The Liberty League

Perhaps the most well-known group on the right of the political spectrum that challenged the New Deal was the Liberty League, which was founded in 1934. Their beliefs were similar to those of many Republicans: they were concerned that the legislation reduced individual liberty. Most worryingly for Roosevelt, two Democrats – Alfred Smith and John Davis – were members. The League argued that since the New Deal had achieved its original aim of saving capitalism, it was time to once again encourage private property and enterprise unregulated by law. In this respect they viewed Roosevelt as a traitor, abandoning those who had made their fortunes through private enterprise and not relied on the state. There were even rumours in 1934 that the far right planned to overthrow Roosevelt's government.

# Other opposition

Opposition did not just come from mainstream political opponents, but from a range of individuals, particularly on the left of the political spectrum, who wanted further change. In many instances, these individuals and groups did not complain about government intervention, but argued that the measures had not gone far enough in tackling the problems.

One of the most prominent critics of the New Deal was Father Charles Coughlin (see page 213), a priest whose radio programme 'The Golden Hour of the Little Flower' attracted audiences of 30–40 million (more than the audiences for Roosevelt's broadcasts). At first, Coughlin argued that 'The New Deal is Christ's Deal', but he later became convinced that the banking reforms did not go far enough and that the New Deal had failed to provide social justice. In 1934, he founded the National Union for Social Justice with the aim of redistributing wealth. It had a membership of some 7 million. Coughlin later became more radical and anti-Semitic, and this led to a decline in his influence.

In a similar vein to Coughlin, the retired doctor Francis Townsend proposed that every American who was unemployed and over the age of 60 should be given $200 per month, provided they spent it all. Townsend argued that this would boost the economy, as it would stimulate demand for goods and production. He also thought it would encourage people to retire at 60 and therefore free up jobs for younger people. The scheme was to be funded by a 2 per cent tax on business transactions; however, this was not practical, as payments would have amounted to some 50 per cent of national income. Despite these concerns, various 'Townsend Clubs' were set up and membership reached 500,000. The scheme, known as 'Old Age Revolving Pensions Ltd', collapsed when Townsend's partner was found guilty of stealing money from the funds. Yet it was pressure from such groups that influenced the passing of the Social Security Act in the Second New Deal (see page 84) and suggested that more radical ideas were needed.

# Huey Long

Probably the most serious individual challenge to Roosevelt came from Huey Long, governor and senator of Louisiana. Long ran the state of Louisiana without opposition, and some of his methods were corrupt. There was no doubt that he used strong-arm tactics, even though he improved public services in the state by taxing big corporations and businesses and using the money to build schools and hospitals.

As a professional politician, Long presented a serious challenge to Roosevelt. Initially, he had supported the New Deal, but soon believed that the schemes were too cautious and too complex. Long produced a radical plan, known as 'Share our Wealth'.

Through this national scheme he planned to confiscate individual wealth over $3 million and limit income to a maximum of $1 million. He proposed to use the proceeds to allow everyone to buy a home, car and radio. Long also wanted the government to provide free education and pensions, as well as buy up surplus agricultural produce and sell it at a low price to those who most needed it.

With such far-reaching offers, Long's popularity grew, particularly among the poorer elements in society who saw him as an ally against the wealthy (who seemed to be doing well from the First New Deal). It was therefore not surprising that Long decided to run against Roosevelt in the 1936 presidential election. However, he was assassinated in 1935, which removed probably the greatest challenge to Roosevelt securing a second term. Despite his death, Long's radical policies and those of Townsend were influential in ensuring that the Second New Deal focused more on the disadvantaged.

## Other alternatives to the New Deal

Long demonstrated in Louisiana one approach to the problems of the Depression, but his was not the only alternative solution. In California, there emerged the 'End Poverty in California' organisation led by the novelist **Upton Sinclair**. Sinclair proposed that the unemployed should work in state-run co-operatives and be paid in a currency that could only be spent in other co-operatives. This scheme gained credibility and Sinclair won the Democratic nomination for the state governorship. Yet, opposition, particularly among the Hollywood élite, ensured that he was defeated.

**Upton Sinclair (1878–1968)** Sinclair was born in Baltimore, but later moved to California where he founded the Californian section of the American Civil Liberties Union. He wrote nearly 100 books, the most famous of which was *The Jungle*, published in 1906, which describes the lives of US immigrants and the terrible working conditions of those in the meat-packing industry. His 'End Poverty in California' campaign won him the support of the Democrats as governor, but his plan was very controversial, particularly after large numbers of migrants arrived in the state to escape the dust bowl (see page 85). Sinclair's opponents portrayed him as a communist, and he lost the election and returned to his former career as an author.

Other opposition took more sinister forms. Employers often used scare tactics to discourage their workers from supporting the schemes, and argued that they would never be implemented. Some focused their attacks on President Roosevelt's personal life rather than his policies, suggesting that his disability was not the result of polio but a sexually transmitted disease.

Despite concerns at the time, the opposition to the New Deal and the alternative movements were not a serious threat to Roosevelt's presidency. Yet, in Roosevelt's view, they reflected large-scale support for more radical measures to combat the impact of the Depression. However, the results of the mid-term Congressional elections in 1934 may have eased Roosevelt's fears, as the Democrats made gains in both houses and in the Senate gained their biggest majority to date.

## Activity

Complete a chart like this to summarise opposition to the New Deal.

| Group or individual? | What was the criticism of the New Deal? | How much support did they have? | What was the impact? |
|---|---|---|---|
|  |  |  |  |
|  |  |  |  |

# The Supreme Court

The greatest challenge to the New Deal came from the Supreme Court. The Court had supported legislation during the crisis days, but increasingly it declared the legislation unconstitutional (against the principles of the United States Constitution). In the 140 years before 1935, the Supreme Court had found only 60 laws unconstitutional, but in the 18 months during 1935 and 1936, the Court found 11 laws to be so.

The matter reached a crisis on 27 May 1935, which became known as 'Black Monday'. On this day, the Court attacked the New Deal in several ways.

- First, it found the Farm Mortgage Act unconstitutional, arguing that the removal of a trade commissioner was not the responsibility of the president, but of Congress.
- More importantly, the Supreme Court found the National Industrial Recovery Act to be unconstitutional as a result of the 'sick chicken' case. The Schechter Poultry Corporation had been found guilty of breaking National Recovery Administration (NRA) regulations as they sold diseased chickens, filed false sales claims, exploited workers and threatened government inspectors. The firm appealed to the Supreme Court, who ruled that the NRA had no right to prosecute them as the NIRA was unconstitutional. This ruling meant that, in practice, the federal government had no right to interfere in internal state issues, and if the federal government could not prosecute individual firms for breaking NRA codes, all these codes must be unconstitutional.

The Supreme Court's ruling suggested that the government had no powers to oversee nationwide economic affairs, undermining much of the New Deal legislation. Roosevelt attempted to tackle the problem by reforming the Court, increasing the number of judges from nine to fifteen. However, this plan was a rare misjudgement as it gave opponents the opportunity to portray him as a dictator interfering in the legal process, and he was forced to back down.

# How successful were the Second and Third New Deals?

## The reasons for the Second New Deal

The Second New Deal was more radical than the first as it tried to reform areas that affected ordinary people, such as union rights, security in old age, providing cheap electricity and reducing unemployment. A particular aim was to improve the position of the poor. The Second New Deal also sought to help small businesses, as the focus of the First New Deal had been on those businesses that employed the largest number and would therefore have the greatest impact. It was described by a journalist as 'the most comprehensive programme of reform ever achieved in this country by any administration'.

The scale of the measures may have been an attempt to address critics such as Huey Long, who argued that the First New Deal had not gone far enough. At the same time, Roosevelt was in a much stronger political position following the 1934 mid-term elections. The USA appeared to be more divided electorally, with the left making large gains, and it can be argued that Roosevelt wanted to realign himself with this development. He was also disillusioned with the two groups in the USA that opposed his measures – big business and the Supreme Court. This encouraged a more radical outlook because Roosevelt needed to bring in new measures to replace those that had been declared unconstitutional.

### The measures of the Second New Deal

When Roosevelt met Democrat senators on 14 May 1935, the recovery in the USA was much slower than that in Europe and even post-war Germany (perhaps because the Depression had been so deep), so the senators put pressure on Roosevelt to take radical steps.

A month later, Roosevelt summoned Congress and listed the measures he wanted passed; within 88 days, he had implemented most of his legislative programme.

## The National Labor Relations Act

The first major Act was the National Labor Relations Act, also known as the Wagner Act, which was passed in July 1935. Roosevelt was reluctant to become involved in labour relations and did not initiate this Act, only giving it his support when it had passed the Senate and was likely to become law.

The National Labor Relations Act was a landmark in US history as:

- it forced employers to recognise unions
- it forbade the sacking of workers for being union members
- it gave workers some legal protection
- it established the National Labor Relations Board, which allowed unions to negotiate wages and conditions.

The Act helped to create a peaceful way to solve industrial disputes and end the violence that had characterised industrial unrest in the United States. Its success can be seen in the rise in union membership, which grew from 3.7 million in 1935 to 8.5 million by 1940.

## The Works Progress Administration (WPA)

At the same time as protecting those in work, Roosevelt continued to provide schemes for those who were out of work. This was done through the establishment of the Works Progress Administration (WPA) in April 1935, which was known from 1939 as the Works Project Administration.

The WPA brought together all agencies involved in the administration of job creation schemes, with a budget of $45.5 billion. It found work for some eight million Americans over the next eight years and was the biggest employer in the USA. Its construction projects included La Guardia airport in New York. It also found short-term community work for unskilled workers, often in the construction industry, as well as office workers, actors, artists and photographers. Some examples of WPA work schemes are:

- unemployed writers produced guides on cities and states
- artists produced pictures for public buildings
- actors toured the country
- photographers produced a set of images depicting the United States in the 1930s (like the one shown here).

*A woman doing laundry at a migrant worker camp, California, photographed by Dorothea Lange in 1937*

To avoid criticism, the WPA was not allowed to compete with private firms or build private housing.

In a similar way, the National Youth Administration (NYA) was set up in 1935 to encourage the education and training of young people so they could find jobs more easily.

## The Social Security Act (SSA)

Perhaps most controversial of all the measures was the Social Security Act (SSA), as this brought the federal government into new areas of responsibility and widened its role. The USA was far behind Europe in terms of welfare provision, with only Wisconsin providing unemployment benefit. As a result of the SSA:

* federal government worked with state governments to provide help for the needy
* a national insurance scheme was established
* pensions, unemployment benefits and support for those with disabilities were provided through contributions from workers, employers and government.

The scheme was dependent upon contributions from workers and employers, so nothing was paid out until 1942 and even then payment was low, with no sickness benefits. Farm labourers, casual workers and domestic servants – all of whom were in need of such help – were excluded. However, the Social Security Act represented a major new area of government responsibility.

## Supporting farmers

The 1933 Agricultural Adjustment Act (AAA) was ruled unconstitutional by the Supreme Court in 1936, so new measures during the Second New Deal aimed to tackle the continuing agricultural problems.

* Farmers were offered help through the Resettlement Administration (RA), established in April 1935. From 1935 to 1938, the RA assisted poor farmers in purchasing equipment and provided grants for soil conservation. It also planned to move 500,000 families to more fertile land through the Farm Security Administration (FSA), established in 1935; however, only 4441 families were moved. This low figure was partly a result of the costs, yet it also reflected farmers' reluctance to move to new areas.
* The government also paid farmers a subsidy, through the Soil Conservation and Domestic Allotment Act of 1936, to those who were willing to devote part of their land to growing soil-conserving crops such as grass. By 1940, some 6 million famers had joined and were earning an extra $100 per year.

However, the problems of farmers were made worse by the droughts of the 1930s that affected much of the US and Canadian farming lands. The droughts resulted in millions of tonnes of topsoil being blown away, leaving the land barren and creating severe dust storms. The effects of the dust bowl were so great that some homes were partially buried and the tops of fence posts could hardly be seen.

*Photo by Arthur Rothstein of a farmer and his sons walking in a dust storm, Cimarron County, Oklahoma, April 1936*

## Other measures

- In order to improve the lives of ordinary people, the Rural Electrification Administration (REA) was established in May 1935. The REA provided low interest loans to companies and farming co-operatives to extend electricity to rural areas. In 1935, only 10 per cent of farms had electricity, but this had grown to 40 per cent by 1940 and 90 per cent by 1950.
- Other legislation increased the control of the Federal Reserve Board over banks to prevent a repetition of the banking crisis of 1933 and increase public confidence.
- The Revenue Act of 1935 raised taxes on higher-level incomes so that the wealthy contributed more.

## Summary

The Second New Deal brought in much that was new and radical to the United States, with a greater emphasis on reform than the First New Deal. Although some measures were limited in their effectiveness, Roosevelt's administration was still seen to be acting and tackling the problems of the Depression. Some of the issues that affected the daily lives of Americans were addressed, and – in the long term – permanent changes were brought about.

## Activity

With reference to this chapter and Chapter 6, complete a chart like this to show the benefits and limits of the New Deal for different groups in the United States.

| Group | Benefits from the New Deal | Limits of the New Deal |
|---|---|---|
| African-Americans | | |
| Native Americans | | |
| Women | | |
| Long-term unemployed | | |
| Farmers | | |
| Industrial workers | | |
| Sharecroppers and tenant farmers | | |

The Second New Deal is often seen as being more radical than the First New Deal as it tackled major inequalities in the USA. Is this true?

# A Third New Deal?

Roosevelt won the 1936 US presidential election easily, with 60.8 per cent of the vote. His Republican opponent, **Alf Landon**, polled only 36.5 per cent, which was less than Herbert Hoover polled in 1932.

**Alf Landon (1887–1987)** Landon became a millionaire through his work in the oil industry. He was elected governor of Kansas in 1932 and re-elected in 1934, winning much support for his policies of reduced taxes and balanced budgets. He won the Republican nomination for the 1936 US presidential election. Although he supported many parts of the New Deal, he disapproved of the labour legislation. However, he was a poor campaigner; he lost the popular vote by more than 10 million and was even defeated in his home state.

Roosevelt's second term in office was characterised more by his battles with the Supreme Court than by the introduction of new legislation. It could even be argued that there was no New Deal in this period, as the USA went into recession in 1937–38. This economic downturn was due, at least in part, to cuts in government expenditure. Also, no government measures were introduced after January 1939, as the United States was preparing for a second world war that seemed inevitable.

In the 1936 presidential election, Roosevelt won all states except Maine and Vermont. In the Senate, the Democrats won three-quarters of the seats and four-fifths of the seats in the House of Representatives.

In 1937, two major pieces of legislation were passed: the Wagner–Steagall Act and the Farm Tenancy Act.

- The Wagner–Steagall Act established the US Housing Authority, provided money for low-cost housing and made available loans of up to 100 per cent. However, Congress allocated only half of the money requested and no more than 10 per cent could be spent in one state. This meant that many of the northeastern states that desperately needed new housing stock missed out.
- The Farm Tenancy Act established the Farm Security Administration. It provided loans for poor sharecroppers and tenants to buy land and heavy farm machinery. It established 30 camps for families who had been displaced by eviction, and it set up medical and dental centres.

However, little positive legislation was passed. Opposition to the levels of public spending grew and Roosevelt, believing that the country was coming out of the Depression, responded by cutting spending.

## The USA goes back into recession

However, with the upturn in the economy, pressure to cut spending brought measures to a halt in 1937. The effects were catastrophic.

- Employment in manufacturing dropped 23 per cent.
- Employment in the car industry fell 50 per cent.
- National income dropped 13 per cent.
- The Federal Reserve Board's index of production lost 66 per cent of the gains made during the New Deal. The fall in its index – from 117 in August 1937 to 76 in May 1938 – was faster than at the height of the Depression.
- Farmers who had made some recovery saw their prices fall by 20 per cent.

In order to get the United States out of recession, there was little choice but to return to deficit financing and the introduction of further measures. However, it was now much harder for Roosevelt to introduce legislation due to Republican gains in Congress.

- A second Agricultural Adjustment Act was introduced in 1938; it provided subsidies for food products and soil conservation. Most importantly, it established procedures to store surplus produce to distribute in poor years and imposed quotas in five staple crops.
- The Fair Labor Standards Act of 1938 was a clear indication of the difficulties faced by the government. Although the Act established maximum hours and minimum wages for workers engaged in inter-state commerce and regulated child labour, it struggled to pass. Southern conservatives argued that it was excessive government interference that would impact on southern competitiveness, which depended upon paying low wages.

As Roosevelt came towards the end of his second term in office, like Hoover before him, he was becoming a 'lame duck' president. He wanted to encourage more private housing and establish seven more planning authorities similar to the TVA, but nothing happened. Many measures did not pass Congress due to increased concern about the level of government spending. The piecemeal nature of the reforms during this period suggests that the idea of a Third New Deal is hardly sustainable, and many Americans were becoming more concerned with foreign affairs than domestic issues. Ironically, the Second World War would finally solve the USA's unemployment problem and provide US industry with the recovery it so desperately sought.

## Activity

List *five* reasons why the New Deal appeared to end by 1939. Rank these reasons in order of importance.

## Conclusion

In any assessment of the New Deal, it is essential that you decide on the aims of President Roosevelt and his government and take care not to impose other criteria on your judgement. The measures introduced by the Roosevelt administration restored faith in the government and preserved the capitalist system and democracy. Both the banking and business systems were saved as the number of failures declined rapidly, helping to bring about some stability. The government took on new roles, on a scale never previously seen, and there were no scandals despite the large sums invested.

However, Roosevelt's 'New Deals' divided the United States, challenged traditional values such as self-help, and failed to bring about an economic miracle.

Unemployment was eased as jobs were created, but how many of those jobs were real jobs? As Source O shows, unemployment did not go away. Although unemployment dropped by over half from the 1932 level by 1941, critics might suggest that the decline was the result of the natural recovery in trade. Others argue that the only substantial fall in unemployment came with rearmament and the outbreak of the Second World War in 1939.

### SOURCE O

US unemployment, 1929–41

| Year | Unemployment (millions) |
| --- | --- |
| 1929 | 5.2 |
| 1930 | 8.7 |
| 1931 | 15.9 |
| 1932 | 23.6 |
| 1933 | 24.9 |
| 1934 | 21.7 |
| 1935 | 20.1 |
| 1936 | 16.9 |
| 1937 | 14.3 |
| 1938 | 19.0 |
| 1939 | 17.2 |
| 1940 | 14.6 |
| 1941 | 9.9 |

With regards to the poorest elements of society, it can be argued that the New Deal was at worst a failure and at best did not go far enough. Although the New Deal prevented starvation and provided jobs for many, total personal income fell from $86 billion in 1929 to $73 billion in 1939, wages were lower in 1939 than in 1929, and one in five Americans was on relief in 1939. It is therefore difficult to argue that life had improved. Roosevelt also failed to redistribute income so that the poorest sectors of society gained, although this was not his aim. The position of African-Americans, Native Americans and women also saw little if any improvement (their position is discussed in greater depth in Chapter 6).

The situation of some farmers recovered, though this was often limited to those with large farms. The small farmers, labourers and sharecroppers gained little benefit from the measures, and those living in Kansas, Oklahoma, Texas and Colorado were further challenged by the impact of the dust bowl.

The position of those within industry improved when the unions gained greater control; even General Motors and Ford – who had been anti-union – recognised workers' rights. For those in employment there were other gains – prices had fallen faster than wages and therefore the employed were better off.

The return to a period of recession in 1937–38, and the decline in support for Roosevelt from 62.1 per cent in December 1937 to 54 per cent in November 1938, suggests that the USA's economic recovery was very limited. This prompted Ed Johnson, the Democrat governor of Colorado, to describe the New Deal as the 'worst fraud ever perpetrated on the American people.' Yet despite this, some saw Roosevelt as their saviour. Source P suggests the gratitude that many ordinary American people felt as a result of the policies of Roosevelt's presidency.

SOURCE P

Dear Mr President,

This is just to tell you everything is all right now. The man you sent found our house all right and we went down to the bank with him and the mortgage can go a while longer. You remember I wrote to you about losing the furniture too. Well, your man got it back for us. I never heard of a president like you, Mr Roosevelt. Mrs — and I are old folks and don't amount to much, but we are joined with those millions of others in praying for you every night. God bless you, Mr Roosevelt.

*A letter written to President Roosevelt in 1933.*

# End of chapter activities

## Paper 3 exam practice

### Question

How radical were the policies of the New Deal?
[20 marks]

### Skill focus

Writing an introductory paragraph

### Examiner's tips

Once you have planned your answer to a question (as described in Chapter 1), you should be able to begin writing a clear introductory paragraph. This needs to set out your main line of argument and to outline **briefly** the key points you intend to make (and support with relevant and precise own knowledge) in the main body of your essay. 'To what extent...?' and 'How far...?' questions clearly require you to analyse opposing arguments and reach a judgement. If, after writing your plan, you think you will be able to make a clear final judgement, it's a good idea to state in your introductory paragraph what overall line of argument/judgement you intend to make.

Depending on the wording of the question, you may also find it useful to define in your introductory paragraph what you understand by any 'key terms'. For example, 'radical' can mean different things. It could mean that:

- the reforms were far-reaching in terms of government activities and extended government intervention into new spheres
- the measures introduced new ideas for tackling the problems faced in the United States
- the New Deal challenged established values and systems.

For this question, you should:

- define the terms of the question
- consider arguments for and against the radical nature of the New Deal policies
- write an introductory paragraph that sets out your judgement.

You need to refer to different New Deal policies and consider how radical they were. You might mention:

- the US government became involved in social welfare through the Social Security Act, but the Act did not include all elements of society
- the powers of the unions were strengthened by collective bargaining
- relief schemes were provided for the unemployed through the WPA and FERA; previously relief had been left to the individual states
- farmers were paid to destroy crops, reduce production and change crops that were grown; these measures aimed to force prices up and conserve soil
- the reforms covered a wide range of issues
- the measures challenged the United States Constitution, and the Supreme Court declared many of them illegal; however, some critics argued that the reforms were not radical enough
- the Second New Deal might be seen as more radical than the First New Deal, which was more concerned with saving the system; the later measures were more concerned with long-term reform and changing the USA.

Setting out this approach in your introductory paragraph will help you keep the demands of the question in mind. Remember to refer back to your introduction after every couple of paragraphs in your main answer.

## Common mistake

A common mistake (which might suggest to an examiner that a candidate hasn't thought deeply about what's required) is to fail to write an introductory paragraph at all. This is often done by candidates who rush into writing **before** analysing the question and writing a plan. The result may well be that they fail to focus on the word 'radical' and give a long introductory account of US government policies and their achievements. This approach may result in a narrative of events from 1933 to 1939. Even if the answer is full of detailed and accurate own knowledge, this will **not** answer the question, and so will not score highly.

Remember to refer to the simplified Paper 3 markscheme on page 219.

## Sample student introductory paragraph

The New Deal affected almost every aspect of life, extending government activity and creating a range of departments, called the Alphabet Agencies. Yet Roosevelt, at least initially, would have been shocked to see the measures described as radical. In the First New Deal, his aim was to save capitalism and democracy, not radically change society. His concern was to provide relief for those suffering the worst aspects of the Depression and set the country on the road to recovery. However, by the Second New Deal, the obstruction of the Supreme Court and growing opposition from people such as Huey Long may have persuaded Roosevelt to pursue a more radical approach and introduce long-term changes to society by bringing aid to the vulnerable and challenging American values such as self-help.

This is a good introduction, as it shows a good grasp of the topic, and sets out a clear and logical plan that is clearly focused on the demands of the question. It shows a sound appreciation of the fact that, to assess success, it is first necessary to identify aims. It also explicitly demonstrates to the examiner what aspects the candidate intends to address. This indicates that the answer – if it remains analytical, and is well supported – is likely to be a high-scoring one.

## Activity

In this chapter, the focus is on writing a useful introductory paragraph. Using the information from this chapter and any other sources of information available to you, write introductory paragraphs for at least two of the following Paper 3 practice questions.

## Paper 3 practice questions

1   Assess the reasons why Hoover was so unpopular by 1932.

2   How effective were the New Deals in restoring economic prosperity to the USA?

3   To what extent was the New Deal more beneficial to farmers than to industrialists?

4   Assess the impact of opposition on the policies pursued by Roosevelt.

5   How far did the New Deal change the role of government in the USA?

6   'The First New Deal was more successful than the Second in achieving its aims.' How far do you agree with this view?

# 4 Canada and the ministries of Mackenzie King and R.B. Bennett 1929–39

## Timeline

**1929** income of Prairie Provinces $450 million; unemployment 116,000

**1930** export of Canadian cattle and dairy to USA hit by Harley–Smoot Tariff Act

**Jul:** Liberal government under Mackenzie King defeated in general election

**1931** income of Prairie Provinces falls to under $100 million; Unemployment and Farm Relief Bill; collapse of the wheat pools' central selling agency

**1932** Ottawa Conference

**Aug:** foundation of the Co-operative Commonwealth Federation in Calgary

**1933** unemployment reaches 826,000

**1934** Bank of Canada established; Natural Products Marketing Act; Commission on Price Spreads and Mass Buying established; Liberal victory in provincial elections in Ontario and Saskatchewan

**1935** Bennett announces Canadian 'New Deal' in a series of radio broadcasts; Wheat Board re-established; 'On to Ottawa' march led by Arthur Evans is stopped at Regina; Conservative government under Bennett defeated in general election

**1937** Padlock Act

**1938** unemployment at 522,000

## Key questions

- What was the impact of the Great Depression on Canada?
- Why did Mackenzie King and the Liberals lose the 1930 election?
- How successfully did the Conservative government of R. B. Bennett deal with the problems caused by the Depression?
- How successful were provincial responses to the problems caused by the Depression?
- How far did the Mackenzie King government of 1935 solve the problems caused by the Depression?

The chapter examines the impact of the Great Depression on Canada, which experienced a severe economic decline from which recovery was slow. The export market collapsed and unemployment reached record levels. However, the response of the federal government was limited, as for most of the time both Liberal and Conservative administrations followed a policy of non-intervention. When Conservative prime minister R. B. Bennett offered Canadians a 'New Deal', not only was he defeated electorally but the measures were ruled unconstitutional. There were attempts by provincial governments to bring in reforms, some of which were quite far-reaching; however, they often had limited impact. As a result, it would take the outbreak of the Second World War in 1939 to stimulate the Canadian economy.

## Overview

- The causes and consequences of the Great Depression in Canada were very similar to those of the Depression in the USA. Although there were regional variations, decline was severe and recovery was slow, ending only with the start of the Second World War.
- The Liberal government of Mackenzie King did little to address the crisis and was defeated in the 1930 election. However, Bennett's Conservative government offered only tariff reform, which worsened the crisis by damaging exports.
- In 1935, Bennett appeared to change direction and offered a 'New Deal', however this did not prevent his electoral defeat and the measures were also declared unconstitutional in 1936.
- Some new radical groups emerged at a provincial level, and this meant that more radical measures were introduced to tackle the crisis.

## What was the impact of the Great Depression on Canada?

### The causes of the Canadian depression

Robert Bothwell (*The Penguin History of Canada*, 2006) argues that Canada suffered the second most serious economic decline of all the western nations. Canada had benefited economically from the First World War, when demand for food led to an increase in the amount of land cultivated and greater demand for raw materials. This resulted in an expansion in Canadian industries and increased trade with the United States. This economic 'boom' continued into the 1920s, but was based on the export of raw materials and food to the USA and the British Empire, most notably wheat, pulp, paper and minerals. The availability of easy loans to start farming after the First World War also meant that production spread into marginal prairie lands. As a result, by the mid 1920s, Canadian grain production outstripped demand. By 1928, provinces such as Saskatchewan were producing record levels of grain, but with overproduction, wheat prices fell from 1925 onwards, reaching an all-time low in 1932. The situation left most Canadian farmers facing poverty.

*Canada's provinces and major cities*

## Comparison with the causes of the Depression in the USA

It is often assumed that Canada's economic depression, which was intense until 1933 and saw slow-moving recovery until the Second World War, had similar causes to that of the United States. As the USA received 35–45 per cent of Canada's exports in 1929, a drastic reduction in trade and spending by the USA was a major cause. In both countries there was overproduction in the agricultural sectors, and a sudden drop in demand hit farmers who were already facing falling prices. Canadian wheat production, like that of US cereals, had to adapt to changing eating patterns in Europe and North America, and the development of railways in Canada and improved machinery, such as tractors and combine harvesters, contributed to this overproduction.

The Canadian states tried to help farmers and protect them with tariffs, as in the USA. In the Canadian west, wheat pools were set up, with farmers forming huge co-operatives to store, transport and sell grain. **Mackenzie King**'s government in the 1920s completed the railway from Winnipeg to Port Churchill, which cut transport costs for wheat. To appease the Maritime Provinces (New Brunswick, Nova Scotia and Prince Edward Island), the federal government offered subsidies. Yet Canada's economic growth, like the USA's, tended to overproduction so was vulnerable to falling demand.

**William Lyon Mackenzie King (1874–1950)** Mackenzie King is the longest-serving Canadian prime minister. He trained in law and social work, a background that was reflected in his motto, 'Help those who cannot help themselves'. He led Canada throughout most of the 1920s to the 1940s, with a period of four years out of office following his defeat in the 1930 election. This domination of Canadian politics is surprising, as he lacked charisma and public-speaking skills and did not shine in radio or newsreel broadcasts. Many contemporaries saw him as cold and tactless, but he understood the Canadian temperament, and as a moderniser and compromiser he was able to guide Canada through difficult periods.

The First World War changed the context in which Canada traded, ending currency stability and the regulation of the Gold Standard. As in the United States, Canada saw an increase in stock market activity and investment in the 1920s; the Canadian federal government and state authorities also failed to establish sufficient controls on corporate finance and share dealing. Like the USA, Canada experienced a consumer boom, at least in parts of the country – generally, the eastern Maritime Provinces did not enjoy the same prosperity. Canada for the first time had a larger urban than rural population, and its urban consumer-based expansion paralleled that of the USA – with some of the same accompanying dangers:

- a considerable gap between rich and poor
- weak demand in many areas, with decline in agriculture and some regional heavy industry
- over-dependence on trade.

Rising tariffs, in the USA and the world generally, were therefore a major concern. The problem was that, with the extra output, Canada was dependent on foreign trade. The export of grain, raw materials and semi-finished goods meant that Canada was closer to a colonial economy than the massive manufacturing country of the USA.

In Canada, the degree of speculation and financial collapse in 1929 was less than in the United States. There were fewer investors and the Canadian banks had not become so uncontrolled. The massive bank failures that characterised the US crash and subsequent economic slump did not have a parallel in Canada.

Canada was also part of a larger economic network, and the Ottawa Economic Conference in 1932 lowered tariff barriers with Britain and other Commonwealth countries. However, the Canadian policy of raising tariffs by nearly 50 per cent increased the cost of imports and restricted trade. Like the USA, by increasing tariffs, Canada damaged the chances of a trade-based recovery. The Canadian dollar remained high and Canada went into a trade deficit of $125 million by 1930.

The effects of the Great Depression therefore seemed similar in the United States and Canada. Source A shows that the effects of the Great Depression on both the USA and Canada in terms of GDP, consumption, investment and exports are quite similar. This might suggest that the causes of economic depression were similar.

## SOURCE A

US and Canadian GDP, consumption, investment and exports, 1929–34

| Year | GDP | | Consumption | | Investment | | Exports | |
|------|--------|-------|--------|-------|--------|-------|--------|-------|
|      | Canada | USA   | Canada | USA   | Canada | USA   | Canada | USA   |
| 1929 | 100.0  | 100.0 | 100.0  | 100.0 | 100.0  | 100.0 | 100.0  | 100.0 |
| 1930 | 91.6   | 87.7  | 92.6   | 89.7  | 85.0   | 69.2  | 77.0   | 85.2  |
| 1931 | 77.0   | 79.7  | 81.9   | 83.8  | 50.5   | 46.1  | 58.7   | 70.5  |
| 1932 | 66.5   | 65.9  | 73.4   | 74.2  | 24.8   | 22.2  | 97.0   | 97.2  |
| 1933 | 59.6   | 62.0  | 66.9   | 70.4  | 15.2   | 21.8  | 51.9   | 52.7  |
| 1934 | 64.5   | 65.3  | 67.7   | 70.5  | 28.5   | 27.9  | 52.7   | 48.0  |

Statistics Canada, www.statcan.gc.ca/

## Activity

Draw a spider diagram to show the causes of the Great Depression in Canada. Include an explanation of how each factor caused the Depression. Finally, place the factors in order of importance and justify your choice.

However, some historians disagree with this traditional explanation, arguing that US productivity improved faster and Canadian unemployment became less severe in the 1930s. Pedro Amarol and James McGee (2002) propose that:

- the bank failures that were important in reducing the money supply in the USA did not occur in Canada
- policy shocks such as tariffs were modified in Canada by links with the British Empire
- there was a degree of federal relief, though not so much as in Roosevelt's New Deal as to delay recovery in productivity

- the farming failures were not so significant given the already depressed sector and the existing problems with bad weather creating prairie dust bowls
- there was not a dramatic stock market collapse in Canada as there had been on Wall Street
- while the economic hardships were common to both countries, the USA witnessed more long-term unemployment and less long-term decline in productivity than Canada.

SOURCE B

Can the usual explanations of the Great Depression account for the depression in Canada? Our answer is no. Money shocks, policy shocks, and terms of trade shocks cannot account for the ten-year depression. Explanations based on these shocks fail because they are quantitatively too small to explain the Great Depression.

*Pedro, A. & McGee, J. 2002. 'The Great Depression in Canada and the United States: A Neoclassical Perspective.'* Review of Economic Dynamics, *Elsevier for the Society for Economic Dynamics, vol. 5(1), January, pp. 45–72.*

## Activity

Re-read the section and complete a table like this.

| Similar causes of the Depression in Canada and USA | Brief explanation | Differences between causes of the Depression in Canada and USA | Brief explanation |
|---|---|---|---|
|  |  |  |  |
|  |  |  |  |

Then write a paragraph on whether there were more similarities or more differences in the causes of the Great Depression in Canada and the USA.

## The impact of the Depression on Canada

The decline in the Canadian economy was intense between 1929 and 1933. This was followed by a slow recovery until the outbreak of the Second World War in 1939.

### Unemployment

This economic weakening is reflected in the levels of unemployment. At its worst, unemployment rose from 4 per cent in 1929 to 27 per cent (meaning that more than 1 in 4 Canadians were unemployed) by 1933.

Canadian unemployment
figures, 1929–38

| Year | Number unemployed |
|------|-------------------|
| 1929 | 116,000 |
| 1933 | 826,000 |
| 1938 | 522,000 |

However, the official unemployment figures ignore the fairly high levels of underemployment, which may have doubled the numbers. The severity of the problem is also reflected in the numbers dependent upon relief handouts, which reached 2 million out of a population of 10 million (one in five).

## Industrial output

Canada's economic decline is reflected in virtually every set of industrial figures available. In the period 1929 to 1932, income fell by about 50 per cent, imports by 55 per cent and exports by 25 per cent. Figures for industrial production show that in 1932, production was 58 per cent of the 1929 level and was the second lowest level in the world after the United States. The same was true of the total national income: by 1932 it was only 55 per cent of the 1929 level and was the second worst behind the United States.

## Trade

As a nation of exporters, Canada was badly hit by tariffs, especially those imposed by the USA. The Harley–Smoot Tariff of 1930 virtually halted the export of Canadian cattle and dairy produce to the United States. However, the situation was made worse by the fact that two of Canada's main export markets, Britain and the USA, also dramatically reduced their imports.

## Regional differences

The impact of the Depression varied from province to province: the Prairie Provinces (Alberta, Saskatchewan and Manitoba) were the worst hit.

### Prairie lands

Wheat prices were already falling and exports were in decline, but tariffs only made the situation worse. Levels of production hit record heights in 1928, with prices at $2 per bushel, but in 1929 prices halved, falling to 35 cents a bushel in 1932. The downturn left farmers in need of relief. Added to this, some areas were also hit by severe drought, most notably south Saskatchewan and the adjoining corners of Alberta and Manitoba, which would experience virtually no rain for seven years; the area became a dust bowl as topsoil was lost in dust storms.

This disaster was followed by a plague of grasshoppers that devoured crops. Yields fell from 23.5 bushels per acre in 1928 to 6.4 bushels per acre by 1937, and the income of the Prairie Provinces fell from $450 million in 1928 to under $100 million by 1931.

The consequences of this were severe. Some 200,000 people left their farms in the 1930s, and in Saskatchewan province, per capita income fell 71 per cent in three years, with two-thirds of the population living on public assistance. This trend was repeated in Alberta, where income fell 61 per cent between 1929 and 1933. The wheat pools responsible for selling grain and making loans to farmers were unable to cope. They faced mounting debts and had to appeal to the provincial governments for support; however, the provincial governments were unable to meet their needs and the wheat pools had to appeal to the federal government in Ottawa for financial aid.

## Activity

The impact of the Depression on Canada varied from province to province. Working in a group, consider a range of provinces, with each student researching one province to find out how badly it was hit by the Depression during the early 1930s. You could consider:

- unemployment
- production levels
- the numbers on relief
- income.

Many histories of Canada, such as *Canada, 1900–1945* (1990) by Ian Drummond, Robert Bothwell and John English, or *Canada's First Century* (1970) by Donald Creighton, have sections on the impact of the Depression on the various provinces.

### Industrial regions

Hard times fell not just in the agricultural sector. Industrial production also dropped dramatically as the following statistics show.

- Rail production declined 88 per cent between 1929 and 1933–34.
- Washing machine sales dropped 42 per cent and sales of stoves by 61 per cent between 1929 and 1933.
- Car production fell significantly – from 128,496 in 1929 to just 30,606 in 1933.
- Investment in new businesses dropped 79 per cent between 1929 and 1933.
- Capital expenditure on new construction, machinery and equipment declined by 70 per cent between 1929 and 1932.

In many ways, the working classes were worse hit than the farmers, as they were unable to live off the land and so became more dependent upon charity and benefits. In the Canadian House of Commons, the socialist party leader J. S. Woodsworth portrayed the impact of the Depression on Canada's cities in stark terms:

SOURCE D

In the old days we could send people from the cities to the country. If they went out today they would meet another army of unemployed coming back from the country to the city; that outlet is closed. What can these people do? They have been driven from our parks; they have been driven from our streets; they have been driven from our buildings, and in this city [Ottawa] they actually took refuge on the garbage heaps.

*James Shaver Woodsworth, leader of the socialist Co-operative Commonwealth Federation (CCF), speaking to the Canadian parliament in 1931.*

This industrial decline was reflected in virtually every industry.

- The newsprint industry operated at 53 per cent of its capacity.
- Mineral prices fell; the export value of non-ferrous metals dropped 60 per cent between 1929 and 1932.
- National income dropped 45 per cent between October 1929 and 1932, and reached its lowest recorded level.

The western provinces suffered the most from this industrial decline. Canada was hit by what some economists describe as the 'multiple accelerator process', where there is a decline because of a contraction in various parts of the economy – plant, equipment, residential construction, inventories and exports – but recovery depends upon the revival of these same elements. Recovery was slow because the export market did not revive and business did not invest.

The provincial governments struggled to cope with this decline. They had expanded their social commitments and services throughout the growth period of the 1920s, but were now unable to pay relief, which cost $1 billion between 1930 and 1937.

Barry Broadfoot (*Ten Lost Years, 1929–1939*, McClelland & Stewart, 1997) is one of several historians who describe this period in Canada's history as a lost decade. Robert Bothwell, Ian Drummond and John English (*Canada, 1900–1945*) refer to it as 'a decade of desperation, anger and broken dreams'. Even the recovery was limited, with per capita output in 1938 ($1480) remaining lower than it had been in 1929 ($1680).

However, for those who remained in work, the decade was not as bleak: real wages rose as prices fell faster than wages. This may have benefited those in the cities, but the collapse in agricultural prices was so great that no farmers benefited from it.

### Discussion point

Which do you think was more severely hit by the Depression – Canadian agriculture or industry? Explain your point of view fully.

## Why did Mackenzie King and the Liberals lose the 1930 election?

The Liberal government of Mackenzie King suffered a severe defeat in the 1930 election, winning 91 seats compared to the Conservatives' 137. It was hardly surprising that the government in power when the Depression began should suffer at the hands of the electorate, particularly as it had done so little to tackle the deepening crisis.

Mackenzie King had been Liberal leader since 1919, so was experienced in government. However, as with most politicians of the time, he was baffled by the events of 1929 and 1930; at the opening of the 1930 parliament he boasted that employment levels were at a record high and that the recent decline was no more than 'seasonal slackness'. Despite concerns expressed by the Conservative opposition about unemployment and the need to help the provincial governments with relief, Mackenzie King stated that relief payments were extravagant and unnecessary, as there was no sign of an emergency.

As the crisis deepened, Mackenzie King offered no programme for recovery, only an increase in tariffs to protect industry, which served to make the economic situation worse. He essentially followed a similar policy to that associated with US president Herbert Hoover – namely 'rugged individualism'.

Throughout the 1920s, the Liberal government made reducing debt after the First World War and tax cuts their main concerns, and they were determined to continue this policy. As most politicians did not understand either the causes or the depth of the financial crisis, it is not surprising that the Liberal government did not consider increasing spending to try to stimulate the economy.

Mackenzie King was unwilling to provide help to the provinces, as he believed they would use the funds for purposes other than tackling unemployment. He also believed that if there was a problem – and it was a long time before he actually acknowledged that there *was* a problem – then it was the responsibility of the provinces to deal with it. He even stated that he would not give 'a five cent piece' of relief money to any province with a Conservative government. Since provincial governments were unable to cope, they passed the problem of relief on to the municipalities, which increasingly relied on church groups and local charities; the government believed that its intervention would only damage this system and make matters worse.

Despite Mackenzie King's wish to ignore the worst effects of the crisis, the Conservative leader **R. B. Bennett** was determined to make the economy the central piece of his election campaign. He argued that the Liberal attitude towards the crisis showed their corrupt and uncaring views, accusing the government of 'timidity' in allowing the Canadian economy to weaken. Bennett stated that he would end unemployment or 'perish in the attempt', promising to increase public works, take over the provinces' responsibility for old age pensions, and raise tariffs on goods entering Canada unless other countries agreed to lower tariffs on goods from Canada.

**Richard Bedford Bennett (1870–1947)** Bennett worked as a lawyer and businessman before becoming a politician. He grew up in poverty on a small family farm, and from this he developed his habit of thrift. In 1897, he moved to Alberta, becoming the first leader of the Alberta Conservative Party in 1905. He was a loner who never married, living in hotels and boarding houses; his social life revolved around the church. Bennett was Canadian minister of finance in the short-lived Conservative administration of Arthur Meighen in 1926. When the Conservatives lost the election, Meighen resigned and was replaced by Bennett as leader. He served as Canada's prime minister between 1930 and 1935. He retired to Britain in 1938.

Bennett's most famous attack on the Mackenzie King government is shown in Source E.

### SOURCE E

Mackenzie King promises you conferences; I promise you action. He promises consideration of the problem of unemployment; I promise to end unemployment. Which plan do you like best?

*R. B. Bennett speaking in the 1930 election campaign.*

The answer the electorate gave to Bennett's question was clear: the Conservatives ended a period of Liberal dominance, winning 48.5 per cent of the popular vote while the Liberals polled only 45.2 per cent. Mackenzie King's lack of understanding contributed to the Liberals' electoral defeat. Mackenzie King's diary entry (Source F) suggests an even clearer view of his attitude towards the problem:

### SOURCE F

The truth is I feel I do not much care, the load is very heavy and I would gladly do literary work for a while.

*Diary entry by Mackenzie King following electoral defeat in 1930.*

### Activity

Write a newspaper front page for the day after the 1930 Canadian election. It should explain and give reasons for the scale of the Conservative victory.

## How successfully did the Conservative government of R. B. Bennett deal with the problems caused by the Depression?

Despite Bennett's promises to end unemployment and introduce social acts, he was a firm believer in capitalism and free enterprise. Bennett was therefore reluctant to increase government intervention to stem the growing crisis. He introduced very few measures to tackle unemployment, and initial actions were focused on the preservation of order. However, it would be unfair to ignore the fact that one of Bennett's first acts upon becoming prime minister was to put aside $20 million for emergency relief out of a total budget of $500 million (equivalent to 4 per cent of the budget). This amount was wholly inadequate given the extent of the economic crisis. Mackenzie King described it as financially irresponsible, as he believed it was not the government's responsibility to use taxes to fund relief.

### The preservation of law and order

Bennett's early policies were dominated by the preservation of law and order, and appeared distinctly repressive:

- he used spies to report back on union meetings
- unemployed marchers were dispersed

- agitators were randomly arrested and deported under an amendment to the Immigration Act
- radical periodicals and books were censored.

The culmination of these measures was the establishment of government work camps for unemployed, unmarried men, who Bennett feared would cause unrest. The Department of National Defence organised the camps, paying the men 20 cents a day, a low amount even during the Depression years. The members of these camps became known as the 'Royal Twenty Centers', but there was nothing appealing about the camps, which were described by its members as 'slave camps'.

*Road workers from the Canadian labour camps pose proudly, 1931; they cleared a stretch of highway in Ontario that would later be a link in the Trans-Canada Highway*

### The 'On to Ottawa' protest

By 1935, there were strikes led by the radical trade unionist **Arthur Evans** (see page 106). Former camp members boarded trains in Vancouver and headed for Ottawa to present their complaints, in what became known as the 'On to Ottawa' protest. Initially, there were about 1000 protestors, but by the time they had reached Regina, numbers had grown to 1500. Bennett was determined to stop the protestors reaching Ottawa and invited Evans for talks, but they failed.

Evans returned to his supporters more determined than ever, while Bennett called in the Royal Canadian Mounted Police (RCMP) and the Regina Police Service, who seized the leaders of the protest. This resulted in riots on 1 July 1935, with a policeman killed, many more injured and 130 arrests. The riot marked the end of the march, which was the most serious direct challenge to Bennett's government.

**Arthur Evans (1890–1944)** Arthur 'Slim' Evans was born in Toronto. A colourful character, he led various mining unions and was sentenced to time in prison for striking. He was also a member of the Communist Party. He achieved his greatest prominence with the 'On to Ottawa' march, which – although it was dispersed – resulted in the reform of the camps and may have helped defeat R. B. Bennett in the 1935 elections.

*Unemployed men at a relief camp in Calgary, Alberta, prepare to board boxcars destined for Ottawa, Ontario, to demand jobs at decent wages from the federal government, June 1935*

## Relief

In 1931, Bennett introduced the Unemployment and Farm Relief Bill, which authorised spending of unlimited amounts for relief. The Bill also gave the authorities special powers to combat unrest based on 'pernicious' (harmful) revolutionary doctrines.

During the 1920s, the rights of provincial governments grew, and they had defended the North America Act, which made them responsible for welfare and relief costs. However, the depth of the crisis meant that the provincial governments were heading towards bankruptcy. The provinces and municipalities had inadequate revenues and they had borrowed large sums in the 1920s when the economy was expanding, so they were unable to cope when the economy contracted.

Through the Unemployment Relief Act of 1931, central government contributed towards relief funds, although Bennett expected the municipalities to contribute 50 per cent, which was an unrealistic figure. When the Canadian prairie province of Manitoba asked the government to contribute 80 per cent, a further Relief Act was brought in – during August 1931 – to deal with the crisis. However, the relief funds were still not enough, and Manitoba had to cut the wages of its civil servants and ask for additional government funds to meet its old age pension payments.

As the crisis deepened, provincial governments moved towards bankruptcy, which would have had a catastrophic impact on Canadian credit. The federal government therefore intervened to bail out the provinces. Bennett could not allow the provinces to default on payments on loans, but he was reluctant to support them financially. When British Columbia tried to spend its way out of the crisis by increasing relief and grants on mining and fishing, the national government declined to aid them. However, British Columbia's provincial government was able to argue for 'equality of treatment', noting that other states had been helped.

By January 1934, Bennett was telling the provinces that they 'were wasteful and extravagant.' He even told Ontario and Quebec that they were rich enough to manage their own problems. In this way, the crisis focused attention on the relationship between the national government in Ottawa and the provincial governments. It could be argued that, until the very end of Bennett's ministry, it was the provinces that put forward the more radical proposals and not the federal government. (The role of the provincial governments will be examined in detail on pages 112–17.) Meanwhile, Bennett's measures were viewed as little more than gestures designed to preserve law and order and pay unemployment benefit, rather than actions designed to tackle the causes of the problems head-on.

## Tariff reform

The major policy that Bennett introduced was reform to the tariff system. He promised to 'blast a way into the markets of the world', arguing that the reforms would take Canada back into the export market on which it depended heavily. Certainly, Bennett needed to increase revenue from tariffs at a time when Ottawa's federal government took on responsibility for paying the unemployed. He therefore raised tariffs on imports by nearly 50 per cent, and although this protected domestic industry and ended the trade deficit, it hit Canadian imports. In the long run, therefore, it did more harm than good, damaging the export sector on which Canada relied. The tariffs also impacted on the domestic market, as Canadian products were expensive and therefore the buying power of Canadians declined.

*Cartoon titled 'Blame it on Bennett' by Arthur George Racey, published in the* Montreal Star, *21 March 1931*

## Other measures

Bennett introduced other measures during his ministry.

- In 1932, he launched the Canadian Radio Broadcasting Commission.
- Also in 1932, Bennett established a basis for a national air transport system; it was partly a relief construction project designed to provide work for the unemployed.
- In 1934, the Bank of Canada was created to regulate currency, monetary policy and advise the government. However, its impact was limited, as those who ran it did not release credit.
- In 1934, the Natural Products Marketing Act established a nationwide network through which farmers would have to sell their goods. This met with limited success, though, as individual provinces, such as British Columbia, introduced their own laws and the government was forced to exempt provincial marketing boards.
- In 1931, the wheat pools' central selling agency collapsed. Bennett appointed John A. MacFarland as the agency's general manager, and attempts were made to restore some level to the price of grain. Then, in 1935, Bennett established a new Canadian Wheat Board.

None of these policies had a profound impact, and they did little to dispel the sense of crisis that gripped Canada. Bennett became the scapegoat for frustrated Canadians. He had promised much in the 1930 election campaign, but failed to deliver. Consequently his name became synonymous with failure: broken-down cars were known as 'Bennett buggies'; hot water and barley became 'Bennett tea'; shanty towns were 'Bennett-burghs' (the Canadian equivalent of 'Hoovervilles'); abandoned farms were 'Bennett barnyards'. The collapse of the Canadian economy was such that in places the usual forms of trade were replaced by exchange – a doctor in Ontario reported that farmers could no longer afford to pay for healthcare and that in the winter of 1933–34 he had received 'over twenty chickens, several ducks, geese, a turkey, potatoes and wood on account'. At the same time, many workers became transient in their search for employment. Many moved west towards Vancouver, where at least the climate was better. Immigrants on relief were deported; some 30,000 were sent back to Europe in the 1930s.

## A more radical response?

In 1934, Bennett established a select committee on price spreads and mass buying. Many felt that big stores were abusing their buying power and forcing manufacturers to sell at drastically reduced prices. This kept wages down and resulted in poor conditions in factories. The committee was the result of a speech made by **Harry Stevens**, the minister for trade and commerce. His previous proposals for action had been rejected, but in January 1934 he addressed a convention of boot and shoe manufacturers in Toronto and attacked working conditions in clothing trades and meat-packing firms. Bennett told him to make a public retraction; Stevens refused and resigned, but Bennett ignored his resignation and decided that the charges needed to be investigated. Stevens was appointed to chair the committee, with the power to investigate the causes and consequences of the large difference between product and consumer prices. This investigation appeared to change the fortunes of the Conservative party, who now seemed to be working on the side of the shop assistants, workers, farmers and small merchants.

**Henry 'Harry' Stevens (1878–1973)** Stevens was born in Bristol, England, but went to live in Canada at the age of nine. He entered politics following a personal anti-crime crusade in Vancouver where he reported on the seedy behaviour in many nightclubs. He became an MP in 1911 and was appointed minister of trade in 1930 by R. B. Bennett. He chaired the Royal Commission on Price Spreads and Mass Buying, but when many of its recommendations were ignored he resigned from the Cabinet. Despite having support within the Conservative Party, he refused to challenge Bennett for the leadership and instead founded the Reconstruction Party, although he was the only candidate elected. In 1938, he rejoined the Conservative Party, but failed to win election after 1940.

This was not the only consequence of the select committee. Historians such as Donald Creighton (*Canada's First Century*, 1970) argue that these revelations were the final part of Bennett's transformation from laissez-faire individualism to policies that increased state power, regulation and control. According to Creighton, this led Bennett to call for a Canadian 'New Deal', which he announced to the nation in a series of radio broadcasts in January 1935. Creighton argues that it was Bennett's Christianity that provided him with a social conscience, and that he was troubled by the evidence from the select committee. In perhaps his most telling remark, Bennett stated in January 1935, 'if we cannot abolish the dole, we should abolish the system'. According to Creighton, Bennett became convinced that the evils of capitalism could be cured by government controls and services. It is also possible that Roosevelt's 'New Deal' influenced him, heightening his belief in the need for action and the possibility of introducing a similar programme in Canada. After all, Roosevelt was able to silence his opponents; it might be possible for Bennett to do the same in Canada.

For many contemporary observers, Bennett's proposed 'New Deal' was an about-turn; he appeared to have abandoned his long-held belief in individualism. The announcement came as a surprise to many; Bennett had even failed to inform his own cabinet in advance of his proposals.

Bennett announced a series of measures in January 1935 that he wanted the pre-election parliamentary session to pass. They included:

- unemployment insurance
- a minimum wage
- a limit on the number of hours that could be worked
- the extension of federally backed farm credit
- fair trade and anti-monopoly legislation
- farm rehabilitation measures to deal with soil erosion and water conservation
- reorganisation of the Wheat Board to oversee and control prices
- amendments to the Combines Act and the Companies Act
- a review of price spreads by the Criminal Code and Industry Commission.

## SOURCE G

In the anxious years through which you have passed, you have been the witness of grave defects and abuses in the capitalist system. Unemployment and waste are the proof of these. Great changes are taking place about us. New conditions prevail. These require modifications in the capitalist system to enable that system more effectively to serve the people.

*R. B. Bennett speaking in 1935.*

This sudden conversion to state intervention left Bennett open to charges of political opportunism as the 1935 election approached. It also destroyed his image as a hard-line Conservative. Bennett's critics argue that it was a 'deathbed conversion': Bennett was not sincere and simply wanted to win an election. James Gray (*R. B. Bennett*, University of Toronto Press, 1991) and P. B. Waite (*In Search of R. B. Bennett*, McGill-Queen's University Press, 2012) counter this view, supporting Creighton's argument that Bennett gradually recognised the weaknesses of the capitalist system and became committed to reform based on government regulation. On the other hand, historians such as Robert Bothwell (*Canada, 1900–1945*, 1990) suggest that Bennett embarked on this course to regain popularity. They argue that Bennett feared the growing popularity of Harry Stevens following his work on the select committee on price spreads and mass buying; that therefore he was trying to save his leadership of the party and his political career.

Bennett's proposals divided the cabinet, although the measures were enacted. Within parliament, the most significant attacks on Bennett's 'New Deal' came from Mackenzie King, who questioned whether parliament had the legal power to authorise the measures:

## SOURCE A

Tell this House whether as leader of the government, knowing that a question will come up immediately as to the jurisdiction of this Parliament, and of the provincial legislatures in matters of social legislation, he has secured an opinion from the law officers of the Crown or from the Supreme Court of Canada which will be a sufficient guarantee to this House to proceed with these measures as being without question within its jurisdiction.

*Mackenzie King speaking in 1935.*

Mackenzie King went on the offensive, portraying Bennett as a dictator who was undermining the Canadian constitution in order to remain in power. The Liberals also argued that high tariffs had prolonged rather than eased the economic problems and made recovery much harder. Mackenzie King was therefore able to launch the 1935 Liberal election campaign under the slogan 'King or Chaos?'

Moreover, during disputes within the cabinet, Bennett failed to support Harry Stevens, even though many of the proposals were Stevens' ideas. This gave further weight to the argument that Bennett was concerned about the growing influence of Stevens and was willing to abandon him to save his own position. Stevens resigned his office again, this time setting up the Reconstruction Party. This only served to further weaken the Conservative Party in the run-up to the 1935 election.

It appeared that Bennett only produced a far-reaching programme for change as the 1935 election approached. The measures he introduced beforehand were very limited in scope and were nowhere near as far-reaching as President Roosevelt's New Deal. It seemed that Bennett's Conservative government were waiting for the natural trade cycle of growth and recession to recover without government intervention, while ministers struggled to abandon their long-held liberal beliefs.

It is therefore not surprising that many onlookers were sceptical about Bennett's proposals. Furthermore, the measures were subject to legal challenges as they interfered with the powers and responsibilities of the provincial governments.

Yet, at the same time, if Canada's federal government failed to produce an innovative response to the crisis, some provincial legislatures went much further. They introduced, or attempted to introduce, reforms that conflicted with the ideals of the national government. This led to disputes between the two over their legality and desirability, as discussed in the next section.

## Activity

Create a balance sheet like this to show the successes and failures of Bennett's administration in terms of dealing with the social and economic problems it faced.

| Problem | Evidence of success | Evidence of failure |
|---|---|---|
| Unemployment | | |
| Agriculture | | |
| | | |

# How successful were provincial responses to the problems caused by the Depression?

If the response of the Canadian federal government to the crisis of the Great Depression was somewhat limited, the response of some of Canada's provincial governments was more radical.

## Radical responses

There was an increase in radicalism in Canadian politics after the First World War.

## Communism

The Canadian Communist Party was founded in 1921, but it was virtually banned during the Depression, as both federal and provincial governments took strong measures against any organisation they considered to be a threat to the established order. The party's leader Tim Buck and eight other prominent communists were arrested in August 1931 in a raid on the party headquarters. They were not charged with any crimes, but were held as political prisoners; a clear indication of the almost hysterical reaction of the government that followed on from Bennett's promise to crush communism. Buck was jailed for five years; while in jail, guards fired into his cell. Although he survived, there was an attempted cover up, and when the story eventually broke, the minister of justice Hugh Guthrie defended the guards' actions, stating that the shots were 'only to frighten him'.

Such measures did not prevent a number of provinces producing or electing more radical parties with more far-reaching proposals to deal with Canada's severe economic decline.

## Canada's socialist party: the CCF

The only party to successfully challenge the established economic and social order at a federal level was the Co-operative Commonwealth Federation (CCF), which formed in Calgary, Alberta, in August 1932. It developed from farmers' parties and labour unions and encouraged a policy of 'democratic socialism'.

In 1933, the CCF issued the Regina Manifesto, which called for a new social order. This would be reflected in the nationalisation of key industries and banks, a national minimum wage, a free health service, child allowance, unemployment benefits and state-owned farms. The desire for a socialist state was very clear in the final sentence of its manifesto:

### SOURCE 1

No CCF Government will rest content until it has eradicated capitalism and put into operation a full programme of socialised planning which will lead to the establishment in Canada of the Co-operative Commonwealth.

*Extract from the Regina Manifesto, 1933.*

The appeal of the party was reflected in its electoral success, with seven CCF MPs elected in 1935. Moreover, the party became the official opposition in British Columbia and Saskatchewan, but was unable to make significant progress in the Maritime Provinces.

Although the CCF was not able to win control of any provincial government, it provided the Canadian people with an alternative to the traditional Liberal and Conservative parties. However, it was after the Depression, in 1944, that the party had its greatest triumph when Tommy Douglas, a Baptist minister and labour activist, became the premier of Saskatchewan and head of the first socialist government in Canada.

## The Social Credit Party

In Alberta in 1932, **William Aberhart**, better known as 'Bible Bill', proposed his theory of social credit. He put forward the very simple view that consumers simply did not have enough money to spend. In order to overcome this problem, the government would provide them with cash vouchers, called social dividends or credit, to overcome the difference and fuel a recovery.

**William Aberhart (1878–1943)** Aberhart was known as 'Bible Bill' because of his outspoken Baptist views. He was born in Ontario and later trained as a teacher. He became involved with politics with the onset of the Depression, and founded the Social Credit Party. This won him widespread appeal and the party gained 54 per cent of the popular vote in 1935. Although the Supreme Court overturned Aberhart's programme, he was able to introduce public works and some poor relief. He was premier of Alberta from 1935 to 1943. The Social Credit Party remained in power in the province until 1971, though it abandoned Aberhart's economic theories after his death.

Aberhart stood for election to the Alberta provincial parliament in 1935, promising payments of $25 per month to every adult. Given this commitment, it is hardly surprising that he won a landslide victory. He introduced some of the more innovative reforms: bills to freeze debt collection; a government-sponsored crop insurance scheme; reform to labour and welfare programmes.

'Social credit' presented a different challenge, however. People were soon queuing outside government offices wanting their $25, and although Aberhart tried to avoid the issue, his own backbenchers forced him to act. In 1937, the Alberta Provincial Parliament brought in legislation that allowed the issuing of social credit. However, monetary policy was a federal responsibility and the federal government in Ottawa disallowed it, while Canada's Supreme Court declared it unconstitutional. Despite this, the Social Credit Party had some electoral success, with 17 Social Credit MPs elected in 1935. The party continued to do well in provincial elections in both Alberta and British Columbia until 1965, when it won only five seats in the federal election.

## Union Nationale

In the province of Quebec, the Liberals were defeated in 1936 by a coalition known as Union Nationale, led by **Maurice Duplessis**. Some reforms were introduced, most notably to provide rural credit and extend farm aid to help agriculture. However, the Union Nationale was more conservative in its outlook and took a strong line in dealing with protests, unions and radicalism. This was demonstrated most clearly with the 1937 'Padlock Act', which allowed the government to arrest anyone from any location that was suspected of being used by communists. The government was also able to jail anyone for a year for publishing, printing or distributing communist material without the right to appeal. What made the Act so severe was the lack of definition of communism – this effectively meant the government could remove anyone it did not like!

*Cartoon of social credit, 1936, by cartoonist Arch Dale, published in the Winnipeg Free Press*

**Maurice Duplessis (1890–1959)** Duplessis trained as a lawyer. He entered politics in 1927 and became the Conservative Party leader in 1933. In 1936 the Conservative Party merged with Action Libérale Nationale (ALN) to became the Union Nationale, winning a large majority. Duplessis was premier of Quebec from 1936–39 and again from 1944–59. His time in office was known as 'The Great Darkness' because of widespread corruption. Duplessis championed provincial rights and anti-communism.

# Moves to increase provincial rights

It was not just from new groupings that the Canadian government faced challenges. This was seen most clearly in Ontario and British Columbia.

In Ontario, **Mitchell 'Mitch' Hepburn** (see page 116) was elected on a reform programme; however, his policies were hard-line and repressive. This was seen most clearly in his handling of the Oshawa car plant strike in 1937. He asked Mackenzie King to send in the Royal Canadian Mounted Police (RCMP) but was refused, so Hepburn put together his own force of vigilantes.

**Mitchell Hepburn (1896–1953)** Hepburn wanted to pursue a legal career, but he left school after he was accused of throwing an apple at a visiting dignitary. He worked as a bank clerk, joined the Liberal Party and was elected to the Canadian parliament in 1926. In the same year he became leader of the party in Ontario. As premier of Ontario (1934–42), he followed an austerity policy that involved firing a large number of civil servants.

In British Columbia, **Thomas Dufferin 'Duff' Pattullo** engaged in a similar struggle. Pattullo wanted to extend provincial rights so that he could introduce a range of relief schemes. The province endured growing labour unrest and Pattullo was determined to set up his 'little New Deal' specifically to meet the needs of British Columbia. Pattullo was able to bring in what has been described as the most progressive system of social services in Canada, but he failed to bring in Canada's first public healthcare system, as doctors blocked it.

**Thomas Dufferin Patullo (1873–1956)** Patullo was born in Ontario, where he initially worked as a journalist. He later moved to Prince Rupert, British Columbia, where he was elected mayor. He was elected to the provincial government in 1916 as a Liberal, and following their defeat in 1928 he became Liberal Party leader. In 1933 he led the Liberals back into government. He tried to extend government services and relief to help tackle the Depression. The Liberal Party was re-elected in 1937 on a programme of 'socialised capitalism', but failed to win a majority in 1941. Patullo's leadership ended when he refused to form a coalition government.

Even in states such as Nova Scotia, where little appeared to be done to tackle the effects of the Depression, the provincial premier Donald Macdonald set up a Royal Commission of Enquiry into the economic condition of the province as the first step to reform.

## Conclusion

Attempts to bring about Canada's economic revival can be found in the provinces more than at a federal level, as only Bennett's 1935 'New Deal' attempted a wide-ranging plan for recovery. However, as the next section will show, that plan was declared unconstitutional and therefore much depended upon provincial action.

Although some new groupings were formed, in other provinces Liberal provincial politicians offered measures to stop the abuses of laissez-faire capitalism and attempted to introduce state regulation and public services. These attempts were reflected in an electoral shift towards the left in many provinces. For example, in Ontario, the Liberals ended 29 years of Conservative rule in 1934; and there was a Liberal victory in Saskatchewan in 1934, with the CCF replacing the Conservatives as the main opposition.

These provincial election results suggest the disillusionment of many Canadians at the failings of Bennett's Conservative government. This was reflected in Bennett's crushing defeat in the 1935 federal election.

## Activity

Create a summary chart like this to show what each Canadian province did to tackle the problems caused by the Depression.

| Province | Measures taken | Successes | Failures | Overall judgement /10 |
|---|---|---|---|---|
| Alberta | | | | |
| Quebec | | | | |
| Ontario | | | | |
| British Columbia | | | | |
| | | | | |

Next, analyse the measures taken to determine their success. In light of your analysis, award each province a mark out of 10 depending upon their level of success – the higher the mark, the greater the level of success.

# How far did the Mackenzie King government of 1935 solve the problems caused by the Depression?

The Conservative Party paid the price for its half-hearted response to the Depression. In the 1935 federal elections, its share of the vote collapsed to 29 per cent. However, the election result also showed that the Canadian public had rejected the reforming programmes proposed by R. B. Bennett and Harry Stevens, as well as the more radical and socialist ideas of the CCF. Victory went to the Liberals, the party with the least to offer in terms of welfare support, as Mackenzie King simply promised a return to free trade. However, it should be noted that the Social Credit Party winning all the seats in Alberta and the CCF winning seven seats nationally aided the scale of Mackenzie King's victory, as the Liberals failed to win a majority of the popular vote.

## Conservative policy after 1935

Mackenzie King was fortunate to be returned to power at the same time as the economy started to show signs of improvement with the recovery of the natural trade cycle. This economic revival was very slow, however, and required assistance. Recovery was more sluggish in the Prairie States than in the Maritime Provinces or Quebec, where there was greater economic diversity.

Mackenzie King followed a cautious policy, described by A. R. M. Lower (*Colony to Nation: A History of Canada,* Longmans, Green & Company, 1946) as 'the politics of fear.' Lower described the Conservative government as 'the huddling together of frightened people uncertain of their way in a chaotic world'. Mackenzie King was elected in 1935 with no proposals to improve the situation; rather, his victory reflected Bennett's unpopularity and Mackenzie King's claims that Bennett was a tyrant who threatened the Canadian Constitution and way of life.

## Reversing Bennett's 'New Deal'

One of Mackenzie King's first acts was to refer much of Bennett's 'New Deal' legislation to the Supreme Court. By 1936, the legislation was ruled unconstitutional as it infringed provincial authority, particularly the right of the provinces to deal with matters of property and civil rights. The Supreme Court denied that the Depression was a national emergency that justified a wide interpretation of federal powers in matters of trade and allowed the federal government's intervention. This raises the question of what was necessary before the Supreme Court considered a national emergency to have occurred. It could be argued that the Constitution of Canada had become a block to better social services.

### Activity

Imagine you are Mackenzie King. Write a speech to parliament explaining why you are referring the Bennett legislation to the Supreme Court.

## Provincial resistance to financial reforms

Despite reversing Bennett's programme for reform, the federal government still had to bail out the provinces; it had become the 'bank of the last resort'. In order to manage this problem, in December 1935 Mackenzie King proposed the setting up of a Loan Council for each province. This idea was rejected by Alberta, which saw it as another way for the federal government to influence the provinces. As a result, the federal government abandoned its loan policy and, on 1 April 1936, Alberta became the first province to default on its payments.

Alberta had tried to reduce the interest it paid, but the courts ruled that this was not permissible. Manitoba also appeared as if it would default, but this time the federal government intervened. The more impoverished provinces, such as Nova Scotia, New Brunswick, Prince Edward Island, Saskatchewan and Manitoba, were more willing to accept a reduction in their powers; the exception was Alberta, where the Social Credit Party was unwilling to relinquish control.

A similar problem arose when Mackenzie King attempted to introduce a national scheme of unemployment insurance. This would have given equal benefits across the whole country, but the proposal was defeated because of provincial opposition. The wealthier provincial governments, such as Ontario and Quebec, were concerned that they would have to contribute more, and that the principle would be extended to other services. It is therefore hardly surprising that there was little positive achievement in dealing with the problems created by the Depression, as provinces appeared more concerned to protect their rights than co-operate with the federal government.

## The Royal Commission on Dominion–Provincial Relations

As a consequence of these problems, a Royal Commission on Dominion–Provincial Relations was established in 1937, although its report was not published until 1940. However, the Commission did eventually help to resolve some of the problems of the Depression. Its aim was to ensure that there would be 'normal Canadian services with no more than normal Canadian taxation'. When the provinces were unable to provide, the federal government would offer assistance through National Adjustment Grants. The Commission also accepted that the federal government had exclusive taxation powers and would finance unemployment insurance and old age pensions (two of the issues that had caused the provinces such financial difficulties during the 1930s).

### Activity

Find out more details about the Royal Commission on Dominion–Provincial Relations. Consider why it was established, when it reported, why it took so long and how its findings affected the Canadian Constitution.

# Conclusion

Despite the failure of two Canadian governments to introduce a programme of welfare and economic reforms, by 1935 seven of the provinces were ruled by Liberal governments and it was only Alberta, with the Social Credit Party, that was anti-liberal. Canada also had the same prime minister at the end of the period as at the start; the Constitution had not changed; the same political parties still represented the nation. In this sense, despite the difficulties, the population had rejected the alternatives, limited though they were, and returned to a party and leader that offered little state help. It would not be government policies that solved the problems caused by the Depression, but an upturn in the trade cycle and, most importantly, the outbreak of the Second World War in 1939. Many of the volunteers who fought in the war were from Canada's relief camps and work projects.

# End of chapter activities

## Paper 3 exam practice

### Question

Assess the success of the provincial governments' response to the problems of the Depression.
[20 marks]

### Skill focus

Avoiding irrelevance

### Examiner's tips

Do not waste valuable writing time on irrelevant material. If it's irrelevant, it won't gain you any marks. This problem can arise because:

- the candidate does not look carefully enough at the wording of the question (see pages 45–46)
- the candidate ignores the fact that the questions require selection of facts, an analytical approach and a final judgement; instead, the candidate just writes down all they know about a topic (relevant or not) and hopes the examiner will do the analysis and make the judgement
- the candidate has unwisely restricted their revision. For example, if a question crops up on the success of the provincial governments in dealing with the problems of the Depression, a candidate may write about the response of the federal government, because that was the topic they wanted to write about!

Whatever the reason, such responses rarely address any of the demands of the question.

For this question, you will need to look at:

- the problems and difficulties faced by the provincial governments
- the measures they introduced
- how far the measures they introduced addressed the problems
- the successes and failures in different provinces
- the longer-term changes.

You also need to discuss views about the extent of failure and disappointment, and how far the federal government blocked any measures.

# Common mistakes

One common error with this type of question is for candidates to write about material they know well, rather than material directly related to the question.

Another mistake candidates often make is to present too much general information, instead of material that is specific to the person, period and command terms.

Finally, candidates often elaborate too much on events outside the dates given in the question.

Remember to refer to the simplified Paper 3 markscheme on page 219.

# Sample paragraphs of irrelevant focus/material

Before looking at the effectiveness of the provincial government response and analysing their success, it is important to examine federal government measures and whether they addressed the problems caused by the Depression. The policies of both Mackenzie King and R. B. Bennett were very limited in scope and did not do a great deal to address the serious economic decline that affected Canada. As unemployment rose, the government failed to introduce measures that reduced levels or tackled the declining industries.

This is an example of a weak answer. Although a brief comment on the measures taken by the federal government might be helpful to show what areas the provincial governments still needed to address, there is no need for detail about the response of the federal government. Therefore, much of the material shown is irrelevant (particularly the underlined paragraph on page 1??), and will not score any marks. In addition, the candidate is using up valuable writing time, which should have been spent on providing relevant points and supporting knowledge.

> Bennett believed in capitalism and individualism and only attempted to introduce any significant measures to deal with the Depression at the end of his term in office, offering a 'New Deal' in a radio broadcast in 1935. The only significant measure that he introduced before that was tariff reform to try and boost Canadian exports. Mackenzie King followed a very similar approach in both of his ministries, as he was unwilling to support federal governments paying relief to those who were unemployed and used the Supreme Court to block the measures that Bennett had proposed before the 1935 election.

## Activity

In this chapter, the focus is on avoiding writing answers that contain irrelevant material. Using the information from this chapter, and any other sources of information available to you, write an answer to one of the following Paper 3 practice questions, keeping your answer fully focused on the question asked. Remember: writing a plan first can help you maintain this focus.

## Paper 3 practice questions

1   How serious was the impact of the Depression on the Canadian economy and society?

2   Why did the Canadian federal governments of the 1930s introduce so little social and economic legislation to deal with the problems caused by the Depression?

3   Assess the view that the response of Canadian governments in the 1930s to the problems of the Depression was limited.

4   'Provincial governments did more to tackle the problems caused by the Depression than federal governments in the 1930s.' How far do you agree with this view?

5   Assess the view that neither Mackenzie King nor R. B. Bennett offered the Canadian people a coherent policy to tackle the problems they faced in the 1930s.

6   How radical were the solutions of the provincial governments to the problems caused by the Depression?

# 5 Latin America and the Depression

## Timeline

**1910–20** Mexican revolution and civil war

**1928** fall in Cuban sugar prices begins

**1929** **24–29 Oct:** Wall Street Crash

**1929–30** value of Argentina's exports falls by 40 per cent; Brazilian coffee prices fall

**1930** **May–Sep:** strikes and violence in Cuba lead to dictatorship of Fulgencio Batista

**6 Sep:** Argentinean army overthrows president Hipólito Yrigoyen

**24 Oct:** Getúlio Vargas comes to power in Brazil with military support

**1931** **Mar:** populist leader Luís Miguel Sánchez Cerro elected in Peru

**July:** following depression and cuts in spending, Chilean president Carlos Ibáñez del Campo is forced from power; a series of military coups follows

**1931–32** beginning of recovery in Latin American countries

**1932** revolt against dictatorship of Getúlio Vargas in Brazil

**1933** National Department for Coffee established in Brazil

**Apr:** assassination of Sánchez Cerro

**1934** **July:** Lázaro Cárdenas elected president of Mexico

**1936** major land reforms in Mexico

**1937** Brazil nationalises railways; coup by Getúlio Vargas, who declares a national state of emergency and issues the Estado Novo ('New State')

**1938** **1 May:** Mexico nationalises oil industry

**1940** Volta Redonda steelworks open in Brazil

**Nov:** end of Lázaro Cárdenas's presidency

## Key questions

- What were the causes of the Great Depression in Latin America?
- What was the economic situation in Latin America by 1930?
- How and with what success did Vargas attempt to deal with the effects of the Great Depression in Brazil?
- What was ISI and how successful was it?
- How and with what success did the Cárdenas regime deal with the effects of the Great Depression in Mexico?

This chapter looks at the causes of the Great Depression in Latin America, in particular the dependency of countries in the region on a limited range of cash crops. Unlike the USA, Latin American countries did not have a developed financial system and a large middle class with money to invest. Furthermore, because there was large-scale production for the North American market, when that market collapsed, Latin American countries were affected by a severe economic decline. This chapter explores the argument that the underlying reason for the Depression in Latin American countries was, therefore, a failure to diversify by producing a wider range of agricultural produce and manufactured goods for alternative markets.

This chapter also looks at how two Latin American regimes under two dynamic leaders responded to the effects of the Depression. The first is Brazil, where the regime of Getúlio Vargas after 1934 became increasingly authoritarian and was influenced by fascist ideas from Europe, in particular from Italy. By contrast, the reforming regime of Lázaro Cárdenas in Mexico after 1934 was influenced by socialist theories. The work of both regimes in bringing about greater diversification and support for workers and peasants is assessed.

The central part of the chapter considers the general development of alternatives to basic cash crop agricultural production in many areas of Latin America. Various Latin American countries followed the import substitution industrialisation (ISI) strategy in the 1930s, which was widely adopted in the post-war period. However, ISI has been severely criticised, especially by economists and commentators who are opposed to government intervention and favour free trade and individual enterprise. ISI's principles and effectiveness are still debated today. The case study on Mexico (see pages 152–57) assesses some of the more progressive policies that the Cárdenas government implemented after 1934.

*Latin American countries*

# Overview

- Leading Latin American countries depended heavily on exporting a small number of cash crops, such as coffee or cattle. To reduce their dependence on these staple crops, there were various attempts to diversify (to sell to a wider range of markets and industrialise to reduce imports, and to encourage wider employment by having more manufactured products and agricultural development). However, economic reforms were limited until the far-reaching changes introduced during the 1930s in response to the Depression.

- The growth in agricultural production during the First World War (1914–18) and fluctuating exchange rates created the long-term problem of overproduction. The dollar was strong in relation to other currencies, making imports cheaper in the United States and increasing demand for them. However, Latin American producers subsequently saw their profits decline and became dependent on US markets. This contributed to the problems affecting Latin American countries when the USA economy crashed in 1929.

- The Depression brought into question the existing political, social and economic policies of Brazil and the army installed a reforming leader, Getúlio Vargas, in 1930. Vargas launched ambitious policies of industrialisation and social reforms, which were based loosely on the theories of the corporate state in fascist Italy.

- Brazilian policies in the 1930s aimed to end dependence on the main export crop of coffee. These policies were part of a general movement in Latin American countries to restrict 'colonial style' economies, whereby expensive goods from developed industrial countries, particularly the USA, were purchased through the sale of cheap raw materials and foodstuffs. Later attempts to increase Brazil's industrial output and implement import substitution industrialisation (ISI) were partly a response to the impact of the Depression and the emergence of different and more radical leaders.

- In Mexico in 1934, the radical leader Lázaro Cárdenas won popular support for his commitment to land reform. This reflected the impact of the Depression and the extent of rural distress, and echoed policies from an earlier revolutionary period in Mexico. Cárdenas's reforms attempted more for the peasants than Brazilian policies, yet their momentum was difficult to maintain and so the results were mixed.

## What were the causes of the Great Depression in Latin America?

### Problems of over-dependence in Latin American markets

In general terms, Latin American countries had less diversification than Canada and even greater dependence on exports. The main export markets were the United States, Britain, France and Germany. This meant that Latin American countries were very vulnerable to changes in world trade – for example, they were severely affected by tariff policies and the effects of the First World War on the global economy, in a similar way to the USA (see pages 25–27). However, there were also regional variations.

In some Latin American countries, there was a dependence on exporting a single crop – such as sugar, which was very profitable and dominated the economy – to a restricted group of countries. This dependence had prevented change and progress since the 1820s. It was easy for Latin American leaders to enjoy the profits from trade without encouraging the economic diversity that would make the primary producers less vulnerable.

During the First World War, the price of sugar rose dramatically. The USA imported most of its sugar from Cuba, and European markets for Cuban sugar declined as the war and naval blockades disrupted international trade. Cuban sugar production rose from 2.78 million tons in 1913 to 4.4 million tons in 1919. As a result, some 300,000 emigrant workers from Haiti, Jamaica, Barbados and other Caribbean countries came to Cuba between 1913 and 1928, mainly to the eastern provinces. Thus, the collapse of US demand and prices in 1929 proved catastrophic to Cuba, as it was over-dependent on one crop. Using all available land for sugar production and importing labour had created a crisis of overproduction.

French advert for Latin American coffee from the 1900s

The overproduction of basic crops and the failure to develop home demand caused problems before the Great Crash, and the prices of key primary products began to fall in the late 1920s. In Brazil, for example, the price of coffee – the main export crop – began to fall from March 1929. In Cuba, where sugar was also a dominant crop, a decline in demand was evident from March 1928.

In countries that were less dependent on a single export crop, such as Mexico, the effects of overproduction and the falling price of exports were less obvious. Some Latin American countries managed to maintain their export markets even with rising production: demand for Venezuelan oil, for instance, remained buoyant, as did markets for bananas from Honduras. However, foreign companies that managed sales and markets efficiently generally controlled these products.

The crisis in Latin American countries was intensified by the Wall Street Crash of October 1929, the subsequent economic depression, the fall in demand, the growth in tariff barriers and the fluctuating exchange rates as major currencies abandoned the Gold Standard (see page 14). It was an export-led crisis in economies that lacked the development and sophistication of the US economy. From 1928 to 1932, Latin American exports lost half their value.

However, the economic decline in Latin American countries began before 1929, as can be seen from the example of the Brazilian cotton industry.

## Case study: the decline in the Brazilian cotton industry

Brazil was unusual in Latin America for having a reasonably large manufacturing base that was not connected with processing mass-produced agricultural products such as cattle and coffee. There was a cotton textile industry, but it was in decline by the late 1920s – most factories had closed by 1931 or were in difficulties. The period 1923–26 saw problems because of increased coffee exports and high interest and exchange rates.

The rise in the value of the dollar against South American currencies made imports cheaper for Americans. Cotton exports rose as US import prices fell by 38 per cent in 1923–26; the US market share of imported cotton rose from 5.6 per cent to 17 per cent. There was a further 25 per cent fall in prices of cotton before a change in the exchange rate in 1927 helped domestic producers, and a new tariff was put on foreign imports in 1929. The Brazilian cotton industry was therefore already weak when the Wall Street Crash of 1929 caused a sudden fall in demand.

Another factor that affected the Brazilian cotton industry was the long-term fall in commodity prices – the staple exports of coffee and sugar. While these fell sharply after 1929, they had already started falling during the late 1920s. The fall in commodity prices in turn affected Brazil's railways, ports and banks, which transported the commodities and financed them. This in turn affected the demand for home-produced cotton.

Brazil is a good example of the problems caused in Latin America by participation in the global expansion of world trade after 1870. The demand for primary products such as coffee, sugar and rubber resulted in a huge expansion of exports – in 1870, exports amounted to £1.3 per head; this figure more than doubled to £2.83 by 1928. This growth was financed by increasing amounts of foreign capital, which rose from £53 million in 1870 to £385 million by the 1920s. To support this rise in export trade, there was increased immigration, urbanisation and the construction of better transport facilities, which further contributed to the overproduction. By 1928, the problems of overproduction were emerging; by 1930, they reached crisis proportions when the price of coffee fell sharply, causing a dramatic rise in unemployment.

The policies of Brazil's ruling élite can be seen to have contributed to the country's economic decline in a number of ways. The country gained independence from Portugal in 1808, but was ruled by emperors in alliance with the dominant landowners until 1891. The region of São Paolo and the coffee growers dominated the new Republic. Those with land and wealth controlled the politicians, and democracy and equal rights for the different regions were limited.

- The leaders of Brazil's 'Old Republic' were happy to receive the profits from the country's exports without worrying about the dependence of the economy on a few key crops. They kept prices artificially high by a process known as 'valorisation' – that is, withholding supplies from the world market in order to maintain prices (the more product on the market, the cheaper it is). This approach was adopted intermittently before 1914 and regularly after 1925. However, as the coffee went into government warehouses, foreign importers simply sought out cheaper supplies.
- Brazil's rulers allowed considerable variations of income to develop between regions and classes. They also did little to support the poorer provinces, and the southeast was favoured at the expense of the rest of the country. Nothing was done to help workers maintain their living standards or the peasants to overcome financial problems.
- The 'Old Republic' also failed to develop a reliable internal market – the result of limited home production and low wages. Thus, Brazil's economy was increasingly dependent on foreign markets, and it was this dependency that led to economic collapse with the start of the Great Depression after 1929.

After 1929, Brazil's gross national product (GNP) fell 14 per cent and the country needed a change of regime under Getúlio Vargas (see page 136) to bring about economic reforms.

 ## Theory of knowledge

The blame game

The above analysis is critical of Brazil's ruling élite and its failures. How important is this type of analysis for a historian? Is there a danger that a historian will try to allocate blame too much? How important is it for a historian to compare events in different countries to avoid seeing national history in isolation?

### Activity

Compare the causes of the Great Depression in Brazil with those in the United States. Start by making a list of the causes of the Depression in each country. Then identify whether there are any similarities, and whether some points apply only to Brazil or only to the USA.

## The causes of the Depression in Latin America and the USA: a comparison

Common factors in causing the Depression in the USA and Latin American countries were:

- the First World War, which brought US economic supremacy without the commitment to stability that accompanied Britain's economic dominance in the previous century
- the increase in production, which exceeded demand by the late 1920s
- the spread of tariffs and trade restrictions in the 1920s
- the effects of the US stock market crash.

The United States' economic power was accompanied by increasing influence and control over Latin America. This included the threat or actual use of military intervention. Thus, when the US economy went into crisis, it dragged the Latin American countries that depended on US trade down with it. The Wall Street Crash of October 1929 was a major cause of economic depression among the USA's Latin American clients and customers.

As with the USA, Latin American governments can be blamed for being short-sighted about profits and developing over-dependence on a limited semi-colonial trade. Furthermore, poverty in much of Latin America and unequal distribution of wealth restricted domestic demand. Thus, domestic sales could not make up for lack of income from foreign trade on which states had become too dependent.

Yet bank collapses and business disasters were not so common in Latin America. This was partly due to banking reforms in the 1920s; it also reflected the different nature of Latin American banks, which had not made loans for share investment or invested heavily and unsuccessfully. As with Canada, the banking sector remained stable and helped both governments and the recovery in the later 1930s. Financial crash and instability was a cause of economic depression in Latin America, but one that was imported from the USA and not home-grown.

Latin American states failed to anticipate and prepare for the Depression – they were unable to prevent the development of long-term regional dependence on the giant US economy that appeared after the First World War. Rather, Latin American governments allowed three export products to account for 50 per cent of foreign exchange and a small group of industrial countries to be the main markets. This has no parallel in the USA, though not all Latin American countries became as dependent as Cuba was on sugar or Brazil was on coffee. As a result, there were considerable efforts by Latin American states in the 1930s to introduce reforms and support economic diversification, for example by import substitution industrialisation (ISI). As with the USA, if these reforms had been made earlier, then the people might have been spared hardships.

## Activity

Imagine that you are a journalist confronting a panel of government representatives of Latin American states in 1929. What accusations would you put to them about their economic policies?

How important were governments in the Americas in causing the Great Depression?

# What was the economic situation in Latin America by 1930?

Though the Latin American economies were starting to diversify and expand before 1929, the sudden downturn following the collapse of the US economy caused a catastrophic fall in the price of agricultural exports. This resulted in further attempts to diversify economic activity in many countries, for example by moving from a reliance on a few cash crops to increased production of industrial and agricultural goods. However, the economic inequalities, the low standards of living (and hence low domestic purchasing power) and reliance on large-scale exploitation of a restricted number of cash crops made this process difficult.

The economic term for the increased diversification in Latin American economies is import substitution industrialisation (ISI). The attempt here was to move away from a basic 'colonial model' of reliance on export of a few key raw materials such as sugar, cotton and coffee. Rather, Latin American states sought to imitate more advanced economies in the USA and Europe – by developing industries, a greater range of agricultural products, urban growth and more modern welfare policies. This laid the basis for Latin America's later economic development. It was accompanied in some countries by political developments that increased the power and responsibility of the state and gave rise to dictatorial regimes.

There is some debate about whether the Wall Street Crash of 1929 merely exacerbated the underlying economic problems of Latin American countries or actually triggered their decline. There is also the question of whether the leaders of the new political regimes were 'Depression dictators', and whether their dictatorial rule was necessary to implement policies that had been under consideration since the end of the First World War. Finally, there is discussion about the effectiveness and success of measures to modernise the Latin American economies and introduce social welfare.

## The international context

It is important to put the developments in Latin America into context. Post-war economic suffering had given rise to dictatorial regimes in Europe, particularly in Italy with the rise of **Benito Mussolini** from 1922.

**Benito Mussolini (1883–1945)** Mussolini was the son of a blacksmith from Forlí in Italy. He became a radical journalist and passionate nationalist. He formed the Fascist Party, whose aims were to defeat communism and set up a new corporate state that united Italy under a single party and dominant leader. As the 'Duce', or dictator, Mussolini attempted a radical social and economic new order. He changed Italy into a one-party state and was successful in adding to its empire, but joining the Second World War on Hitler's side brought him down. He was overthrown in 1943 and killed by his communist captors in 1945.

The Catholic Church and traditional élites supported Mussolini's dictatorship, which offered mass support and implemented 'corporatist' theories. Corporatist theories were based upon the belief that there could be natural harmony between owners and workers in different sectors of the economy if the state intervened to ensure good conditions, fairness and joint effort on behalf of the national community. The so-called corporate state was a feature of fascist Italy; it included a ministry of corporations and organisations for different productive elements within the state. There were also sports and welfare organisations for the workers called *dopolavoro* ('after work').

This approach was later copied in Nazi Germany with the 'Strength through Joy' movement, which introduced benefits such as subsidised holidays to workers. Corporate ideas were discussed in Spain and Portugal and were widely known in Latin America; a version of corporatism even appeared in China in the 1930s with the Nationalist Kuomintang movement. In each of these countries, the state did not take over the economy but was prepared to intervene to ensure social justice, finance vital economic developments and ensure full employment. In effect, there was an alliance between the state and the industrial middle classes. Strikes, unrest and socialism were suppressed, and there were limited measures to improve the lives of the working classes and to set up a system for discussing conditions. However, actual practice in these countries was often very different from the theory, and state interventions were largely designed to prevent workers' interests from interfering with owners' profits.

## Brazil and the Depression

The First World War, which Brazil joined on the Allied side in 1917, disrupted the country's trade patterns. German U-boats (submarines) attacked trading vessels and Allied blockades prevented trade with Europe. German and British investment and trade were much reduced, and so Brazil relied more on trade with the United States. The USA invested $50 million in Brazil in 1914; by 1930, US investment in Brazil was $557 million.

The most important of Brazil's exports was coffee. After an initial post-war slump in prices and trade, Brazil's position improved in 1923 when world demand increased; trade doubled from its pre-war level by 1925. On the back of its coffee wealth, Brazil was able to increase its imports and diversify its economy to some extent. However, coffee remained the main export – by 1929, 72 per cent of Brazil's foreign exchange came from coffee. The effects of the US stock market collapse in the USA and on world trade and payments were felt quickly: coffee prices fell between September 1929 and January 1930. A mixture of very good harvests in 1928–29 and falling demand led to severe overproduction.

Even without the Wall Street Crash and subsequent economic downturn, there would have been problems with falling prices. The Depression made matters worse. Brazil's wealth was very dependent on the sales of coffee. When they fell sharply, there was not enough money in the country for people to buy industrial goods produced for internal consumption. Declining markets in other parts of South America also reduced the export markets for Brazil's industrial goods. This meant that Brazil's industrial areas, largely in the south of the country, went into decline as both internal and external demand fell. Other export raw materials, such as sugar and cotton, were also affected.

By 1930, the Depression had caused significant difficulties for Brazil.

*   Markets for agricultural products declined, yet most of Brazil's population depended on the income from agricultural produce. The planters, who were central to Brazil's economy, faced ruin.
*   The industrial cities – largely in the south of the country – had high levels of unemployment. This reduced a vital part of the home market and created the potential for unrest.
*   Long-term inequalities in income distribution meant that most people had under 0.8 per cent of their income left for consumer spending after food and shelter. Wealthier Brazilians were affected by the decline in prices and trade and their income also fell at a time when it was sorely needed. Thus key industrial sectors – mainly food processing, textiles, clothing mining, chemicals and wood products – were also in decline.
*   Because income from exports had fallen, Brazil did not have the foreign currency, for example US dollars, that these sales earned. Therefore the country could not afford to import goods that had to be paid for in foreign currency, and trade generally declined.
*   As Brazil's economic performance was weak, foreign investors did not want to hold Brazilian currency. To avoid a large number of investors selling off currency, which would devalue it, the government imposed restrictions on the exchange of currency. Payments on debt were suspended in September 1931 and only the Banco do Brasil (Brazil's national bank) had the right to exchange currency. This badly affected international trade.

Even before 1929, Brazil had long-term economic problems: there was regional imbalance; the First World War disrupted normal trade patterns; imports of industrial goods were restricted. Although Brazil's internal and local trade increased, there was a lack of machine tools and little industrial modernisation and development. While there was industrial development in some regions, such as Minas Gerais, Rio de Janiero state and São Paulo, the northeast of Brazil was heavily dependent on agriculture and sugar. The Amazon basin had not recovered from the slump in rubber prices and production after 1912. Many areas had low productivity, low skills and populations suffering from malnutrition and deprivation. Thus Brazil's domestic market was not able to absorb the decline of international trade after 1929.

## Activity

The army was influential in Brazilian politics and installed Getúlio Vargas as ruler (see page 136). Many officers were concerned about Brazil's economic problems.

As a group, act out a role play in which you are Brazilian army officers discussing the options available to the nation at a time of financial crisis. Should you take power and install a new government? What are the arguments for and against a military coup?

## Brazilian politics

Brazil's Constitution of 1891 gave wide powers to each state. These were not only the customary powers of internal policy (such as those found in the federal constitutions of the USA), but the power of each state to raise its own army. These 'states within states' contributed little to Brazil's economic development and remained largely in private hands; there was limited regulation by federal government due to a strong belief in laissez-faire (see page 22). In some areas, landlords supported by armed gangs kept wages and therefore demand low. In the southern industrial areas, there was little welfare provision, along with overcrowding, malnutrition and poverty.

Despite the substantial profits from coffee, there was little attempt to regulate production and prepare for difficulty when the market declined. Furthermore, although investment was now starting to diversify into industry, the federal government provided little overall direction and its authority was weakened by accusations of corruption.

The most developed state of São Paolo dominated the politics of the 1920s, with two presidents, **Artur Bernardes** (in office from 1922–26) and **Washington Luís Pereira de Sousa** (in office from 1926–30) representing the key economic interests.

**Artur Benardes (1875–1955)** Bernades was a president of Minas Gerais state and came under pressure from the army during his troubled presidency of Brazil. He faced a civil war in 1924 in Rio Grande and was required to use force against rebel officers in São Paolo.

**Washington Luís Pereira de Sousa (1869–1957)** Washington Luís was a lawyer and politician. He was governor of São Paolo state, becoming president of Brazil in 1926. He attempted to deal with economic problems through liberal and orthodox policies and was the last president before a military coup in 1930.

Over two-thirds of Brazilians lived in rural areas, and large plantations manned by workers on low wages were the lifeblood of the Brazilian economy. Furthermore, Brazil's transport and communication infrastructure was weak. This left the Brazilian economy and state vulnerable to sudden economic downturn. Brazil's gross domestic product, or GDP (the value of all goods and services produced), fell by 4 per cent between 1929 and 1930 and another 5 per cent between 1930 and 1931.

## The reaction of governments in Brazil to the Depression

The Washington Luís administration by and large followed the established approach to economic management. Governments all over the world were told that, with falling trade and falling revenue, the priority was to keep a balanced budget to prevent inflation and to maintain confidence. Thus, cuts in spending were important. The business cycle would 'bottom out' – that is, reach its lowest level – before rising again, and the natural cycle of capitalism would lead to recovery. What had to be avoided were raising prices and the collapse of currencies. However, the scale of economic depression and crisis was such that this advice could not always be followed.

In Brazil, the Depression had important political effects. From the early 1920s, there was a rise in opposition to the traditional liberal ruling class that had dominated Brazil's politics since the 1880s. Its most significant and active group within the armed forces was led by the *tenentes* – younger army officers who saw in their own lack of equipment and proper military preparedness the results of a failure to modernise the state, society and economy. The *tenentes* compared Brazil's less dynamic semi-colonial economy with that of Argentina, where there was stronger economic growth, and the USA, where there was apparent boom. They saw the increasing independence of the provinces from federal control as the root cause of Brazil's national decline. The obvious corruption of elections, the lack of forward-looking policies and the threat of communism drove them to action. In 1922, there was a riot at the base at Copacabana in Rio; in 1924, there were further disturbances in São Paolo and Rio Grande do Sul. The latter proved impossible to suppress and, under the captainship of **Luís Prestes**, lasted until 1927. This civil war was a humiliating reminder of the weakness of the central government and eroded confidence in investment.

**Luís Prestes (1898–1990)** Prestes was a heroic opposition figure in Brazil and led a long rebellion from 1922–27. He opposed Vargas, who had Prestes's German–Jewish wife deported to Germany, where she died in a concentration camp.

# How and with what success did Vargas attempt to deal with the effects of the Great Depression in Brazil?

In Rio Grande, there were signs of change under a dynamic governor Getúlio Vargas. At a local level there were economic reforms, though at a national level little happened.

## The Depression and the revolution of 1930

**Getúlio Vargas** came to office in 1930 following a revolution against president Washington Luís, who wanted to promote another politician from São Paolo to succeed him. Luís was going against the usual practice in Brazilian politics by failing to handover to a leader from the state of Minas Gerais. Also, while Luís's conventional taxation and economic policies aimed to protect the Brazilian currency, they brought together a diverse group of opponents.

- The local leaders of the states of Rio Grande do Sul and Minas Gerais blamed São Paolo for the effects of the Depression in their areas.
- Rebellious army officers sought wider reforms and a national revival.
- Left-wing reformers in the Partido Democratico do São Paolo objected to the limited action taken to relieve poverty and unemployment in their home state.
- A united pressure group of coffee planters turned against the conservative politicians of the 1920s and demanded direct help when faced with a sudden price collapse.

Vargas aimed to please this wide-ranging group of protestors.

**Getúlio Dornelles Vargas (1882–1954)** Vargas was born in Bras in the state of Rio Grande do Sul to a family of wealthy landowners with a role in local politics. He served in the army then studied law. Vargas entered politics in 1908 and rose up through state politics. In 1922, he became a member of the national assembly and served as finance minister under President Washington Luís Pereira de Sousa. In 1928, he returned to his home state as governor. He campaigned in the election of 1930 against the president's nominee, another São Paulian, Julio Prestes. Although Vargas lost the election, in October 1930 the army installed him as provisional president and he remained in office until 1945, when the army overthrew him.

*President Getúlio Vargas of Brazil gives a speech of welcome to delegates from 21 American republics, Rio de Janeiro, January 1942*

# Vargas's Depression policies

## Tackling coffee overproduction

Provincial governors were already fulfilling the terms of an agreement made with coffee planters in 1906, which stated that they would buy up surplus coffee to prevent a fall in prices. The new government extended this policy: large amounts of coffee were bought and destroyed to prevent a further fall in prices. The less coffee there was on the world market, the higher the price. However, without government action the planters and their workers faced ruin, so the government provided a subsidy and the planters grew coffee in order to be bought and destroyed. In total, Brazil destroyed 78 million sacks of coffee between 1931 and 1944. What began as an emergency measure to help an area of special concern to Brazil and to maintain the support of influential landowners and planters became a fixed economic policy. In all, the equivalent to world coffee consumption for three years was destroyed.

*A railway worker shovels a mixture of surplus coffee and tar into the boiler of a train engine in Brazil, 1932; this was a more productive way of dealing with the coffee surplus of the early 1930s than simply destroying it*

The expense of buying the coffee meant this was not a conventional financial policy. Subsidising coffee required a great deal of government spending, which involved borrowing and printing money. More money in circulation led to higher prices (inflation) and the need to control the exchange of currency (as foreigners are unwilling to hold reserves of a currency that is losing value). Subsequently, inflation rose and was a fairly continuous problem for Vargas and his government until 1944.

The coffee producers were not the only group that Vargas tried to help. Under the strain of the economic crisis, he introduced a variety of measures, beginning with the creation of a new ministry of Labour, Industry and Communications in November 1930. Centrally appointed officials, called interventions, replaced the provincial governments. The federal government gained new extensive powers to control prices, wages and labour relations.

## The political impact of Vargas's Depression policies

Like F. D. Roosevelt in the USA, Vargas found that federal intervention was resented at state level. Both Roosevelt and Vargas faced the problem of achieving economic and social reform within a federal structure. Unlike Roosevelt, Vargas ended local government and, unlike Roosevelt, he faced revolution.

In 1932, São Paolo rose up against its loss of local rights and influence, and for three weeks Vargas's army surrounded the capital. The revolt failed and Vargas introduced a new constitution in 1934, with a central government with specific responsibility for economic development and social welfare. Thus the Depression brought far-reaching political change to Brazil, which was based on a different view of the scope and responsibilities of government.

As in Europe, the Depression also saw the rise of political protest from both right and left in Brazil. Vargas suppressed the protests from both sides: a communist revolt was crushed in 1935, as was an attack on Vargas's presidential palace by the semi-fascist Integralistas. In 1937, Vargas launched a coup against the new Chamber of Deputies and declared dictatorial rule. It seemed that another 'Depression dictator' had emerged.

However, the roots of Vargas's dictatorship lie in the demand for modernisation by the military reformers – the *tenentes* – in the 1920s (see page 135), as much as in the experience of the Depression. The desire to prevent the break-up of Brazil into separate provinces, to improve defence and introduce social modernisation and economic diversity pre-dates the US stock market crash of 1929. Also, Vargas was not a typical dictatorial figure; he was more a 'front man' for the army. Brazilian economic policy depended on US financial support and so Brazil did not seek the sort of economic self-sufficiency that Hitler and Mussolini did. Furthermore, Vargas did not want to align himself with the European dictators, and Brazil joined the Second World War on the Allies' side in 1942. As with Mussolini, Vargas forged an alliance with the élites – the Church, the army and the large industrialists and landowners.

**Activity**

In pairs or a small group, research the background and rise of Getúlio Vargas. Prepare a five-minute presentation entitled, 'Vargas – the rise of a dictator'. Look at historical perspectives on Vargas and include summaries in your presentation.

## Vargas's Depression policies: the historical debate

Rosemary Thorp (*Latin America in the 1930s*, 1984) argues against the established view that many of Vargas's policies were a response to the economic problems of the 1920s. In her view, the Depression did not cause but accelerated the decline of the Old Republic that emerged between 1888 and 1894. However, Jens Hentschke, in *Vargas and Brazil: New Perspectives* (Palgrave Macmillan, 2006), argues that the military coup of 1930 did, in the long run, become more of a revolution.

Alan Knight, in the *Oxford History of the Twentieth Century* (1998), proposes that in much of Latin America there was an understanding of economic problems before the Depression. There was a dilemma in that voters expected rewards in terms of more goods (often imported) and higher wages, but the economies needed investment at a time when traditional markets, such as Britain, dried up.

**SOURCE A**

In South America, the shift to authoritarianism, though less of a break with the past, was clearly evident in the 1920s as countries fell under the sway of authoritarian modernisers who sought to solve the consumption/investment dilemma by executive action.

Knight, A. 1998. Oxford History of the Twentieth Century. *Oxford, UK. Oxford University Press. p. 284.*

Here, the 'authoritarian modernisers' (and periods of rule) that Knight refers to are:

- Peru's Augusti B. Leguía (1919–30)
- Cuba's Gerardo Machado (1925–33)
- Venezuela's Juan Vicente Gómez (1908–13; 1922–29; 1931–35)
- Chile's Carlos Ibáñez del Campo (1927–31)
- Ecuador's Isidro Ayora (1926–31).

In Knight's view, Vargas was part of that tradition – a ruler who addressed established problems and was not merely motivated by the need to tackle a prolonged economic depression. This argument is supported by the fact that Brazil's economic crisis, as opposed to its long-term economic problems, did not last as long as that of the USA. The injection of financial support and the measures taken, such as high external tariffs, protected key elements in the economy. Vargas's defeat of opponents between 1932 and 1938, and the fact that Brazil did not go into a prolonged civil war, may be a result of early government action alleviating the worst effects of the financial crisis.

## What policies did Vargas follow?

### Industrialisation

Brazil led the way in industrialisation aimed at import substitution. ISI was a major feature in Latin American economic policy after the Second World War. The aim was to restrict foreign imports via tariffs in order to develop internal production. In this way, it was hoped that Brazil's industrial sector would develop sufficiently to meet the demands of the home markets. This would free the Brazilian economy from its dependence on world markets, and hence its vulnerability to the fluctuations of external markets. ISI was therefore a reaction to the liberal, free-market policies followed by Brazil's old ruling élite.

State intervention increased after 1930.

- In 1933, the Departamento Nacional do Café was established to control the prices and marketing of coffee.
- US oil refineries were placed under Brazilian control in 1938.
- In 1942, the Central Office for Co-ordination of Economic Mobilization was established.

The Vargas administration offered incentives to investment by guaranteeing private ownership of industries. The government also promoted industrial steel production, with the setting up of the Volta Rotunda steelworks in collaboration with private enterprise.

*The Volta Redonda steelworks, built between 1941 and 1946*

The Volta Rotunda steelworks was a symbol of the Vargas era. It was planned and begun in 1940–41 with a mixture of public capital and US support. It produced 300,000 tons of steel a year from 1946.

The Vargas administration made industrialisation the subject of a propaganda campaign to boost its importance and attract workers. Industrial growth was seen as the key to a sort of rebirth of the country, much as it was in Stalin's Russia. Vargas was portrayed as 'the number one worker of Brazil', and posters urged 'the renovation of the political and economic order'. Industrialisation was accompanied by social reforms that encouraged a healthier workforce.

Brazil's industrial growth was largely in the south, in Minas Gerais, Rio de Janiero state and São Paolo. The extent of industrialisation should not be exaggerated, as two-thirds of the Brazilian population were still working on the land in 1940. Yet in 1920, agriculture was 79 per cent of gross national product and industry 21 per cent, and by 1940 agriculture was 57 per cent and industry 43 per cent. There was considerable industrial growth in the period 1933–39, though less so in the years that followed. The main growth areas were metallurgy, mechanical engineering and electrical engineering. These were relatively new industries and their growth doubled in the inter-war period. Chemicals and pharmaceuticals grew even faster, tripling their output between 1919 and 1939. The older industries linked to the land – such as textiles, clothing, food and tobacco – fell from 70 per cent to 60 per cent of the total industrial output in this period. Thus growth tended to be limited to a few sectors in some parts of the country.

With industrial growth came the associated growth of infrastructure, such as the development of hydroelectric power and improvements in roads and railways. Together with high tariffs and population growth, this boosted internal sales for home produced products. Statistics show quite an impressive rate of growth:

- cement manufacture rose from 87,000 tons in 1930 to 700,000 tons in 1940
- caustic soda production increased from 13,000 tons in 1936 to 27,000 tons in 1938
- iron and steel production rose from 90,000 tons in 1929 to 150,000 tons in 1940.

Foreign investors were attracted to Brazil by the seeming political stability of the Vargas state and the lack of strikes. In all, there was a threefold increase in industrial growth and the numbers working in factories between 1920 and 1940. By 1940, there were 50,000 factories and 780,000 factory workers, and the value of industrial production had risen by 600 per cent since 1920. Between 1920 and 1940, the percentage of workers in industry rose from 1 per cent to 2 per cent of the population; at the same time, Brazil's population increased from 30.6 million to 42 million.

In actual terms rather than terms of growth, the largest industries by 1940 were food processing, which made up a third of the total value, followed by textiles and clothing, then mining, refining and metallurgy, the three of which together amounted to only 10 per cent of the whole.

State control over oil refineries was established in April 1938, despite US investment in oil since 1935. This was modified in 1943 when the US was a valued ally and buying considerable amounts of rubber, quartz and metals, and Brazilian industry was producing weapons for the Allies.

In the same way as in the USA, the Second World War accelerated previous changes and stimulated growth. The policies of the 1930s prepared Brazil's economy for the opportunities to supply the Allies and Brazil's industrial base expanded. Foreign investment during the war was important – it was used to buy machinery for Brazil's factories, which led to a much more modern post-war industrial economy.

## Activity

Prepare a presentation on the main economic policies of Brazil under Getúlio Vargas and the main economic policies of the United States under F. D. Roosevelt. How similar were the policies?

## Social policy and Estado Novo

Brazil's industrialisation has to be seen in the context of a range of quite ambitious social policies and the theory of corporatism, which was explained and developed by the lawyer Francisco José de Oliveira Viana, a leading Brazilian intellectual.

In November 1930, the Ministry of Labour, Industry and Communications was established to mediate between workers and employers and to control trade unions. The aim was to offer a context of peaceful industrial relations to attract investment and growth. As industry and cities grew, the state intervened to avoid social and industrial unrest. This was accompanied by welfare developments and a growth in education, overseen by the minister of education and health. There were campaigns against illiteracy and moves to ensure better higher education, such as the setting up of a university in São Paolo. In the 1930s, school attendance rose from 9 per cent to 21 per cent at elementary level, and adult illiteracy fell from 70 per cent to 57 per cent.

During the election campaign of 1937, there was a communist plot to overthrow the government. Vargas used the situation to declare emergency measures and acquire dictatorial powers, which he held for the next seven years. His new powers in place, Vargas closed Brazil's Congress and announced a new parliamentary assembly –

Estado Novo. This 'new state' would intervene in the economy and promote nationalism. In this respect, Estado Novo has similarities with Mussolini's Fascist state in Italy and Hitler's Nazi state in Germany, and reflects fascist ideas in Spain and Portugal. Brazil's social and economic policy was formalised as part of this new state.

Brazil was generally a repressive political state with secret police and concentration camps. Yet, the corporatist policies depended on some social reforms and progress for industrial workers. The state took responsibility for improving labour relations and conditions, family life and social stability, and education, and it promoted activities for the young and sport. The quality of life became the state's concern: the nation was urged to 'drink more milk' in 1938. The Brazilian Youth Corps, established in 1940, helped instruct the young in nationalism, as well as in a healthy diet and lifestyle. There were price controls on foods and a ban on exports of key foods, such as rice, as well as penalties for speculating in food. In 1943, the state took over slaughterhouses and flourmills to cut out the profits of the 'middle man' and keep prices down. The state's Social Welfare Food Service of 1941 provided cheap restaurants in urban centres and industrial lunchrooms.

For each part of the industrial and commercial economy, syndicates (associations) were established to represent both employers and employees. There were also state labour unions at lower levels that were co-ordinated by the ministry of labour, which collected the subscriptions paid by workers to be members of unions. After 1937, strikes were illegal and state labour courts settled disputes. By 1943, there was a national Confederation of Industry. The National Service for Industrial Training was set up in January 1942.

### Activity

How similar were Vargas's social policies to those of Roosevelt's New Deal in the USA?

These reforming ideas predated the Depression, however it is unlikely that such ambitious social and economic policies could have been introduced without the stimulus of major economic change. By the mid 1940s, Brazil had embarked on a major economic policy that the historian Rollie E. Peppino (Brazil: The Land and the People, 1973) described as 'a new chapter in the economic history of Brazil', and which continued after Vargas's fall in 1945. The pressure to avoid dependence on raw material exports to pay for imported industrial goods led to the growth of domestic industries. In order to ease the social strain of a larger industrial workforce, a well-developed social policy based on contemporary corporatist ideology was introduced.

There were undoubted social gains in terms of education and a considerable expansion of state responsibilities for different aspects of the well-being of the workforce. Statistics show the growth of industry and the increase in the relative importance of the industrial sector in the Brazilian economy. The role of government changed considerably, and so did its aspirations. Vargas had the nickname 'The Father of the Poor' and enjoyed a considerable reputation as a reformer in his lifetime.

## SOURCE B

What is government, papa?
Government is an organisation that directs and orientates the destiny of the country, attending to its needs and progress. Everyone needs a guide, governor, a dictator who makes things run smoothly!

*Extract from a Brazilian primary school textbook of the 1930s.*

## SOURCE C

Getúlio Vargas was everything to me. I wouldn't let anyone say anything against him. Whenever he spoke on the radio, I was thrilled. He always gave us benefits; I am a worker. He gave me so many benefits.

*Interview with Rita de Casia Rossi, published 1998.*

*The construction of the statue of Christ the Redeemer at Rio de Janeiro, 1931; the 710-metre-tall statue stands on top of Corcovado Mountain overlooking the city and is the most famous legacy of Vargas and his public works programme*

**Activity**

What do the following terms mean?

- GDP
- Estado Novo
- Corporatism
- ISI economic diversification
- Depression dictator

## The outcomes of the Brazilian policies

It is always difficult to assess ambitious projects in countries with low levels of economic development and considerable poverty, malnutrition and poor education, such as Brazil, especially when there are profound inequalities of income distribution. Highly publicised programmes give historians plenty of ammunition to show the gap between aspirations and reality. There is no doubt that many aspects of Brazilian life did not change very significantly despite the rhetoric of Estado Novo. The same criticisms have been made of the New Deal in the USA and Mussolini's Corporate State. In the case of Brazil and the USA, there were many shortcomings with state intervention, and the economic opportunities provided by the Second World War were probably as significant as government policy. However, viewed from the perspective of the 1920s and the Depression, the positive achievements may have seemed greater. Vargas raised hopes and expectations in Brazil and moved the economy away from its dangerous dependence on raw materials and a fluctuating world market.

In terms of the overall development of industry, traditional industries rather than the new chemical and metal industries continued to dominate. Brazil remained a mostly agricultural country and the real wages of industrial workers stayed relatively low. In the 1930s, workers had only 0.8 per cent of their wages left for anything other than food or shelter. This restricted their purchasing power for the import substitution industries and the appeal of industrial work. Despite changes in Brazil's infrastructure, the census of 1940 revealed that 50 per cent of urban dwellers had no electricity.

A skilled workforce was slow to emerge. Programmes such as the national service for industrial training benefited a minority. For most industrial workers, low wages and high prices were the norm. High levels of spending and the limited availability of goods led to inflation, which ran at 56 per cent per year by the 1940s. The view from the British consul in 1945 was that 'the rich are richer than ever and the poor are poorer'. The uneven distribution of income was a major problem in generating sustained economic growth.

Also, the Estado Novo was more concerned with modernising the economy and urban areas. Little was done in the countryside, where two-thirds of Brazilians lived. The corporatist state did not extend to rural areas and so the different regions of Brazil experienced very different growth rates. Subsidies protected coffee growers from the worst effects of the Depression.

There was new state development, such as the *Companhia Siderúrgica Nacional* (CSN) (National Steel Company), and construction begun in July 1940 of the national steelworks at Volta Redonda. However, this depended on a mixture of US loans and technology, state co-operation and private investment.

Brutal repression by Vargas's chief of police, **Filinto Müller** (a keen student of Hitler's Gestapo and SS), together with suppression of private unions and cheap labour made Brazil a low-cost economy. However, the state's inability to control inflation and the weakness of internal demand led to a fall in economic growth by 1942.

**Filinto Müller (1900–73)** Müller was the son of German immigrants. He joined the army and became a reformer – a *tenente*. He was Vargas's chief of police, and in 1937 he visited Germany and worked with the Gestapo. He lost favour when Brazil joined the Allies in 1942. He remained active politically after the Second World War and was killed in a plane crash in 1973.

There was a heavy dependence on state agricultural controls and subsidies, and social policies met with variable success. The considerable efforts to improve nutrition, for example, were only moderately effective – and only in urban centres such as São Paolo; surveys of 1944 revealed extensive malnutrition in the nation as a whole. By 1945, only a quarter of industrial workers enjoyed a basic standard of living, and living conditions in the countryside were worse. Educational campaigns about hygiene depended on available water supply and refrigeration, yet these were often absent. The traditional discrimination against women workers was largely ignored, and women earned 58 per cent less than men. In these respects, Brazil's modernisation had its limits.

SOURCE D

Institutes, autonomous agencies and consultative councils proliferated. This remained a rather ramshackle and jerry-built structure, lacking methods for effective co-ordination.

*Schneider, R. 1996. Brazil. Nashville, USA. Westview Press. p. 65.*

## Activity

Prepare for a debate about Getúlio Vargas. One 'team' argues that Vargas benefited Brazil and deserves to be seen as attempting to modernise and meet the needs of his people. The other 'team' prepares to defend the view that Vargas was an ambitious but ineffective dictator, more concerned with power and publicity than his people.

 ## Theory of knowledge

### Historians and moral judgements

Getúlio Vargas restricted political freedom, but he also introduced measures to help the poor. Should historians offer moral judgements or restrict themselves to assessing the effectiveness of Vargas's social and economic policy? How much judgement should a historian make about the morality of trading with Nazi Germany, for example, and activities such as suppressing opposition and allowing torture and persecution?

# What was ISI and how successful was it?

## The broader context

Import substitution industrialisation (ISI) is the term for economic policies pursued by a number of countries in the post-war period. Though some countries were Latin American – Brazil, Chile, Peru, Mexico, Argentina and Ecuador, the policy was followed in Africa and Asia as well. The strategy replaced predominantly free trade economic policies. Latin American countries had exported raw materials and cash crops, but even before the Great Depression some countries were concerned by their dependence on world markets. The Wall Street Crash of 1929 revealed a dangerous dependence on US markets and on the export of a restricted number of staple products.

*Banana harvesting in Guatemala, 1925*

Generally, the value of Latin American exports fell by 50 per cent between 1928 and 1932. This led to serious trade imbalances and loss of foreign earnings, making it difficult for Latin American countries to import manufactured goods from Europe and the USA, which further increased the problems of poor world trade and delayed recovery. There was a shift in Latin American countries away from the free market towards closed economic systems with high tariffs, direct control of imports through quotas or limits, and control of foreign exchange. Importers could no longer access unlimited foreign money to pay for imports because there were central bank controls and government licenses to restrict available foreign currency. With foreign competition restricted, there was a shortage of important industrial goods in Latin American countries. This provided an incentive for entrepreneurs and native firms either to start to manufacture industrial goods or to increase production.

## Economic assumptions behind ISI

Behind the economic policies of protection there was the assumption that the major manufacturing powers in the world had had their early industries protected from foreign competition. Free trade had helped well-developed economies, but was a threat to developing industry. If there was protection, then home-grown industries of different sorts could develop.

In order to achieve this, states used some public enterprise, some domestic firms and enterprises and some foreign companies, particularly from the USA. Thus the ISI strategy led to greater state investment, because in most countries there was not enough private capital available for large-scale production.

### Activity

Imagine you are an economic analyst in 1930. Write a paper explaining why you think ISI is the way forward for Latin America. The paper is intended for busy, non-specialist political leaders, so make clear bullet points with brief explanations.

## The effects of ISI

In some cases, there was a rapid economic growth in terms of certain industries. For example, in Brazil there were large-scale iron and steelworks. Incentives for these home industries enlarged the industrial working class. Brazil also developed a new middle class – the industrialists. These new entrepreneurs benefited from freedom from competition, a cheap and readily available labour force, a more developed and secure financial sector and the government civil service, which administered the controls necessary for the system to work.

The end of free-market policies resulted in a considerable increase in state subsidies and controls. There were means of preventing strikes and initiatives to maintain social peace. This approach required new administrators and bureaucrats, and so the role and size of government increased. The development of state-protected industry also increased the size of urban populations and led to a rising middle class. This made housing dearer, and there was a marked increase in suburban and shanty development on the outskirts of cities.

Economic analyses revealed problems, however. As ISI developed, there was the need to import more capital goods. Latin American countries could not build the new factories and power stations needed for the new industries, so technology had to be imported. This occurred in Brazil in the 1940s rather than the 1930s, but was linked to the earlier developments. In most countries, there was not a closing but a widening of the gap between rich and poor. To ensure the success of the strategies, wages were kept down and generally prices rose, thereby squeezing the real wages of the poorer workers. Quite independently of government policies, population growth added to both inflation and to the slump in wages.

## Analysis: was ISI a success?

It is worth considering how ISI strategies pioneered in the 1930s impacted on later Latin American development. The US economist Werner Baer (*The Brazilian Economy: Growth and Development*, Greenwood Publishing Group, 2001) argued that countries that industrialised after Britain all had to rely on a form of ISI to protect their industries against the dominant British economy. Thus policies pursued in Brazil and Chile in the period were not so much dictatorial policies, but essential to the development of industries. He also points out that ISI was essential in developing economic diversity, without which economies would have been vulnerable.

The debate as to the success of ISI focuses on its relative importance in the short term and its long-term significance. In the short term, there was a marked increase in the annual industrial growth rate in some Latin American countries in the 1930s.

- In the highest performing economies – Brazil, Mexico, Cuba, Peru, Venezuela, Costa Rica and Guatemala – GDP rose by 50 per cent or more between 1931 and 1939.
- In medium performing economies – Colombia, El Salvador, the Dominican Republic, Bolivia, Ecuador and Haiti – GDP rose between 20 and 50 per cent.
- Weaker recovery of less than 20 per cent was seen in Honduras, Nicaragua, Paraguay, Panama and Uruguay.

Industrial growth rate (average per cent rise) in Latin America, 1930–39

| Argentina | 7.3 |
|-----------|------|
| Brazil | 7.6 |
| Chile | 7.7 |
| Colombia | 11.8 |
| Mexico | 11.9 |
| Peru | 6.4 |
| Uruguay | 5.3 |

**Activity**

What do the statistics on page 149 and in Source E suggest about the role of industrialisation in achieving economic growth in Latin America?

- Which countries experienced industrial growth and a large rise in GDP?

- Which countries experienced a weak rise in GDP but growth of industry?

- Which countries experienced no great rise in industrial growth yet a rise in GDP?

## Assessing the role of other factors

The promotion of ISI was one way for Latin American countries to relinquish their dependence on exports of primary produce. However, ISI is only one factor that explains the general recovery and growth of the Latin American economies in the 1930s.

After the downturn of 1930–32, world trade grew for most of the 1930s. The US government softened the harsh tariffs imposed by Congress in 1930 through individual trade agreements with Latin American countries. Excluding Argentina and Mexico, the average increase in trade in Latin American countries as a result of softer tariffs was 53 per cent. Argentina did less well, as it was over-dependent on exports to Britain, and Mexico suffered from the hostile reactions of foreign countries to its oil nationalisation in 1938. However, what was exported was basically the same produce as before 1939. The recovery of traditional exports led to a recovery in home demand, which in turn stimulated the process of ISI, but overall recovery would have happened without ISI.

ISI was dependent on other factors for its success. The easing of traditional controls on the money supply meant that Latin American governments accepted budget deficits – they spent more than they were gaining in revenue. They used the funds to encourage the growth of infrastructure, particularly roads, hydroelectricity and public buildings. Though this brought inflation, it also increased employment and boosted demand for goods. This demand was not met by foreign imports in the 1920s, so it encouraged ISI.

Thus, recovery in traditional exports and home demand were key elements that brought about ISI. Yet ISI was not necessarily the prime element in recovery. Uruguay developed some import substitution industries, but these failed to stimulate much growth. In Cuba, Guatemala and Venezuela, there were no import substitution industries and other factors linked to the export of primary produce led to recovery.

It is also important to keep the ISI policies in perspective: in many countries they were a continuation of existing industrial development and were limited by the lack of investment available to develop large-scale factories or modern equipment. Such developments occurred mostly in the period after the 1940s and 1950s. In the majority countries, ISI depended on outdated machinery and labour-intensive factories.

## SOURCE F

The average number of people employed in industrial establishments by 1939

| Argentina | 13 |
| Brazil | 20 |
| Chile | 25 |
| Colombia | 32 |
| Mexico | 20 |
| Uruguay | 7 |

Is there any relation between Source E on page 150 and Source F? Explain your answer.

### Activity

Research another country that was industrialising in the 1930s (such as the USSR). Find out about the size of its industrial enterprises and compare this with the figures above.

In addition, the circumstances that gave rise to import substitution industrialisation also gave rise to ISA – import substitution agriculture. Many Latin American countries imported foodstuffs and raw materials in the 1920s, and these imports were replaced in the 1930s by home-grown produce.

While it is true that almost no country relied on ISI for its recovery, ISI nevertheless did have considerable long-term significance in moving Latin American countries away from their previous dependence on exports. It also developed the role of industry and government economic management. In the period from the 1940s to the 1970s, there was a shift in Latin American economies from exporting raw materials or agricultural products towards more self-reliant industrial development. This was able to happen because of the foundations laid by the economic policies of the 1930s. However, the Second World War and the growth in economic co-operation between Latin American countries and the USA were also major factors in bringing about economic change.

**Theory of knowledge**

### Historical guidance

Can the study of previous economic and social policies be a guide to present actions, or are such studies purely academic and of little relevance? How important is economic history in the study of economics?

## How and with what success did the Cárdenas regime deal with the effects of the Great Depression in Mexico?

## Mexico and the Depression

In contrast to Brazil's political unrest during the 1930s, Mexico did not experience military coup or regime change. From 1910 to 1920, the history of Mexico was turbulent and violent, with costly and disruptive civil wars until peace was restored in 1920. The subsequent presidents mostly followed liberal economic policies, though there were some attempts at agrarian reform and to promote industry.

After 1930 and the fall in prices and exports, the government introduced various moderate changes. However, the election in 1934 of **Lázaro Cárdenas del Río** as president brought about the radical change associated with Latin American dictators and leaders.

As with the rest of Latin America, Mexico was dependent on exports – the three main ones were oil, silver and copper. However, unlike Cuba and Brazil, Mexico did not have one dominant export commodity. There was some development of domestic industries, such as textiles, and some attempts at land reform. However, in 1929, Mexico was still largely rural; there had been limited reform of the large-scale farms and only modest industrial growth.

**Lazáro Cárdenas del Río (1895–1970)** Cárdenas was born in Michoacán in
May 1895. His background was lower middle class. He became involved in the civil wars in
Mexico against the repressive forces of General José Victoriano Huerta Márquez. He rose
to be a lieutenant colonel by 1915 under the command of the future president, General
Plutarco Calles. In 1920, the wars ended when General Álvaro Obregón, supported by Calles,
became president. By 25 years of age, Cárdenas was a general. He helped to suppress
opposition and in 1928 became governor of Michoacán. He pursued progressive policies
of land reform and distribution, and promoted schools, roads and irrigation projects,
anticipating his later national policies. He was known for his opposition to corruption.
Calles was president until 1928 and then ruled through 'puppets' (those loyal to him). In
1934, Cárdenas was chosen by Calles to act as president because he was loyal and popular in
his own right as an incorruptible politician, a reformer and a successful general.

In the mid 1920s, Mexico experienced falling export prices, deflation
and declining trade. The free-market economic policies of the 1920s
had not involved direct action to tackle low growth rates, which fell to
1.6 per cent after 1925. Furthermore, Mexican population growth was
around 1.8 per cent per annum.

The financial problems worsened when the Depression took hold and
unemployment in the United States rose; as a result, the USA expelled
over 300,000 Mexican workers between 1930 and 1933. In addition, US
import restrictions hit Mexican export farming, and unemployment in
Mexico rose threefold after 1930.

The worst years of the Depression in Mexico were 1931–32, with low
export prices, poor food production and an increasing labour force with
limited jobs. Between 1929 and 1932, foreign trade fell by two-thirds, and
there were poor harvests in 1929–30. GDP fell by 16 per cent between
1929 and 1932, and real wages also fell. This decline was accompanied by
a rise in rural land seizures, demonstrations and strikes.

However, there were some factors that softened the effects of the
Depression on Mexico.

- The opening up of more oil fields and the recovery of oil prices
  prevented too much unemployment, though the domination of
  oil production by foreign firms stopped the benefits from reaching
  Mexicans directly.
- The Mexican government's policy of increasing the money supply
  and deficit finance prevented excessive deflation. This meant
  that government spending cushioned people from the effects of
  falling trade.
- The recovery of international trade from 1932 reduced hardships,
  and as people's incomes recovered, internal demand grew. There
  was already some domestic industry, and the circumstances
  supported the growth of manufacturers for the domestic market.

## Land reform

In 1933, the ruling party, the PNR (National Republican Party), adopted a six-year plan. It had been conceived under Calles, but was promoted by the new presidential candidate Cárdenas, who had ruled behind the scenes since 1928. The plan reflected a commitment to land reform and greater government intervention to develop the economy.

Cárdenas introduced extensive land reform to control what was happening in many areas of Mexico, where peasants were seizing lands and establishing communes. Cárdenas envisaged co-operation with peasant organisations and trade unions as a means of applying government control. The government set up a special agricultural department in 1934 and began to redistribute land from the haciendas (the big estates) to peasants.

*Villagers greet President Lázaro Cárdenas del Río; some Mexicans saw Cárdenas as a saint, and there are poems in local dialects written about him*

Land reform was partly a reaction to depressed prices and rural under-employment after 1930, and partly a return to previous policy. The liberal economic policies of the 1920s favoured private ownership, with land redistribution and the break-up of the larger estates. Cárdenas favoured communes known as *ejidos*. These were experimental co-operatives for the commercial growth of crops, such as cotton and henequen (a plant grown for its fibres, which are used for rope), and were organised on a profit-sharing basis. Individual plots focused more on subsistence crops, such as maize. New government assistance to finance irrigation, seeds, tools and fertilisers was necessary to support the policy and ensure that production was maintained to avoid rising food prices. Two new banks for the co-operatives – the Bank of Agricultural Credit and the Bank of Ejidal Credit – were established.

Mexico was unusual in responding to peasant demands for land reform and redistribution, which intensified due to falling prices, bad harvests, weak trade and disappointment with earlier reforms. By 1940, Cárdenas had redistributed land to some 800,000 people; around 18 million hectares of land were redistributed between 1934 and 1939. The amount of land held in collectives rose from 15 per cent to 47 per cent between 1930 and 1940, and the landless rural population fell from 2.5 million to 1.9 million. The state encouraged peasants to organise themselves, and provided credit and investments. Rather like industrialisation in Brazil, rural reform in Mexico was met with enthusiasm and seen as a progressive crusade.

Sometimes reforms were dramatic. In the Laguna region, following considerable unrest between landlords and peasants, the president ordered 75 per cent of valuable land to be handed over to 30,000 peasants in 300 cooperatives (emits) in 1936. Cotton production rose in 1936–37 and stabilised in the late 1930s, so there were no disastrous economic results from the sudden revolutionary change. Rural minimum wages rose by a third during the 1930s and there was greater efficiency in food production.

Thus, on the face of it, rural reform in Mexico was a success. Yet there remained a considerable amount of low-productivity subsistence farming by 1940. Also, production of crops such as cotton, however democratically organised in cooperatives, depended on world markets and these were uneven; both production and demand declined in the years 1939–41 and 1945. No agrarian reform could guarantee favourable sales. Also, the degree of support provided by the government in the initial phase of land reform was not possible to maintain. Thus, after 1941, the ejidos found it more difficult to obtain capital and farmers had to rely on individual plots. They were also controlled more and more by the officials of the bank that had lent them money.

Re-distribution of land was a complex process and often done in a hurry. The land could not always support the larger families of a growing population, and the fertile and poorer quality lands were not always distributed evenly. There were complaints about corruption and the grant of land to those who were not peasants. Also, the redistribution of land sometimes disrupted traditional and successful means of cultivation, and the ejidos often faced competition from more prosperous landowners who had superior machinery and processing facilities. Peasant indebtedness to the new agrarian banks also became a problem.

The sheer scale of change in the countryside was of enormous importance to the standing and self-esteem of the peasants. It was accompanied by social reforms, such as improvements in education – government spending on education in the 1930s increased from 1 per cent to 20 per cent of the government budget.

A more educated rural population was better able to absorb new farming techniques and better equipped to take advantage of increased work opportunities in cities and factories.

## Rail and oil

State control of key elements in the economy began with the nationalisation of Mexico's railways on 1 May 1938. The handing over of the railways to the railway workers' trade union was a remarkable social experiment that met with mixed success. There were 47,000 railway workers, which made the railways one of Mexico's biggest employers. As with agrarian reform, there was initial enthusiasm and progress, but there was an underlying lack of capital and modernisation. To stay within budgets, the unions alienated their own workers by wage reductions and there were safety issues. Gradually, state administration replaced worker control.

The most dramatic change came with oil nationalisation in 1938. Oil was a significant employer (14,000 people) and a vital resource, but it was largely foreign-owned. The second six-year plan, established in 1939, involved the creation of a state oil company to develop fields that private firms had chosen not to develop. Poor labour relations led to a national oil strike in 1937, and the foreign companies proved unwilling to develop costly new areas, so Cárdenas nationalised the oil industry in May 1938.

*President Cárdenas announces the nationalisation of foreign oil companies, 18 March 1938*

Again, control was given to labour unions, with the government retaining overall control and finance. As foreign countries dominated oil production, this was less a socialist measure than a nationalist assertion of Mexico's economic rights. There were protests at the changes, especially from Britain, but the USA was not prepared to intervene to protect firms that the Mexican state had taken over; rather, the USA restricted trade with Mexico and was less willing to loan Mexico money. Consequently, Mexican oil exports fell at the same time that there was a general drop in prices, from 1937 to 1938. After Mexico joined the Second World War on the side of the USA in 1942, there was a growth of trade with the Allies, at which point the Mexican government agreed to compensate the foreign oil companies.

A lack of investment and high labour costs proved problematic for the alliance between unions and state, and this resulted in cutbacks and wage reductions. The major problem was that industrial reforms depended on high spending and budget deficits, at a time when trade, though increasing, was not keeping pace with government plans. Government spending increased from 265 million pesos in 1934 to 604 million pesos in 1940. Then, when the USA went into a temporary recession between 1937 and 1938, US markets for Mexican exports fell, reducing government revenues. Consequently, deficit finance and the government printing more money resulted in inflation. Food production was disrupted by reforms and Mexico's population was rising, both generally and in cities. This meant a rise in food prices. While guaranteed minimum wages supported many urban workers, higher food prices– the most important element in urban spending – eroded any wage increases.

Despite the initial successes of President Cárdenas's reforms of 1936 to 1938, they were hurried through and ultimately led to various problems in the Mexican economy. In 1938, cutbacks in spending put an end to various plans for road building and public works, and currency devaluation made imports dearer. Inflation was an ongoing problem into the 1940s, with prices two and half times greater in 1945 than they had been in 1939.

## Activity

Create a table like this to help you compare and contrast the policies of Vargas and Cárdenas. List similar policies and then contrasting policies. For example, a similar policy might be deficit finance; a dissimilar policy could be land reform.

| Cárdenas policy | Evaluation | Vargas policy | Evaluation |
|---|---|---|---|
|  |  |  |  |
|  |  |  |  |

# End of chapter activities

## Paper 3 exam practice

### Question

How successful was the response of any one Latin American country to the Depression in the 1930s?
[20 marks]

### Skill focus

Avoiding a narrative-based answer

### Examiner's tips

Even once you have read the question carefully (and so avoided the temptation of including irrelevant material), produced your plan and written your introductory paragraph, it is still possible to go wrong.

By 'writing a narrative answer', history examiners mean providing supporting knowledge that is relevant (and may well be very precise and accurate) **but** which is not clearly linked to the question. Instead of answering the question, it merely **describes** what happened.

The main body of your essay/argument needs to be **analytical**. It must not simply be an 'answer' in which you just 'tell the story'. Your essay must **address the demands/key words of the question**. Ideally, this should be done consistently throughout your essay, by linking each paragraph to the previous one, in order to produce a clear 'joined-up' answer.

You are especially likely to lapse into a narrative answer when answering your final question – and even more so if you are getting short of time. The 'error' here is that, despite all your good work at the start of the exam, you will lose sight of the question, and just produce an *account*, as opposed to an analysis. Even if you are short of time, try to write several analytical paragraphs.

Note that a question that asks you the extent to which you agree with a statement expects you to come to judgements about success/failure or the relative importance of a factor/individual, or the accuracy of a statement. You need to provide a judgement on the views expressed in the statement. Very often, such a question gives you the opportunity to refer to different historians' views (see pages 190–91 for more on this).

A good way of avoiding a narrative approach is to refer back to the question continually, and even to mention it now and again in your answer. That should help you to produce an answer that is focused on the specific aspects of the question – rather than just giving information about the broad topic or period.

For this question, if you choose president Vargas of Brazil, you will need to include:

- the problems that the Great Depression caused for Brazil
- his policy of encouraging ISI
- his policy towards social welfare and helping those hit by the Depression
- his policy of social harmony in the Estado Novo
- his policy towards agriculture and limiting the fall in price of staple products such as coffee
- an overall judgement on how well Vargas dealt with the problems of the Depression.

You will then need to make a judgement in your concluding paragraph.

## Common mistakes

Every year, even candidates who have clearly revised well, and therefore have a good knowledge of the topic and of any historical debate surrounding it, still end up producing a mainly narrative-based or descriptive answer. Very often, this is the result of not having drawn up a proper plan.

The extracts of the student's answer below show an approach that essentially just describes Vargas's policies, without any analysis of the aims or degree of success/failure, and without always focusing on the issue of the Depression.

## Sample paragraphs of narrative-based approach

In 1928, Getúlio Dornelles Vargas was elected governor of Rio Grande do Sul. He became president in 1930 and later became a dictator. He replaced a state known as the Old Republic. He had support from the reforming elements of the army who were concerned about the lack of modernisation in Brazil and the effects of the Depression.

This example shows what examiners mean by a narrative answer – it is something you should **not** copy!

> Vargas made many changes in Brazil and introduced administrative reform and important changes in industrialisation and in labour legislation, creating a minimum wage. He was one of the most popular leaders and was called 'The Father of the Poor'.
>
> The most important policy he followed in the economy was the development of industry...

[The rest of the essay continues in the same way – there are plenty of accurate/relevant facts about Vargas's main policies/actions and the situations he faced, but there is no attempt to answer the question by addressing what the problems facing Brazil were and how well he dealt with them.]

## Activity

In this chapter, the focus is on **avoiding** writing narrative-based answers. Using the information from this chapter, and any other sources of information available to you, try to answer one of the following Paper 3 practice questions in a way that avoids simply describing what happened.

Remember to refer to the simplified Paper 3 markscheme on page 219.

## Paper 3 practice questions

1 Compare the effectiveness of policies introduced to deal with the effects of the Great Depression in any *two* Latin American countries.

2 How successful were the policies of ISI in the 1930s?

3 Why did the Depression lead to political upheaval and change in Latin American countries in the 1930s?

4 To what extent are the policies carried out by any *one* Latin American regime in the 1930s comparable to the US New Deal?

5 Why was there greater economic recovery in some parts of Latin America than others in the 1930s? (You may confine your answer to any *two* states.)

# 6 The impact of the Great Depression on US society: African-Americans, women and minorities

## Key questions

- What was the position of African-Americans and other minority groups in the USA in the late 1920s?
- What was the impact of the Depression on African-Americans and other minority groups within the USA?
- To what extent did the Depression change the position of women in the USA?

This chapter assesses the impact of the Great Depression on African-Americans, other minority groups and women within the United States. It considers their social, economic and political position on the eve of the Great Depression and whether it had changed by 1939. The chapter analyses the impact of the New Deal on these groups and considers whether the measures introduced addressed the issues they faced and improved their political, social and economic position.

## Overview

* African-Americans, other minority groups and women were discriminated against before the Great Depression, and any gains made during the First World War were soon lost.
* The status of African-Americans was worst in the southern states, where there was lynching (mob execution) and racial segregation (enforced separation of African-Americans and whites).
* Minority groups and women were usually the first to lose their jobs when the Depression came. Little specific legislation was aimed at these groups during the New Deal, as Roosevelt was unable to obtain political support for such measures.
* Native Americans saw some improvement in their situation during the 1930s, and it can be argued that they received a New Deal.
* Some individuals within minority groups made progress and provided inspiration for others, but, as a rule, there were few improvements until after the Second World War.

## What was the position of African-Americans and other minority groups in the USA in the late 1920s?

The position of African-Americans and other minority groups, such as Native Americans, Hispanics and Asians, was poor in the late 1920s. In all areas of life, their situation was much worse than that of other Americans.

### Legal position

African-Americans made up approximately 10 per cent of the population of the United States in the 1920s, but 85 per cent lived in the south, the poorest area of the USA. Discrimination dominated every aspect of their lives; this was largely the legacy of slavery and a belief held by many white Americans that African-Americans were inferior. For African-Americans in the southern states, the situation was particularly bad: although discrimination occurred throughout the USA, it was enshrined in law in the south.

## The 'Jim Crow' laws

The 'Jim Crow' laws formed the organisational basis of society in the south, legalising discrimination and racial segregation. Although the facilities provided for African-Americans were supposed to be 'equal' to those provided for whites, in practice the law was interpreted in whatever way the courts desired. As a result, facilities provided for African-Americans were usually inferior. Segregation was seen in transport, churches, theatres, parks and schools.

*Segregated students at the University of Oklahoma in 1948; segregation in the United States persisted well beyond the Depression era*

In the southern states, radical white supremacist groups, such as the Ku Klux Klan, targeted African-Americans and law enforcers provided little protection from their violence. Sometimes there was lynching, usually by hanging, and the culprits generally went unpunished. The absence of a federal police force to protect African-Americans added to their problems. While there was less violence against African-Americans in the northern states, there were also cases of lynching that went unpunished.

## Economic position

Economically, African-Americans had seen little improvement in their situation since the abolition of slavery in 1865, particularly in the southern states. In the south, most former slaves were sharecroppers; they rented small farms by giving half their crop to the landowner as rent. Opportunities for improvement were limited and many tried to escape poverty by moving to the northern cities in search of better-paid work. This migration created racial tensions within northern states, where whites feared increased competition for jobs. However, only 7 per cent of first-generation African-Americans were able to get professional, administrative and managerial ('white-collar') jobs; and this figure rose to only 9 per cent for second generations. Instead, most ended up with the lowest-paid jobs, a position made worse by poor education. As a result, many African-Americans were trapped in a cycle of poverty: a study in Pittsburgh showed that African-Americans remained unskilled because a lack of employment opportunities forced them to rely on casual employment.

Low income also had an impact on African-Americans' ability to engage in political protest – most were too busy working and trying to improve their living conditions. Many were afraid of losing their jobs.

## Social position

Socially, the position of African-Americans was also poor. The First World War provided some African-Americans with the opportunity to experience equality as soldiers and they encountered less racial discrimination when they were posted to Europe. However, in 1919, there were race riots in 25 US cities. The most serious riots were in Chicago, where over two weeks, 38 people were killed, 500 were injured and 1000 were left homeless.

A grand jury investigation, commissioned by the governor of Illinois on the 1919 race riots, called for an end to racial segregation and blamed the riot on the unfair treatment of African-Americans by white law enforcers. The recognition of the mistreatment of African-Americans by the white authorities was a breakthrough, yet little changed in practice – segregation and inferior facilities ensured African-Americans remained disadvantaged. Even in northern states, whites feared the arrival of African-Americans in their neighbourhoods. These racist attitudes had a negative impact on house prices and increased competition for housing. Some northern cities therefore passed segregation laws that resulted in the development of African-American ghettos (slum areas occupied predominantly by African-Americans). In New York, Harlem's African-American population grew from 50,000 in 1914 to 163,000 by 1930, leading to overcrowding and poor living conditions.

## Political position

Slavery was legally abolished in 1865 and, in theory, former slaves had the vote; however, in practice, African-Americans seldom voted in the south due to various restrictions.

- African-Americans had to pass a literacy test (which was deliberately made too hard) before they were allowed to vote. (Illiterate whites could vote.)
- 'Grandfather clauses' limited the right to vote to anyone whose father or grandfather had voted, or had had the right to vote, before the Civil War.
- Ten southern states imposed a poll tax that you had to pay before you could vote – and it was more than most African-Americans could afford.

Where African-Americans did vote, most voted Republican because of the passing of the Emancipation Act by President Lincoln (a Republican). Politically, however, African-Americans had few opportunities to improve their position. Federal governments did little to help, as most local politicians were white; in Congress, southern politicians were able to control Senate Committees and used 'filibustering' (delaying tactics such as giving lengthy speeches) to prevent attempts to improve the position of African-Americans.

*The fear of 'white' jobs going to black people led to riots, injuries and deaths in 1919; here, two white men stone a black man during a race riot*

### Activity

The Declaration of American Independence in 1776 stated that all men were created equal. Read a copy of the Declaration. How might white Americans try and reconcile the wording of the Declaration with their treatment of African-Americans?

## Changes during the 1920s

During the 1920s, there were some signs of change within the African-American community itself. The Harlem Renaissance of the 1920s was a cultural flowering of African-American literature and music that included the jazz musician Louis Armstrong. For many African-Americans, it showed there was a way out of poverty. However, whites owned the nightclubs where African-Americans performed and they were only allowed in as performers.

The inter-war period also witnessed the emergence of key individuals, such as William du Bois, who founded the National Association for the Advancement of Colored People (NAACP), and A. Philip Randolph, who established a black trade union for rail porters. **Marcus Garvey** emphasised racial pride and self-respect among African-Americans, and called for a 'back to Africa' spiritual campaign. In these ways, Garvey helped to create a more positive sense of African-American identity.

**Marcus Garvey (1887–1940)** Garvey was born in Jamaica and moved to Harlem in 1916. He argued that God was black, and put forward ideas of self-help, self-defence and the separation of races. He established the Universal Negro Improvement Association, which had 500,000 members by 1925. However, other African-American leaders disliked Garvey's appeal to the black working class and his belief that 'blacker was better'. He was found guilty of fraud in 1923 and deported in 1927.

While black activism increased and became better organised in the 1920s, most African-Americans were too busy or lacked political consciousness. In the south, many African-Americans feared campaigning for change as it could lead to lynching. Thus, despite some developments in activism and African-American consciousness, the position of African-Americans had changed little when the Depression began in 1929. 'Jim Crow' laws in the southern states enforced discrimination and segregation; in the north, discrimination was reflected in the ghettos and the limited economic opportunities.

## Activity

Create a chart like this. Add to the chart to briefly summarise changes African-Americans experienced after 1880.

| Factor | Changes between 1880 and 1914 | Changes in the 1920s |
|---|---|---|
| Legal | | |
| Social | | |
| Political | | |
| Economic | | |
| Other | | |

Now write a concluding paragraph explaining how far life improved for African-Americans in the 1920s. Do you think life improved enough?

# Other minority groups

## Native Americans

Reservations were lands set aside by the US government for Native Americans so as to free up other lands that white Americans wanted but that were originally inhabited by Native Americans. At first, Native Americans agreed to the move, but later they were forced onto the reservations, where they struggled to make a living from the land and they could no longer maintain their traditional ways of life. Many Native Americans starved as they were deprived of the ability to hunt buffalo. There was some sympathy for the plight of Native Americans in the early 20th century, when their death rate exceeded their birth rate and numbers declined. In 1924, largely as a result of their contribution to the war effort, Native Americans were granted US citizenship. However, progress in other areas was slow and they continued to live in poverty.

*A traditional picture of Native American life; in the early decades of the 20th century, Native American groups were subject to much discrimination*

### Hispanics

The other sizeable ethnic group within the USA were Hispanics. They had not made much progress up the economic or social ladder before the Depression. They were already viewed as a threat to the US labour market, particularly when jobs were in short supply. This created tensions between Americans and Hispanics, as Mexican immigrants were usually agricultural labourers, and the USA was already seeing signs of an agricultural depression. White Americans also often saw the Hispanic lifestyle as conflicting with US values, and subsequently they stereotyped Hispanics as lazy, criminals and carriers of disease. Hispanics faced discrimination and segregation in public places.

### Discussion point

Why do you think minority groups in the USA were treated so badly? Does it matter if minority groups are diminished or disappear? Why?

## What was the impact of the Depression on African-Americans and other minority groups within the USA?

### African-Americans and unemployment

The Depression hit the African-American community harder than that of white Americans. This is most clearly seen in the unemployment figures. The employment opportunities created by the rapid industrial expansion of the 1920s were soon lost, as manufacturing industry in the northern cities was badly hit by the downturn. African-Americans were often the first to lose their jobs, and with racial prejudice and no effective social security, their situation was very bleak. Richard Wright described his childhood during the 1920s in his autobiography Black Boy.

### SOURCE A

Hunger had always been more or less at my elbow when I played, but now I began to wake up at night to find hunger standing at my bedside. The hunger I had known before this had been a normal hunger that had made me beg constantly for bread, and when I ate a crust or two I was satisfied. But this new hunger baffled me, scared me. Whenever I begged for food now, my mother would pour me a cup of tea, which would still the clamour in my stomach for a moment or two.

Wright, R. 1946. Black Boy. London, UK. Victor Gollancz. pp. 14–15.

What does Source A reveal about the experience of African-Americans in US society in the 1920s?

The magazine *Nation* reported in April 1931 that the unemployment rate for African-Americans was between four and six times higher than the unemployment rate for white Americans. The low-paid and menial jobs, such as domestic service and garbage collection, previously done by African-Americans, were now being done by whites, who were willing to take any jobs available. Employers added to the difficulties of African-Americans as they offered work to white people first. The problems were worse in cities, such as Atlanta, where vigilante groups such as the Black Shirts of Atlanta were set up to ensure any employment opportunities were reserved for whites.

## Reactions to migrant workers

In the southern states, African-American sharecroppers were particularly badly hit by the financial crisis. They already lived a very precarious life, but for many the Depression brought utter ruin. As agricultural prices fell further, over two million African-Americans left their farming lands; many went to northern cities in search of work. The Social Security Act and the National Labor Relations Act did not cover sharecroppers, therefore there was no safety net for them and they were forced to seek other employment opportunities. However, with urban unemployment rates already high, the arrival of black migrant workers intensified racial tensions within cities. It also added to the problem of providing relief, as voluntary organisations were already overstretched and so were unable to cope with the influx of large numbers.

### Discussion point

Is the treatment of African-Americans during the Depression similar to the way other minority groups, such as Jews or migrant workers, have been or are being treated? Do you think that a poor economic situation stimulates such behaviour? Why?

## The realities of the 'New Deal'

Despite the very difficult situation for many African-Americans, President Roosevelt was more concerned with saving the US capitalist system than introducing specific legislation to ease their plight. However, even if he had wanted to take specific action, it would have been very difficult. Roosevelt depended upon the votes of southern Democrats to get legislation through Congress, and they would not have approved laws that gave specific benefits to African-Americans over whites.

The legislation that was passed was frequently prejudicial to African-Americans.

- The National Recovery Administration (NRA) codes allowed African-Americans to be paid less than whites for doing the same job. As a result, African-Americans nicknamed the NRA the 'negro-run-around', because of its discriminatory nature.
- The Civilian Conservation Corps (CCC), which was supposed to help unemployed young men, was even more racist that the NRA. The man in charge of the CCC was Robert Fechner, a southern racist who did little to encourage African-Americans to join; and when they did they were subject to a policy of strict segregation.

 ## Theory of knowledge

### History and the individual
Do you think it always takes a long time to change people's attitudes? Why? How have your own attitudes and understanding of the world been shaped by your education?

The shortage of jobs encouraged a hardening of attitudes towards African-Americans and other minority groups, particularly in the south. Any small steps towards racial equality made since the First World War were reversed, as many whites viewed African-Americans as another threat to employment. However, in some ways, the situation had got no worse for African-Americans. According to one contemporary commentator in Georgia, 'most blacks did not know the Great Depression had come. They had always been poor and only thought the whites were catching up.'

## The effects of the Depression on other minority groups

### Hispanics

The Depression added to existing tensions between Americans and Hispanics. Hispanics – largely Mexicans – worked as farm labourers, so the severe agricultural decline meant that they were in need of relief and added to the USA's financial burden. Many white Americans already viewed Hispanics as economic 'parasites' and discriminated against them. High unemployment during the Depression meant that whites started viewing Hispanics as rivals for their jobs, and as a result many were deported: the Mexican population in the USA fell from 600,000 in 1930 to 400,000 in 1940.

### Native Americans

Native Americans were badly hit by the Depression, yet they started from a position of poverty. Also, since there had been some efforts in the 1920s to improve the situation of Native Americans, many white

Americans already accepted that Native Americans needed support and the Depression did little to hinder this progress. A critical aspect in this is perhaps that Native Americans were never seen as a threat to white jobs – they did not even want to be US citizens. Rather, their concern was to preserve their own culture and way of life, as they did not want to live in the cities and find employment there. (This contrasts sharply with the experiences of Asian-Americans, who were seen as a threat to the employment prospects of whites and were therefore resented.)

## Activity

Consider the following two statements:

1   Life during the Depression was harder for African-Americans and other minority groups in the USA.
2   Life during the Depression was just a continuation of the struggles African-Americans and other minority groups were accustomed to.

Which of these statements do you think best describes the position of African-Americans and other minority groups during the Depression? Explain your answer.

Compare the position of African-Americans with that of Native Americans. Who do you think was better off? Why?

# The impact of Roosevelt's New Deal

The New Deal aimed at tackling the problems faced by Americans and not individual groups. In most cases, if marginalised groups – such as African-Americans, Hispanics and Native Americans – benefited from the New Deal, it was because of the wider aims of the measures, and not because the government was concerned with their particular issues.

## The New Deal and African-Americans

Little was done to help African-Americans as part of Roosevelt's New Deal (see pages 169–70). Indeed, many measures worked against African-Americans. For example, the Agricultural Adjustment Administration set quotas for production and encouraged modernisation, but both had the effect of putting farm labourers out of work, and in the southern states the African-Americans were particularly affected. However, the New Deal did encourage wage rises and reductions in working hours, so for African-Americans in work there was some improvement. While anti-lynching bills were introduced in 1934 and 1937, they were defeated as the Democratic Party opposed any changes in racial laws; Roosevelt needed his party's support to get the New Deal legislation passed.

While F. D. Roosevelt was unable to achieve much in terms of civil rights, there were important gestures of support, most notably from his wife, **Eleanor Roosevelt**, who showed a particular interest in the position of African-Americans. In 1938, she attended a bi-racial group meeting in the highly segregated city of Birmingham, Alabama, where she sat between white and African-American delegates. The meeting declared its support for equality before the law, voter registration for the poor and funding for African-American postgraduates. Eleanor also worked behind the scenes to put forward the cause of African-Americans. She persuaded officials running the New Deal into providing non-discriminatory aid to African-Americans and introduced their representatives to the president. The result was that nearly 50 African-Americans obtained senior positions in the federal bureau, giving rise to the term the 'black cabinet'.

**Anna Eleanor Roosevelt (1884–1962)** Eleanor was born in New York. Her maternal grandmother brought her up following the death of her parents. She gained first-hand knowledge of the terrible living conditions of many Americans by working as a volunteer in the East Side slums in New York. She married Franklin Delano Roosevelt, her father's fifth cousin, in 1905. Following his election as US president, she continued her business and speaking agenda. She played an important role for in her husband's presidency, and helped him connect with the USA's African-American population. She was outspoken in her support for civil rights and appointed Mary McLeod Bethune (see below) as head of the Division of Negro Affairs.

The status of African-Americans improved during the Depression period as Roosevelt, encouraged by his wife, displayed some sympathy for their position, declaring, 'We are going to make a country in which no one is left out'. There were also some African-Americans who rose to prominence, for example **Mary Mcleod Bethune** was employed in government. Harry Hopkins (see page 70) and Harold Ickes (see page 72), who were responsible for implementing much of Roosevelt's New Deal, also ensured that African-Americans were included in the relief programmes.

**Mary Jane Mcleod Bethune (1875–1955)** Bethune was the daughter of former slaves, and she worked in the fields from the age of five. However, her interest in education led to her founding a school in Daytona, Florida, which became the Bethune–Cookman School. She was also active in women's clubs and campaigned for the election of Franklin D. Roosevelt. She became part of the 'black cabinet' when Roosevelt appointed her to help with the National Youth Administration (NYA) in 1933. She later became director of the Division of Negro Affairs and was the first black woman to head a federal agency.

## Hispanics and the New Deal

Hispanics did not benefit from the New Deal. Many Mexicans were deported because they were seen as depriving white Americans of employment – and this included Mexican-Americans who were US citizens. Some 16,000 Mexicans were forced to leave the United States in 1931 alone.

## Native American experiences

The policies pursued by John Collier as commissioner for the Bureau of Indian Affairs (BIA) – a federal government agency responsible for the safekeeping of lands assigned to Native Americans – have led some to claim that there was a 'New Deal' for Native Americans. Collier was appointed commissioner for the BIA in 1933. He was a man with a deep interest in traditional Native American communities and the restoration of their rights to self-determination. He was determined to reverse the traditional government policy towards Native Americans, which was based on the Dawes Act of 1887.

The Dawes Act (also known as the General Allotment Act or Dawes Severalty Act) had at its core the twin ideas of assimilation (the integration of Native Americans into American culture) and allotment (the breaking up of Native American reservations into small plots that were then assigned to individuals). As a result, Native Americans were taught in Christian schools and forced to wear western-style dress; tribal units were broken up and reservations divided into family-sized farms of 160 acres, with surplus land sold off. The Act was largely responsible for destroying Native Americans' cultural heritage and ways of life, leaving many living in squalor and idleness. Much of the land allocated to them was barren. Of the 138 million acres allocated to Native Americans in 1887, only 48 million remained by 1932.

Collier helped pass the Wheeler–Howard (Indian Reorganisation) Act of June 1934, which ended the Dawes Act. The Wheeler–Howard Act gave Native Americans a greater role in the administration of their reserves and protected their rights to practise their own religion and assert their cultural identity. Their children were allowed to attend local schools and learn about Native American culture, rather than being forced to assimilate into white western culture. Most importantly, the Act stopped the sale of Native American lands. Native Americans also recovered large amounts of unallocated land, which was used to expand or create reservations. More controversially, Collier persuaded Congress to stop trying to ban the use of peyote, a hallucinatory substance that Native Americans used to produce religious visions. While it was not addictive or violent in its effects, religious missionaries opposed its use; however, peyote was part of the traditional culture and so represented a symbolic victory in the struggle to preserve native traditions.

*A sewing class at a Native American school*

The Indian Reorganisation Act succeeded in affirming and protecting Native American culture. However, opponents accused Collier of encouraging Native Americans to 'go back to the blanket', arguing that instead of protecting and promoting their own culture they should be assimilated into US culture so they could prosper economically. At the same time, Native Americans were given more land, were trained in farming and were provided with better medical services. Land sales on reservations were more strictly controlled, and tribal corporations were established to ensure that resources were better managed. Collier also did his best to ensure that Native Americans benefited from the opportunities offered by the Civilian Conservation Corps and the Public Works Administration.

Yet although Native Americans were given greater control over the reservations, some policies met with resistance. Tribes were organised into self-governing bodies that could vote to adopt constitutions and have their own police and legal systems, but 75 out of 245 tribes voted against these measures. There were concerns that Collier did not understand the real needs of the population or their culture. Furthermore, poverty was not alleviated, and the use of a secret ballot to decide whether Native Americans wanted the Act and to establish democracy on the reservations was unpopular. The democratic process went against the Native American tradition of open voting.

If Native Americans gained a 'New Deal', its implementation was slow and carried out reluctantly. Most were employed by the Bureau of Indian Affairs, but after years of persecution and deprivation of their rights, they were heavily dependent upon it. Therefore, they did not take over the running of their own affairs, as the initial Act envisaged, because they were dependent upon federal aid. Furthermore, much of the land allocated to them was already leased to whites.

In 1948, a review by the Hoover Commission found that the earlier destruction of Native American tribal culture 'appears to have been a mistake'. This supports the view that Native Americans did benefit from the policies pursued in this period.

The historian Hugh Brogan (*The Longman History of the United States of America*, 1985) takes this view further, suggesting that the New Deal represents a real turning point in the fortunes of Native Americans:

### SOURCE B

By the time the enemies of the red man won national power again, after the Second World War, the Indians had recovered so far that they were able to beat off the attackers and begin the slow rise which, with many setbacks, has characterised their history ever since. This was one of the most complete and heart-warming successes of the New Deal.

Brogan, H. 1985. The Longman History of the United States of America. Harlow, UK. Longman.

### Discussion point

Why do you think that Native Americans gained more from Roosevelt's administration than African-Americans?

Does the Indian Reorganisation Act of June 1934 warrant the title 'A New Deal for Native Americans'?

## Political changes

New Deal policies were not aimed specifically at African-Americans, yet many – like white Americans – saw Roosevelt as their saviour. They praised him for his attempts to raise wages and reduce working hours. Given that 30 per cent of African-Americans were on relief (compared with 10 per cent of white Americans), this was a sign that the New Deal policies did make a difference to African-Americans.

Support for Roosevelt's policies is most notable in the change in voting patterns in the north in the period (in the south, barely 5 per cent of African-Americans voted). Traditionally, African-Americans voted Republican because this was the party that fought the Civil War to end slavery. However, this changed in the 1930s.

In 1932, out of fifteen African wards in nine cities, Roosevelt won only four; in 1936, that figure increased to nine; by 1940, he won all fifteen wards. In some areas, support for Roosevelt was very high: he won 85 per cent of the popular vote in Harlem, and a 1936 opinion poll showed that 76 per cent of all African-Americans intended to vote for him. These changes suggest that African-Americans believed that their best hope of improvement was with a Democrat in the White House, particularly one who was prepared to stimulate the economy and create jobs.

## Discrimination

Yet despite these changes, discrimination meant that relief and job opportunities did not reach, or only partially reached, African-Americans or other minority groups. Where schemes benefited minority groups, this was not to the same extent as white Americans benefited. This discrimination is seen clearly in the Civilian Conservation Corps, where African-Americans were put into segregated camps (see Source C). However, around 200,000 African-Americans benefited from the CCC, even if their gains were not as great as those of whites.

### SOURCE C

We reached Camp Dix about 7:30 that evening. As we rolled up in front of headquarters an officer came out to the bus and told us: 'You will double-time as you leave this bus, remove your hat when you hit the door, and when you are asked questions, answer "Yes, sir", and "No, sir".' And here it was that Mr. James Crow first definitely put in his appearance. When my record was taken at Pier I, a 'C' was placed on it. When the busloads were made up at Whitehall street an officer reported as follows: "35, 8 colored." But until now there had been no distinction made. But before we left the bus the officer shouted emphatically: "Colored boys fall out in the rear." The colored from several buses were herded together, and stood in line until after the white boys had been registered and taken to their tents. This seemed to be the established order of procedure at Camp Dix.

Wandall, L. 1935. 'A Negro in the CCC' in Crisis 42. New Deal Network. pp. 244, 253–54.

What evidence is there in Source C that African-Americans were discriminated against? What evidence is there that the situation of African-Americans improved during the New Deal?

# Employment opportunities

There were some advances in the employment opportunities available to African-Americans in the 1930s.

- The number of African-Americans working in the civil service trebled to 150,000 in the period from 1932 to 1941, giving some greater opportunities and more prestigious employment.
- By 1939, over one million African-Americans were employed through the Works Progress Administration (WPA).
- In 1938, the Congress of Industrial Organizations (CIO) banned member unions from discriminating on the grounds of race, making it harder to return to segregation.

However, employment laws often did not apply to areas where African-Americans were heavily employed. For example, the Social Security Act and the minimum wage requirements of the National Labor Relations Act excluded domestic workers, waiters, cooks, janitors and sharecroppers. Also, little was done to help about 200,000 sharecroppers who were displaced by the Agricultural Administration Programme. This forced many African-Americans to travel to towns in search of work, increasing competition for jobs and racial tension.

Southern Democrats refused to support measures that would have specifically helped African-Americans, reflecting the racial prejudice in the southern states (a legacy of the large number of slaves who had worked on plantations in the 19th century). In the south, this pattern of racism did not improve, and lynchings increased from 20 in 1930 to 24 in 1934. A 1936 NAACP (National Association for the Advancement of Colored People) report commented that six million African-Americans working in agriculture received no help from the New Deal, and it was very hard for them to complain about their treatment, particularly in the south, as they risked further discrimination or even violence.

# Social impact

The social impact of the New Deal also brought little benefit to African-Americans. There were more unemployed African-Americans than other groups, and even with the Fair Employment Practices Committee, segregation and discrimination continued. The high levels of unemployment had a negative impact on health and life expectancy, the latter of which was ten years lower for African-Americans than for white Americans. This inequality was also reflected in housing: the Federal Housing Administration refused to give mortgages to enable African-Americans to buy homes in 'white' areas, thereby helping to reinforce segregation. At the same time, the Tennessee Valley Authority built all-white towns, such as Norris.

## The historical debate

Left-wing historians, such as Barton Bernstein ('The New Deal: The Conservative Achievements of Liberal Reform' in *Towards a New Past*, Knopf, 1968), argue that the New Deal brought African-Americans few benefits. However, Tony Badger (*The New Deal*, 1989) and Harvard Sitkoff (*A New Deal for Blacks*, Oxford University Press, 1979) propose that the New Deal did as much for African-Americans as was possible given Roosevelt's dependency upon southern Democrats in Congress, the tradition of states' rights (whereby individual states could pass laws that discriminated against African-Americans) and the indifference of many in the north.

African-Americans received more benefits than before, even if the system still favoured whites. There were places where aid did not reach them, particularly in the south where it was distributed by whites. Yet the change in allegiance of African-American voters suggests that they recognised the benefits of the New Deal, despite the lack of civil rights legislation. Indeed, Roosevelt denounced lynching as murder, even though other members of the Democratic Party did not fully support the two anti-lynching bills (see page 171).

Roosevelt's administration also responded to African-American protests, seen most obviously in the Harlem riots of 1935. Clashes with police over the alleged beating and killing of an African-American shoplifter left one African-American dead and over 200 injured. Although some newspapers tried to blame the incident on communists, a commission recognised the causes as Harlem's poverty and the discrimination in the distribution of relief. In response to the report, racist officials were removed and more African-Americans were employed to administer relief.

Historians such as August Meier and Elliott Rudwick (*From Plantation to Ghetto*, Constable, 1970) see this period as crucial in the development of civil rights, describing it as 'a watershed in Afro-American direct action' that would not reach similar levels until the 1960s. Civil rights had become a political issue: African-Americans were more assertive and were starting to boycott retailers who practised discrimination. Self-help groups formed to help families struggling to survive, and Alpha Kappa Alpha's Mississippi Health Project, which ran each summer from 1935 to 1942, brought healthcare to many poor African-Americans. Many whites blamed Roosevelt for this increased assertiveness, suggesting that Roosevelt had helped to create a climate in which the self-confidence of African-Americans flourished.

## Discussion point

Consider statements a–f. Which statements do you agree with and which do you disagree with? Explain your answers fully.

a   The New Deal did not make life better for African-Americans.
b   The New Deal brought only minimal improvements for African-Americans.
c   The New Deal showed that African-Americans were still discriminated against.
d   The New Deal resulted in economic but not social improvements for African-Americans.
e   The New Deal helped to change attitudes in the United States towards African-Americans.
f   There was still discrimination against African-Americans after the New Deal, particularly in the south.

## Activity

Complete a chart like this to summarise the gains and losses experienced by minority groups as a result of the New Deal.

|  | African-Americans | | Native Americans | | Hispanic Americans | |
|---|---|---|---|---|---|---|
|  | Gains | Losses | Gains | Losses | Gains | Losses |
| Social |  |  |  |  |  |  |
| Political |  |  |  |  |  |  |
| Economic |  |  |  |  |  |  |
| Cultural |  |  |  |  |  |  |
| Other |  |  |  |  |  |  |

Then write a paragraph explaining which group gained the most from the New Deal and which group gained the least.

# Theory of knowledge

### Minority groups: too much or too little attention?

How much attention should historians devote to the study of minority groups? Until quite recently, their history was generally ignored. Why do you think it is studied now? Is it possible to write a balanced account of the experiences of minority groups?

# To what extent did the Depression change the position of women in the USA?

## Women's traditional role

Early 20th-century American women, particularly married women, played a traditional role in society; they were expected to remain at home, look after their husband and raise the family. The First World War did little in the long term to change this traditional role. Although women supported the war effort, as soon as the war ended it was expected that they would return to their domestic role, which was still accepted by most women. The economic prosperity of the 1920s created more job opportunities for unmarried women, and the development of numerous domestic gadgets, such as vacuum cleaners and washing machines, made home life easier for married women. The rapid growth in the sale of such goods, partly as a result of the availability of credit, was a clear indication of the impact they had on daily life. As a result, advertisers targeted women, as they chose items for the home; it was even rumoured that Henry Ford commented that his decision to make cars in colours other than black was the result of women choosing them! However, the lightened domestic load resulting from the new gadgets did not cause women to look for new roles; instead, they tended to spend the extra time with their children.

## Employment

Opportunities for career advancement were limited for women in the early 20th century. Very few women entered the higher-level professions or worked in industry; in the 1920s there were only 150 female dentists, fewer than 100 accountants and even fewer managing directors. Many employed women worked in clerical or sales-based jobs, but most of the work was low paid and menial, with over 700,000 women working as domestic servants. Those who were employed did not get the same pay as men, even if they did the same job.

The economic boom of the 1920s made it more acceptable for women to work, and by 1930 two million more women had joined the workforce. This resulted in 10 million women working – 24 per cent more than in 1920. There were also more married women in employment, with numbers rising in the 1920s from 22.8 per cent to 28.8 per cent, again mostly in clerical jobs. Some women worked in factories, while others were employed in nursing, social work and teaching. Yet even during a period of growth, women were seen as taking work away from men or threatening their wages, which could be kept low since women were paid less. Also, despite the increase in the number of women in employment, there was a 5 per cent fall in the number of women receiving a college education in the 1920s – a decline that would further limit their economic advancement.

**Discussion point**

Why do you think the position of women in the USA had changed little by 1920?

*The popular image of the 1920s 'flapper'; although some women wore dresses with short hemlines, and smoked and drank in public, most were expected to marry and run the home*

# Women's social position

The 1920s saw some improvement in the social position of women.

- The 1921 Sheppard–Towner Act funded healthcare for pregnant women and gave them some control over the clinics that were set up. However, this development angered feminists, who saw the Act as simply reinforcing the traditional role of women as mothers; feminist organisations such as the American Birth Control League were more concerned to make birth control available to women, but despite their efforts there were only ten branches in eight states by 1924.
- There were also moves to stop women working night shifts, but again this angered feminists who complained that women were not being treated equally and were being made more dependent upon men.
- Perhaps the clearest indication of women's greater social mobility and freedom was their reluctance to stay in unhappy marriages. This was reflected in the number of divorces, which doubled – from 100,000 in 1914 to nearly 200,000 by 1929.

# Political changes

In August 1920, the Nineteenth Amendment to the US Constitution gave most American women over the age of 21 the right to vote. (Immigrants who had not been naturalised were excluded.) However, very few women were politically active, and many women voted the same way as their husbands. Nevertheless, in 1928, the League of Women Voters reported that 145 women had seats in state legislatures, although only two of the 435 members of the House of Representatives were women. While political parties wanted the female vote, many male party members did not want women as candidates as they saw them as unelectable. For most women, there was little realisation that the vote empowered them and there was certainly no attempt to organise their voting power. In many cases, women were more concerned about the day-to-day realities of living. Often, African-American women living in the south were unable to take advantage of the right to vote, as – like their male counterparts – they faced intimidation or discrimination.

Some working-class women turned to union activity to protect their position in the workplace. However, unions were not very supportive of women workers as they were seen as a threat to jobs for men and to wages, as they were paid less. As a result, little was achieved, although female membership of unions did increase during the 1930s.

The most exploited of all women workers were African-Americans and Hispanics. Where unions were available for women, they were restricted to whites. Most women from minority groups entered lower-paid jobs, particularly Asian women, who often worked as domestic servants.

Politically, most women remained conservative in outlook; their traditional religious beliefs and domestic values meant that they did not envisage a change in their status. However, young, urban women were more progressive.

### SOURCE D

These large middle classes do their own housework with few of the mechanical aids. Women who live on farms – and they form the largest group in the United States – do a great deal of work besides the labour of caring for their children, washing clothes, caring for the home and cooking; thousands still labour in the fields, help milk the cows.

The other largest group of American women comprises the families of labourers, of the miners, the steel workers, the vast army of unskilled, semi-skilled and skilled workers. The wages of these men are on the whole so small that wives must do double duty – that is, caring for the children and the home and toil on the outside as wage earners.

Doris Fleischman, a feminist writer and publicist, describes the experiences of American women, 1932.

What impression does Fleischman give of the experience of women in this period?

## Activity

Complete a chart on the changing position of women on the eve of the Depression.

| | What improved? | What did not improve? |
|---|---|---|
| Social position | | |
| Economic position | | |
| Political position | | |
| Other | | |

Consider whether the 1920s were a good or bad time for women living in the USA.

# The impact of the Depression on women

## Women and employment

The impact of the Depression on women was very hard, particularly for married women. Opportunities for employment collapsed and women faced the likelihood of managing the family on a reduced income. Women were expected to give up their jobs for men; a 1936 opinion poll suggested that 82 per cent of Americans opposed working women, and in 1930, 75 per cent of school authorities refused to employ married women. Women were often laid off before men, particularly in unskilled trades, but some struggling companies preferred to keep women on as they were paid less. This was particularly hard where females were heads of the household. Many women worked in order to supplement the low income of their husbands, and the loss of employment had a severe impact on families reliant on two incomes.

As unemployment rose to record levels, 26 states attempted to introduce laws that banned married women from working. However, this only became law in Louisiana, and even there it was declared unconstitutional by the Supreme Court and had to be reversed. Where women remained in work, they were often accused of creating unemployment for men; some were even dismissed and replaced by men. Women who sought relief or paid employment risked public scorn for taking jobs or money away from 'more deserving' men. This attitude was summed up by Norman Cousins in 1939:

### SOURCE E

Simply fire the women, who shouldn't be working anyway, and hire the men. Presto! No unemployment. No Depression.

*Norman Cousins, a political journalist, speaking in 1939. Cousins realised that the number of gainfully employed women was roughly equal to the national unemployment figure.*

If the husband was unemployed, some women were forced to try and find work, usually in employment not covered by the National Recovery Association codes (which upheld the principle of lower pay for female workers). In this way, a significant number of women found themselves doing laundry work or other menial jobs. However, during the 1930s, women were fortunate in that traditional areas of female work, most notably clerical, were some of the quickest to recover, so employment opportunities improved. Women also benefited from the increased use of machinery in factories, as this created a greater demand for unskilled labour.

The Depression reversed the growth in female employment of the 1920s. Families accustomed to the extra income from women's jobs found their lifestyle changed as they struggled to make ends meet.

## Domestic life

Although many American women did not go out to work, the Depression continued to affect their lives at home. Many husbands took a pay cut to keep their jobs; if the man then lost his job, the family faced a struggle to survive without relief or losing their possessions. Very often, it was the responsibility of the woman to manage reduced resources; as Eleanor Roosevelt stated, 'Practically every woman, whether she is rich or poor, is facing today a reduction of income'. Women made do, substituting their own labour for things that had been bought, making economies by buying day-old bread or preparing more than one dish at a time to save gas. As one housewife said, 'We had no choice. We just did what had to be done one day at a time.'

> What is meant by the comment, 'We just did what had to be done one day at a time'? Who else might this comment apply to?

Overall, the years of Depression were not good for women, particularly working-class women from minority groups who needed to work to supplement their meagre incomes. While African-American women were poor to begin with, the Depression did make circumstances much harder. In Source F, the novelist and poet Maya Angelou describes the effects of the Depression on black women.

In 1930, 90 per cent of African-American women worked in either agriculture or domestic service. However, many housewives started to do their own housework and no longer hired servants, and some white women who needed to supplement the family income took on jobs that were previously considered too menial.

SOURCE F

The country had been in the throes of the Depression for two years before the Negroes in Stamps [Arkansas] knew it. I think that everyone thought the Depression, like everything else, was for the white folks.

Angelou, M. 1969. I Know Why the Caged Bird Sings. *New York, USA. Random House.*

Hispanic women – who were at the bottom of the economic ladder – faced a similar problem, compounded by the threat of deportation because of fears about job competition or relief.

## Government help for women

The Roosevelt administration did little to directly improve the position of women during the Depression. The government had many pressing concerns, and because women did not vote as a bloc (combine votes for a specific cause), the government gave greater priority to other issues. Women struggled to be treated equally even when they tried to qualify for the new federal programmes.

In practice, some of the legislation that was passed as part of the New Deal worked against women.

- The 1933 Economy Act prevented members of the same family working for the federal government. Many lost their jobs as a result of this law; of those, 75 per cent were women.
- The National Recovery Administration established the principle of lower pay for women in 1933, even for the same job (this decision was reached under the leadership of Frances Perkins – see page 67).
- Some agencies, such as the Civil Works Administration or Civilian Conservation Corps, gave jobs almost entirely to men.

Thus, most of the policies adopted by Roosevelt's administration were biased towards men and did little to improve the position of women in the USA.

### Discussion point

Why do you think there were few direct measures to improve the position of women in the workforce? How far do you think things have improved for women in the workplace today?

However, there were some Acts – not specifically designed for women but aimed at wider issues – that did improve women's position.

- The Social Security Act of 1933 introduced welfare benefits for poor families and therefore helped reduce stress for married women where incomes were low.
- The 1935 Aid for Dependent Children federal assistance programme gave relief to women with children who were unable to work and where there was no male head of the household. However, this programme was not always implemented fairly. It was often only white women who benefited from the aid, and recipients had to go through a humiliating process to get it.
- The Fair Labor Standards Act of 1938 established a minimum wage. Although this resulted in better pay for many women, it did not ensure that women were paid the same as men for doing the same job. In 1939, female teachers were paid 20 per cent less than male teachers and female white-collar or non-manual (clerical) workers received lower pay than male factory workers. The Fair Labor Standards Act also reduced working hours for women (although initially it did not cover major areas of women's employment, such as agricultural work or domestic service), abolished child labour and made it a right for women to join a union, thereby providing them with greater protection at work.
- The Wagner Act of 1935 encouraged a dramatic growth in organised labour as it guaranteed workers the right to collective bargaining and gave unions rights in law. This forced employers for the first time to accept unions. Women took up the protection offered and participated in major CIO (Congress of Industrial Organizations) strikes.

However, the needs of women might have been ignored entirely if it were not for an informal network of female administrators who held important positions within the New Deal agencies. Frances Perkins oversaw many of the welfare initiatives, and **Ellen Sullivan Woodward** supervised many women's relief projects for the Works Progress Administration. Their effectiveness was enhanced by access to Eleanor Roosevelt, who used her position to advance the cause of many minority groups.

**Ellen Sullivan Woodward (1887–1971)** Although born in Mississippi, Woodward was brought up in Washington, where she developed an interest in politics. In 1926, she returned to work in Mississippi for the State Board of Development. Her success led Harry Hopkins to bring her back to Washington as his assistant administrator, and she was put in charge of creating and supervising relief projects to provide work for unemployed women. This role increased with the creation of the Works Progress Administration (WPA).

In some ways, it could be argued that women saw their position enhanced, as their ability to economise was critical to the financial survival of the family unit. It was the man's world that had changed; for women, their home life, with its routines of cooking, cleaning, mending and childcare, remained largely unchanged.

*During the 1920s and 1930s, women were expected to stay at home performing traditional roles that focused on looking after the family*

 **Theory of knowledge**

### History and culture
Why has women's history become a more prominent feature of study in recent years? In what ways do cultural changes affect the way history is written and interpreted?

## Did life for women improve during the 1930s?

The greatest advancement for women during the 1930s was in national government. Women held more posts in government than at any time before the 1990s. The most prominent were the Secretary of Labor, Frances Perkins, and Mary Macleod Bethune, who headed the National Youth Administration. Although she held no official post, Eleanor Roosevelt also played an active role in campaigning for women's rights and she provided an excellent role model for many American women; she joined the League of Women Voters and the Women's Trade Union League, clearly showing her views about women's involvement in politics, and her support of workers' and trade union rights.

Other prominent women of the period who provided positive role models through their own endeavours include:

- Ruth Bryan Owen, who became the first female ambassador and was posted to Denmark
- Nellie Tayloe Ross, the first female director of the Mint
- Florence Allen, the first female judge on the US circuit of appeals.

However, these women often found themselves the victims of attack. Frances Perkins was attacked in the press and accused of being a Soviet spy; at work, she was ignored by many of her colleagues. Such ill-natured behaviour reflects how deeply entrenched traditional views of women were in US society.

A number of women were also prominent in the design of some of the New Deal measures, particularly those that tackled social issues. However, this role declined with the arrival of the Second World War and a change of emphasis in government. The gains made by women were therefore short-term, although women did achieve greater prominence in government during the period.

Most women did not gain from the New Deal. The National Recovery Agency allowed unequal wages to be paid, and the Civilian Conservation Corps barred women from working for it. At a local level, governments often tried to avoid paying social security to women by the introduction of 'special qualifications' – for example, often limiting payment to white families or putting young women through humiliating interviews. By the end of the period, men were still seen as, and expected to be, the main earners, while anything women earned was viewed as a supplement. Where women had been able to find work, it was usually low status and poorly paid; figures indicate that the average wage of women during the 1930s was half that of men.

If the position of women in general scarcely improved during the Depression period, the situation for women from minority groups was even worse. African-American and Hispanic women were still discriminated against, particularly in rural areas. Acts limiting the amount of agricultural production to keep up prices hit small landowners and sharecroppers, lessening the need for female labour. Meanwhile, when unemployed workers from minority groups moved to northern cities, there was little work available for men, and women were forced into low-paid jobs, especially domestic work. The situation was slightly better for Native American women, as they made some gains from the Indian Reorganisation Act of 1934 (see pages 173–75). The Act gave them political rights and provided training for domestic work and as seamstresses. The promotion of native arts and crafts also provided some employment opportunities for Native American women.

**Activity**

Draw a chart to show the gains and losses made by women as a result of the New Deal.

# Summary

You should now have an understanding of the changes to the position of minority groups and women in the United States during the period from 1920 to the outbreak of the Second World War. Although there were some improvements, the gains were usually the result of more general policies aimed at the whole of the nation rather than at specific groups. There were some exceptions, particularly for Native Americans, but there would be no major improvements in general for minority groups and women until the Second World War. Most minority groups were treated as second-class citizens, and they were often the first to lose their jobs as unemployment rose during the Depression. Many found it very hard to obtain relief, and when recovery commenced they were often the last to benefit. However, it might be argued that, because the position of minority groups before the onset of the Depression was one of poverty, they had less to lose, and so the gap between them and other Americans actually narrowed. Even if this view is accepted, you should still be aware that discrimination and prejudice remained for all the groups discussed in this chapter.

**Activity**

Construct a spider diagram to show the reasons why progress in improving the position of minority groups and women was so difficult. What justifications were there for not helping the position of minority groups and women more directly?

Then imagine that you are either President Roosevelt explaining your decision to Congress or a member of Congress opposed to specific measures to aid minority groups and women. What would you say in your speech to Congress? How would you defend your position?

How far had the position of African-Americans, Native Americans, Hispanics and women improved by the outbreak of the Second World War?

# End of chapter activities
## Paper 3 exam practice

### Question

'The New Deal did more for Native Americans than African-Americans.' How far do you agree with this view?
[20 marks]

### Skill focus

Using your own knowledge analytically and combining it with awareness of historical debate

### Examiner's tips

Always remember that historical knowledge and analysis should be the *core* of your answer – aspects of historical debate are desirable extras. However, where it is relevant, the integration of relevant knowledge about historical debates/interpretations, with reference to individual historians, will help push your answer up into the higher bands.

Assuming that you have read the question carefully, drawn up a plan, worked out your line of argument/approach, and written your introductory paragraph, you should be able to avoid both irrelevant material and simple narrative. Your task now is to follow your plan by writing a series of linked paragraphs that contain relevant analysis, precise supporting own knowledge and, where relevant, brief references to historical debate interpretations.

For this question, you will need to:

- consider the aims of the New Deal – 'successes' cannot exist independently of the problems being solved or ambitions met
- supply a brief explanation of the context (the scale of the problems and the attitude of previous governments to these groups)
- outline what happened – the main elements of policy; what measures were taken to improve the position of Native Americans and African-Americans
- provide a consistently analytical examination of the reasons for the introduction, course and development of these events.

A topic like this, which has been the subject of much historical debate, will give you the chance to refer to different historians' views.

## Common mistakes

Some students, being aware of an existing historical debate (and knowing that extra marks can be gained by showing this), simply write: 'Historian X says …, and historian Y says …' However, they make no attempt to **evaluate** the different views (for example, has one historian had access to more/better information than another, perhaps because he/she was writing at a later date?); nor is this information **integrated** into their answer by being pinned to the question. Another weak use of historical debate is to write things like: 'Historian X is biased because she is American.' Such comments will not be given credit.

Remember to refer to the simplified Paper 3 markscheme on page 219.

## Sample paragraphs containing analysis and historical debate

These gains, when compared with the position of African-Americans, suggests that the New Deal did more for Native Americans than African-Americans. Many New Deal agencies discriminated against African-Americans, and unlike the situation for Native Americans, there were no agencies established specifically to look after their interests. This supports the view of left wing historians such as Barton Bernstein, who have argued that the New Deal brought the African-American nothing more than words and gestures. This appears to be valid with the development of all white towns through the TVA. However, it ignores the benefits made by African-Americans from the slum clearance schemes in many northeastern cities. It also ignores the fact that nearly one million jobs were provided for African-Americans and a further 50,000 units of housing and training for some half a million African-American youths.

This is a good example of how to use historians' views. The **main** focus of the answer is properly concerned with using precise own knowledge to address the demands of the question. However, the candidate has also provided some brief but relevant knowledge of historical debate, which is **smoothly integrated** into the answer.

In much the same way as Native Americans were handicapped by the reluctance of officials, the same was often true for African-Americans in the south. However, the achievements should not be dismissed and need to be placed in their historical context. Badger and Sitkoff are right to argue that Roosevelt did as much as he could for African-Americans, as he was dependent upon the support of southern Democrats who would not have approved further legislation aimed purely at African-Americans. It should also be remembered, as Meier and Rudgwick have argued, that the New Deal resulted in civil rights becoming a political issue. As one white southerner noted, 'You ask any [African-American] in the street who's the greatest man in the world: nine out of ten will tell you Franklin Roosevelt.' Therefore, even if the gains were not always obvious in the 1930s, the period was significant in the long term in improving the position of African-Americans and should not be dismissed when compared with the gains of Native Americans.

## Activity

In this chapter, the focus is on writing an answer that is analytical, and well-supported by precise own knowledge, and one which – where relevant – refers to historical interpretations/debates. Using the information from this chapter, and any other sources of information available to you, try to answer one of the following Paper 3 practice questions using these skills.

## Paper 3 practice questions

1   Was there a New Deal for Native Americans?

2   To what extent did the position of African-Americans improve as a result of the New Deal?

3   How seriously affected were African-Americans, Native Americans and women by the Depression?

4   'The New Deal failed to improve the position of minority groups within the United States.' How far do you agree with this view?

5   To what extent did women benefit from the New Deal?

6   'The benefits outweighed the losses.' How far do you agree with this view of the impact of the New Deal on minorities in the USA?

# 7 The Great Depression and the arts in the USA

## Timeline

**1929 Oct:** Wall Street Crash and onset of Depression

**1931** premiere of the movie *Public Enemy*, starring James Cagney

**1932 Nov:** Franklin D. Roosevelt elected president

**1933 12 Mar:** Roosevelt's first radio 'fireside chat'

**Dec:** Public Works of Art Project set up

**1935 Apr:** Works Progress Administration (WPA) established

**Aug:** Federal Theatre Project set up; WPA's Federal Art Project begins; Rural Electrification Administration – more electrification increases radio listening

**1935–37** Farm Security Administration sets up a photographic programme

**1938 Nov:** first issue of *Life* magazine

**1939** publication of John Steinbeck's *The Grapes of Wrath*; the movies *The Wizard of Oz* and *Gone with the Wind* premiere

## Key questions

- How did the Depression influence the development of photography?
- How did the Depression influence the development of the movie industry?
- How were literature and drama affected by the Depression?
- How did the Depression influence the development of the radio industry?

This chapter focuses on the impact of the Great Depression on the arts in the USA. One of the major themes of the chapter is the greater role the US federal government played in promoting the arts. The chapter also considers the impact of new technology, including the growth of radio listening and the increasing technical sophistication of movies. There were significant creative changes in the field of photography, which developed into a distinct art form.

How far the circumstances of the time affected creative artists is always difficult to know. It is possible to trace the impact of official patronage of the arts, and the growth of certain arts, such as photography, Hollywood movies and radio, is indisputable. However, the balance between the impact of technical processes, such as the advent of sound in film-making, and the effects of the Depression in motivating and inspiring artists and creators, is a matter of debate.

The issues in this chapter are very important, and the changing cultural world of the 1930s was a major influence on 20th and 21st century artistic development.

## Overview

- The increased role of the state in the US economy meant there were direct government initiatives to promote the arts. These included grants to theatres and the sponsoring of documentary films and photographs. Some of the most distinctive creations of the 1930s came as a result of New Deal patronage.
- Art during the 1920s and 1930s reflected the Depression in different ways:
  - Some works were created as a direct response to the suffering and conditions that the Depression either caused or intensified. The most famous is probably John Steinbeck's novel *The Grapes of Wrath*, which was filmed in 1940.
  - Some artistic works were influenced by the Depression, but their focus was not economic distress. Some of the more creative photography of the Depression falls into this category, as do some of the more adventurous writing and poetry.
  - Escapist entertainment became particular relevant in the Depression era. This might have been produced even in times of prosperity, but it took on a new importance because reality was harsh and the need for escapist fantasy was intense.
  - Some art appeared to have little direct connection to the Depression, but if seen in the context of the time it can be viewed as a product of the Depression years. For instance, the film *The Wizard of Oz* (1939) is a much-loved fairy tale, yet may also be understood as a sort of parable of Roosevelt's New Deal.

# How did the Depression influence the development of photography?

All creative activity is both part of its time and influenced by the concerns of individual artists, so it is always impossible to determine the exact extent to which external situations influence art. Yet aspects of photography during the Depression were undeniably influenced by the New Deal, since the work was commissioned by federal agencies.

## Resettlement Agency photographers

The New Deal established federal government organisations to promote economic recovery, such as the Resettlement Agency for farmers. These organisations used photography to show the general public the problems they were trying to solve and to publicise their work.

### Dorothea Lange

One of the most famous photographers working under government commission was Dorothea Lange (1895–1965). Lange was part of a team of photographers employed by the Resettlement Agency (later the Farm Security Administration), a New Deal organisation set up to help farmers resettle their land and recover economically from the dust bowl (see page 85) and the financial crisis. Under the leadership of Roy Stryker, the photographers aimed to show the impact of the Depression, farm mechanisation and the dust bowl on American society. The aim was documentary – that is, to provide a record of the United States. The photographers included Walker Evans, Dorothea Lange, Carl Mydans, Arthur Rothstein, Ben Shahn and others. What was innovative about this process was that the federal government was actually taking the initiative in subsidising and patronising the arts.

The photographs produced were widely seen, and Dorothea Lange's 'Migrant Mother' became famous. Lange commented, 'If one picture could sum up the experience of Depression, many think that this would be it.'

*Dorothea Lange's 'Migrant Mother', California, 1936; the photo was one of a series taken by Lange of Florence Owens Thompson and her children*

Other images of the Depression appeared in newspapers, magazines, museums and books. They were produced with the purpose of promoting New Deal policies and educating Americans about their own country. The photographs were more than just a record – they were intended to provoke discussion and often had a distinct social and political agenda.

There were some issues regarding the ethics of the photographs. For instance, Lange made little engagement with Florence Owens Thompson (the woman shown in 'Migrant Mother') – did not ask her name, send her a copy of the photograph or pay her a fee, even though the picture made Lange a celebrity and was widely reproduced. Another issue is whether the art became more important than the message. If we compare 'Migrant Mother' with another photograph taken at the same time (of Florence Owens Thompson nursing her child), the composition and texture of the 'Migrant Mother' photograph is similar to a painting, whereas the photo of Thompson nursing her child seems more random and less appealing.

*Florence Owens Thompson nursing her child*

 ## Theory of knowledge

### Documenting history

What is the moral duty of those who document hardships, such as the plight of Florence Owens Thompson, the mother depicted here? Thompson was a migrant pea picker of Cherokee origin, living a hard life, but she unwittingly did much to promote Lange's career. Did Lange exploit Thompson, or does the attention that Lange's image brought to the plight of migrant workers make this an example of a humane and creative use of a sitter? Should historians use images such as this, and what is their relevance to historical research?

## SOURCE A

I saw and approached the hungry and desperate mother. There she sat in that lean-to tent with her children huddled around her, and seemed to know that my pictures might help her, and so she helped me. There was a sort of equality about it.

*Dorothea Lange's memory of taking the 'Migrant Mother' photograph, given in an interview in 1960.*

### Activity

Read Source A. Do you agree that there was 'a sort of equality' between photographer and subject?

What was controversial, too, was that the images from these official photographers could be used to support a political agenda. For example, photographs of desperation and poor housing could be seen to show the products of Republican policies and neglect, while images of New Deal improvements could be used to portray the Democrats as the party of action.

*This photo by Arthur Rothstein, taken in 1936, neatly contrasts the poster's idealism with the reality of living conditions in a poor area in Birmingham, Alabama*

### Activity

Look at Arthur Rothstein's image from the Depression era. What point is Rothstein making by contrasting the cheerful poster with the poor-quality housing? How do you explain the photograph's importance and message with regard to the New Deal?

## The role of the Works Progress Administration

In addition to the body of work produced by the Resettlement Agency/ FSA, there were the sponsored activities of the Works Progress Administration (WPA). Its aims were to show America to Americans and encourage the arts as a nationally unifying medium. The WPA commissioned some interesting murals and photographers. One of the most celebrated photographers was Berenice Abbott, who produced studies of New York between 1935 and 1938 as part of the WPA's Federal Art Project. Most of the hundreds of photographers employed by the WPA were restricted to relief project documentation, but Abbott was a well-known experimental artist who used her unique perspective and skills to create striking photographs of New York City.

Officially sponsored photography involved the visual recording of different regions. This enabled the Depression's impact across the USA to be seen, and Americans could witness the reality of life in different areas. State aid for artistic photography was restricted by 1938, and eventually ran out. However, the Depression era had an impact on the art of photography in other ways than straightforward patronage.

During the 1930s, there was a growth in new venues for displaying exhibitions and in new mass-produced periodicals. These encouraged high-quality and striking images and greater public awareness of the photograph as a means of artistic expression. There was also a new interest in photographs of ordinary people, rather than famous subjects, which allowed the viewer to engage with the drama and experience of ordinary life.

### Activity

As a class, make up your own exhibition of photographs from the Depression era. Explain why you have chosen particular photographs.

## The appeal of photography during the Depression

The suffering the Depression caused therefore acted as a major artistic stimulus. Photography had been developing as an art form since the 1890s, under pioneers such as Alfred Stieglitz. The 1930s brought together a series of factors: the photographers, the magazines and exhibitions, the dramatic opportunities to portray real life and personal emotion, and a public demand for images.

This new appetite for photography can be explained in several ways.

- Photographs were something lasting and worthwhile at a time when material possessions and wealth were being lost and prosperity appeared short-lived.

- The Depression made Americans more curious about their country and its future. Photographs provided a means of explaining how the Depression came about, how was it affecting other people and what was being done about it. In times of economic and social confidence, energies often turn outwards; in times of decline, they tend to turn inwards and become more reflective – and during the Depression era, photography suited this inward gaze.
- Words seemed to have failed the USA – the talk of the 1920s of prosperity and progress now seemed cheap. The public therefore turned to images, which were more immediate and seemed more reliable.
- During the New Deal, the public sphere became more significant. Americans engaged more with museums and public places, where photography could be displayed. At the San Francisco World Fair of 1940, for instance, photographic exhibitions were extremely popular.
- Technology made cameras more accessible – 50 per cent of American families owned one in the 1930s. Photography therefore became a democratic art form, open to everyone.

### Discussion point

Which, if any, of the above explanations do you find most convincing?
Can the development of any art form be explained by looking at economic circumstances?

There was also a new interest in technology – **Margaret Bourke-White** became famous for her pictures of engineering and industrial sites. Perhaps the closing down of these sites in the depth of the Depression reinforced their importance, as did the New Deal's public works.

**Margaret Bourke-White (1904–71)** Bourke-White was born in New York and became a professional commercial photographer in 1929. She later moved into photojournalism and was the first woman to work for *Life* magazine. She was also the first woman war correspondent and the first female photographer to work in combat zones. She produced vivid photographs of the suffering during the Depression years in the USA and photographed Buchenwald concentration camp in 1945. She travelled extensively and was the first western photographer to make detailed photographic studies of the USSR.

### Activity

Carry out research on photographs of the USA in the 1930s taken by photographers such as Ansel Adams and Maragaret Bourke-White. How far were these photographers influenced by the Depression?

## The impact of *Life* magazine

A key element in the new interest in photography was the decision of the publisher Henry Luce to buy the existing humorous magazine *Life* and turn it into a magazine dedicated to photojournalism. Luce already produced *Time* and *Fortune* magazines, but *Life* (launched in November 1936) was built round the idea of pictures telling the story of current events and developments. With 50 pages of pictures for 10 cents, the magazine became highly popular, reaching sales of a million in four months and employing major photographic talents. It was copied by *Look* in 1937. These weekly magazines satisfied and stimulated a growing demand for high-quality photographs that exposed American life. *Life*'s popularity paralleled the huge growth of the movie industry in the later 1930s (see next section), and both developments were part of a revolution in the accessibility of images.

*Life meets art: Margaret Bourke-White's photograph of a dam on the cover of the first edition of* Life *magazine, 23 November 1936*

### Activity

What impact does the cover of the first edition of *Life* magazine have on you? Why do you think this photograph was chosen for the first edition?

# How did the Depression influence the development of the movie industry?

## Pare Lorentz and documentary filmmaking

As with photography, there was federal patronage of documentary movies during the years of the Depression and the New Deal. These are most associated with the filmmaker **Pare Lorentz**. Lorentz was a former advertising man who despaired of the capitalist system and the ability of the individual to rise through a free economic system. His best-known films are *The River* and *The Plow That Broke the Plains*.

**Pare Lorentz (1905–92)** Lorentz was born in Virginia and worked as a writer, advertising man and film critic in New York. He impressed President Roosevelt with a picture biography of his first year in office, and received federal funding for his documentaries, which were a major success in the 1930s. He worked on documentary films about the war effort and the Nuremberg trials (the post-Second World War trials of Nazi war criminals).

*The Plow That Broke the Plains* (1936) was commissioned by the Department of Agriculture. Its subject matter was the creation and effects of the dust bowl in the Great Plains (the wide open, mostly agricultural lands in the central states of North Dakota, South Dakota, Nebraska, Kansas and Oklahoma). It was a film with a message – individualism had destroyed the natural relationship of man with the land and brought hardships, so better management of natural resources was essential. A similar message was delivered in *The River* (1938). It had a verse commentary and a powerful score by Virgil Thomson, and is regarded as one of the most striking documentaries ever made. *The River* was first screened in the White House, but such was its quality that it was taken by movie theatres after an initial run at the Rialto Theatre in New York.

Hollywood regarded Lorentz's work with suspicion, as the films could be seen as political propaganda and it was hard for movie theatres to get film stock and distribution. Congress objected to funding *The River*, and so Lorentz's film was made on a low budget.

Lorentz's sponsored documentaries, though moving, do not compare in scale with the great age of the Hollywood movie. The Depression years coincided with an enormous expansion of filmmaking. There was the introduction of sound and then of colour film, both of which transformed an already thriving industry. The USA's economic problems did not restrict this growth, and indeed may have stimulated it, since they profoundly affected the subject matter and style of filmmaking.

## Movie styles

The silent films of the mid 1890s to late 1920s were influenced by European moviemaking and built around the importance of the visual image. Public demand in the 1920s was for romantic storylines, visual humour and melodramatic playing. Some silent films attempted to tackle major social topics, but the advent of sound revolutionised the industry and changed acting styles. Silent stars with unfortunate voices gave way to actors who had stage experience. Thus the popularity of stage plays determined a lot of the subject matter of the early 'talkies'. In the later 1920s, gangster plays became popular in theatres, and the actors associated with them were used by Warner Brothers to make a series of powerful gangster movies starring Edward G. Robinson, Paul Muni and James Cagney. With these films, tough dialogue, fast action and very direct emotional comment became new elements in cinema.

## Explaining gangster movies: the historical debate

Morris Dickstein (*Dancing in the Dark*, 2009) argues that this new style of filmmaking was influenced by the Depression. Joel W. Finler (*The Hollywood Story*, Wallflower Press, 2003) puts forward the alternative view generally accepted by film historians – the new film style emerged because the advent of sound meant moviemakers needed a new kind of star. The debate here is whether films about gangsters were a product of the Depression or would still have been made had prosperity continued. Andrew Bergman's study of the gangster film in the context of US society (*We're in the Money*, Harper & Row, 1972) suggests that gangster films reinforced American myths about individual success. The gangsters depicted in the films rose from obscure backgrounds by their own efforts – and with a strong element of risk – to wealth and influence. Dickstein suggests gangster films reflect not the get-rich individualism of the 1920s but a new uncertainty about success and individualism arising from the Depression. The gangsters in *Scarface* (1932), *Little Caesar* (1931) and the better-known *The Public Enemy* (1931) are indeed punished for their success. By pursuing individualism, the gangsters kill others, destroy their loved ones and sacrifice themselves, becoming brutalised. The actors portrayed the gangsters as monstrous figures. Their turbulent, violent world could be compared to the chaos that accompanied the Depression, though none of the movies refer to it.

If the influence of the Depression on moviemaking is accepted, then it created some distinctive high-energy cinema. The gangster film genre was developed later in the 1930s and peaked with the *Godfather* films of the 1970s and 80s. In this respect, the Depression could be said to have started a popular form of moviemaking.

## Escapism

While Depression audiences were thrilled by gangster movies, they also responded to films that offered a means of escape. Audiences wanted a world of wit and to see lavish musical productions in order to momentarily forget the harsh realities of 1930s American life. Musicals were immensely popular, and the advent of sound also gave rise to the fast-talking comedies of the 1930s. These featured sophisticated wisecracks, verbal sparring and bizarre word play from the likes of the Marx Brothers; the sharp dialogue was unusual in stage plays of the time but it was highly suited for films and proved extremely popular. Dick Powell and Myrna Loy played a rapid-fire, high-living husband and wife detective team in *The Thin Man*; Cary Grant was a witty and urbane leading man; Fred Astaire and Ginger Rogers danced and talked at speed, but also with elegance and charm.

A deeper analysis by Dickstein suggests that the precision of massed dancers and elaborate patterns in films such as *42nd Street* (1933) and *Gold Diggers of 1933* (1933), choreographed by Busby Berkeley, represent a move away from individualism to achievement by working together in harmony. Perhaps the speed of the tap dancing and the dialogue represented a freedom and mobility for US citizens that ended with the Depression. In this sense, moviegoers were attracted to films that reminded them of their hopes for the future – of stability, co-operation, freedom and opportunities for change.

## Films about the Depression

In the 1930s, there were also movies that dealt directly with the impact of the Depression. One example is *I am a Fugitive from a Chain Gang* (1932), directed by Mervin Le Roy and starring Paul Muni. It is a powerful story that charts the way in which the poverty brought about by the Depression ended individual hopes and aspirations. The following chart provides a summary of the plot (left column) along with a possible interpretation of how it links to the period (column 2). (Note that another interpretation of this movie is that it was simply based on a popular series that actually predated the stock market crash of 1929.)

| Plot event | Possible interpretation |
|---|---|
| James Allen returns from the First World War to find himself cut off from normal life. | This parallels the changes the war brought to normal economic life. |
| He wants to be an engineer, not work in his old dull factory job. | This projects the restlessness of the Depression years. |
| He leaves and wanders through the country looking for work. | The Depression saw a considerable increase in the numbers of people wandering the country. |
| In Georgia, he gets involved in a robbery led by another hobo and is sentenced to 10 years on a chain gang. | Criminality was common during the Depression, as people struggled to survive. |
| The conditions in the work camp are barbaric and the authorities uncaring and brutal. | Authority is seen in a bad light – echoing the repression of strikes and the demolition of the Hoovervilles. |
| He escapes, moves north, changes his name, gets a job in construction and rises to be an upstanding citizen. He returns south after being promised a pardon. | The USA is still the land of opportunity. |
| The authorities break their word; he becomes a frantic man, escaping on a truckload of dynamite. He becomes a doomed criminal whom society has failed. | Society and unreliable authority destroy individual creativity and progress, just as uncontrolled capitalism and poor government destroy businesses and hope. The story is a representative Depression tale. |

 ## Theory of knowledge

### History in the arts

Movies can provide subtle evidence about the time in which they were made. How useful is film evidence to historians?

## Moviemakers

Hollywood in the 1930s was more strictly organised by powerful individual film studios – MGM, Warner Brothers, Columbia, RKO and Universal – than in the 1920s. The studios controlled the creative artists and increased production of so-called 'B-movies' – lower-quality films intended to supplement the main feature during a double-bill showing. This structured approach can be seen as an industry equivalent to the controls and collectivism of the New Deal. Alternatively, it could be viewed as merely a reflection of the need for greater organisation to manage new technology and to be able to produce films cheaply enough at a time when profits were not very high.

Despite the increased demand for movies, the Depression reduced profits and forced filmmakers to keep prices competitive. The USA's return to recession in 1938 hit film audiences, as there was less money available for entertainment. However, the studios attracted stars, strong writers, excellent musicians and composers, and they also pursued technical advances, especially colour film. As hardship and unemployment continued until the start of the Second World War, there was an on-going need for escapism along with a need for commentary on the times. Historical films and Westerns were popular, and their meaning can be analysed in terms of a comment on the Depression. *Gone With the Wind* (1939) dealt with the demise of the old south and the efforts of the heroine – the former pampered beauty of the plantation, Scarlett O'Hara (played by Vivien Leigh) – to rebuild her life, just as thousands of formerly affluent Americans tried to reconstruct their own lives.

## The Grapes of Wrath

The most powerful cinematic representation of the events of the Depression came with *The Grapes of Wrath*, made by John Ford in 1940 and based on the bestselling novel by John Steinbeck, which had appeared in the previous year. *The Grapes of Wrath* is a film whose subject matter is dominated by the experience of the Depression and whose message is highly influenced by the New Deal. It was made at the end of the Depression years by a filmmaker who was interested in showing the heroic qualities of those who ventured into the unknown, and whose heroes were often tortured individualists. The movie, however, reveals the limitations of individual enterprise.

The hero of the film, Tom Joad, returns from prison to find that the bank has repossessed his family's farm after the dust bowl conditions have ruined the land. The family of 12 piles into an old car converted into a lorry, and with other 'Oakies' (ruined farmers from Oklahoma and the mid-west) sets off for California, where fruit growing has not suffered to the same extent. Grandpa Joad dies on the way.

In the first camp for migrant workers they find starving and desperate migrants; at a second camp the fruit growers, who pay poor wages and control the only available shop, exploit them. In a dispute with a guard, Tom kills the man who has killed his friend, Casy. The family escapes to a third camp run by the Department of Agriculture and encounters the only humanity seen in the film. Tom goes off to fight for justice. His mother has the last words in the film:

## SOURCE B

I ain't never gonna be scared no more. I was, though. For a while it looked as though we was beat. Good and beat. Looked like we didn't have nobody in the whole wide world but enemies. Like nobody was friendly no more. Made me feel kinda bad and scared too, like we was lost and nobody cared... Rich fellas come up and they die, and their kids ain't no good and they die out, but we keep on coming. We're the people that live. They can't wipe us out, they can't lick us. We'll go on forever, Pa, cos we're the people.

*Extract from Nunnally Johnson's film script for John Ford's* The Grapes of Wrath *(1940), based on John Steinbeck's 1939 novel of the same name.*

By 1940, Depression films had moved from the despair evident in some of the movies of the early 1930s to the portrayal of a hope beyond the obvious poverties. For example, in *Wild Boys of the Road* (1933), small-town adolescents suffer hardships but are in the end helped by enlightened adults and a thoughtful judge.

The Great Depression influenced American movies by stimulating an already flourishing industry into using the experiences of men and women facing hardship to produce some powerful works of art. There was also government sponsorship of films illustrating economic problems and solutions. There was a huge rise in demand for movies during the 1930s, partly through the need for emotional escape from the turmoil of the Depression – Hollywood was happy to help with dramas, comedies and musicals starring glamorous and vibrant personalities. However, the need for Americans to see how others were coping with the Depression was considerable, and the financial hardships permeated the movies in all sorts of ways. There were films that dealt directly with Depression issues. There were also movies where a break with the past, an interest in greater community effort and a loss of confidence in traditional self-help and individualism were evident, even if the stories were not specifically about economic and social distress. For example, millions of Americans saw *The Wizard of Oz* (1939) without seeing it as a 'Depression picture'.

The very popular dancers Fred Astaire and Ginger Rogers, and the relaxed and charming singer and actor Bing Crosby, did not appear to be linked with the Depression in the same way that actor Henry Fonda, playing Tom Joad in *The Grapes of Wrath*, so clearly was. However, their pictures still reflect the economic and social conditions of their time, even if only through escapism.

*Fred Astaire and Ginger Rogers dance together in the 1936 musical comedy Swing Time*

## How were literature and drama affected by the Depression?

Unlike photography and moviemaking, the New Deal offered little direct incentive to writing. The dramatic effects of the Depression on the lifestyle of Americans offered a wealth of opportunities for writers to investigate the human condition, and provided a strong context for writing that could be angry and emotional and offer heartfelt protest. Yet the motivations for writing can be so diverse that it may not always be possible to isolate a writer's main motivation. Would some writing have developed in a particular way even if the relative boom years of the 1920s had continued, or did the Depression play a key role in developing literature between 1930 and 1940?

The most remarkable sponsorship of theatre plays came from the WPA's establishment of the Federal Theatre Project in 1935. Harry Hopkins, the head of the WPA, chose the theatrical producer and director Hallie Flanagan to develop a large-scale organisation, employing actors and theatre staff, to bring theatre to the masses. New productions of existing classics were staged and new work commissioned. Writers took current issues and produced 'living newspapers' to educate audiences. Subject matter ranged from the Italian invasion of Ethiopia to the work of the TVA. The entertainment value of these productions may have varied, but there was the excitement of writers taking material that was so current and making instant popular theatre. Some famous names were associated with the project – Elmer Rice, Orson Welles, Arthur Miller and the composer Marc Blitzstein.

Another striking innovation was the Negro Theatre Project. New works were commissioned and produced by African-American writers, such as Frank Wilson's folk drama *Walk Together, Children* (1936), which described the deportation of 100 African-American children from the south to the north to work for low wages.

There was a considerable desire among some writers to depict hardship and poverty, and there was also a tradition of humanitarian protest literature. Rather like the Federal Theatre Project's work, stories of hardship were probably too much a part of their time to become classic literature.

## Writers and the depiction of poverty

Just as photographers were moved to record bad conditions, so some writers investigated and wrote about misery or drew on their experiences of growing up in poverty. Michael Gold (1893–1967) came from an immigrant family that lived in New York's Lower East Side. His stories *Jews without Money* appeared in 1930. The Depression encouraged this sort of writing about life in deprived areas of the USA; certainly there was not much writing on this subject in the 1920s. The same inward-looking desire to record the United States as seen in the photography of the period is found in John Dos Passos's epic trilogy *U.S.A.*, written between 1930 and 1934.

The early stages of the Depression produced a variety of novels depicting political awareness among US workers, stimulated by hardship and poverty. These grim novels, such as Edward Anderson's *Hungry Men* (1935), provided representations of men pushed to their limits. Often, these stories were the result of the author's direct experiences of Depression America. These writers, along with crime writers such as Dashiell Hammett, explored their downbeat subject matter using a concise writing style. The most famous and enduring writer in this tradition was John Steinbeck, whose *Tortilla Flat* was published in 1935 and *The Grapes of Wrath* in 1939.

Some writers found inspiration in groups that were unlikely subjects for conventional novels – such as migrant workers. Erskine Caldwell's *Tobacco Road* (1932) focuses on the poverty-stricken south, which was also the setting for William Faulkner's stories. A new departure in writing about the south came with the publication of Richard Wright's *Native Son* (1940) and *Uncle Tom's Children* (1938). These works are quite unyielding portrayals of oppression and include some disturbingly violent scenes. For example, the son of a black woman has his knees broken and his eardrums burst, while another character is driven by circumstances to kill white men. The desire to stir up audiences was common. The playwright Clifford Odets induced audiences to cry out 'Strike! Strike!' in his political play of 1935, *Waiting For Lefty*.

## Activity

Each member of the class selects a book inspired by the Depression. Select one page and explain to the class how it was influenced by conditions in the 1930s. The page could be photocopied and enlarged and mounted with the commentary on the wall.

## Word and image

The mass circulation of photojournalism meant, to some extent, that images had become more powerful than the written word. This shift from text to image was reflected in the growth of comic books. The most iconic comic book character is Superman, who was conceived in 1934 by Jerry Siegel and Joe Shuster. Siegel's father was killed in a robbery in 1932, and Shuster thought Superman was created in response to Siegel's personal crisis. Superman was a righteous crime-fighting hero who could cope with urban problems while living a 'normal' life as a reporter. As well as hero, Clark Kent is also the common man – highlighting the key New Deal theme of the importance of the individual.

*The first edition of Action Comics (1938), in which Superman made his debut*

In times of anxiety and crisis, did Americans crave the help of a superhero? Was this the Depression's influence on popular culture?

## Discussion point

Is any attempt to relate literature to life – from the most profound poetry to comic book writing – unrealistic? Or can literature only be understood in the context of the time?

# How did the Depression influence the development of the radio industry?

The development of radio in the 1930s was one of the most important cultural events in US history. In *Radio's America* (2007), Bruce Lenthall sees the development of radio as one aspect of the decline of the isolated, self-reliant and independent USA of the 19th century. Radios helped to link the United States in the same way that railroads did after the Civil War (1861–65), the remarkable growth of cities after the 1860s, the development of a rural postal service in the early 20th century and greater circulation of newspapers. The development of cheap motor cars and military service during the First World War were two other major influences that brought Americans together.

Increasingly, Americans were part of a greater world beyond their farm or small town, and so they were affected by events outside their control. They needed to know more of the wider world that affected their individual lives. Radio stations were able to expand and provide that contact with the wider world and the American nation as a whole. Radio met the demand for more information, shared experiences and a national culture. The government helped with rural electrification, and technology enabled mass production of cheap and accessible radios.

## SOURCE C

Ordinary people felt that the New Deal offered them a new self-respect. The common man had come into his own. On the cultural side, radio programmes such as *The Goldbergs*, *I Remember Mama* and even Amos'n'Andy bolstered ethnic pride while creating cultural bonds that helped bring immigrants into the mainstream.

Dickstein, M. 2009. *Dancing In the Dark*. New York, USA. Norton. p. 442.

*A farm couple listening to the radio at home in Hidalgo County, Texas, 1939; the new medium of radio could reach even the most remote regions of the United States*

## Activity

Look at Source C and the image of the farm couple. How useful is each for understanding the impact of radio on Americans in the 1930s?

## The development of radio

Radio developed quickly from the initial patenting of wireless telegraphy by Guglielmo Marconi in 1897. The Westinghouse Electric Company in Pittsburgh experimented with broadcasting to the public in 1920, and this set off a rapid growth in radio technology. By 1922, there were 570 radio stations; and from the mid 1920s they were financed with advertising revenues. The federal government regulated airwaves from 1927 and favoured commercial broadcasting run by large companies (in contrast with the state monopoly of the BBC in Britain after 1926). National broadcasting was established with NBC (National Broadcasting Company) in 1926 and CBS (originally Columbia Broadcasting System) in 1927, and together they controlled 30 per cent of broadcasting stations in the USA.

The Depression did not determine the form of broadcasting. By 1930, there were centralised and powerful networks broadcasting comedies, music, news and political speeches. However, the Depression provided the mass audience and the desire for shared experience that made radio, together with the movies, such an integral part of US popular culture.

In 1930, about 40 per cent of national households owned radios; by 1940, radio ownership was 90 per cent. The creation of the Rural Electrification Administration in 1935, a result of measures to combat the Depression, and the provision of electricity, had a massive impact on this rapid growth in radio ownership. Falling prices were also influential: in 1916, the average price of a radio was $35 and could be as high as $200; by the 1930s, mass production had brought the price of a radio down to $10. It was not unusual for people to share the use of a radio, with neighbours coming to the house of someone who owned one. The average listening time was four to five hours a day, and most listening was devoted to national networks.

In order to exist in a hard financial climate, radio performers sought business sponsorship and musicians were associated with particular companies and products, such as the dance bands of A&P (Atlantic and Pacific Tea Company), Gypsies and The Ipana (a toothpaste brand of the Bristol-Myers Company), and the banjo orchestra the Goodrich Zippers (named after B. F. Goodrich Company). This close relationship between private firms and radio networks was a feature of 1930s radio.

Radio offered opportunities for stardom, and comedians such as Eddie Cantor rose to fame. Quick-fire comedy in front of a live audience offered diversion from economic problems. Entertainment such as the Maxwell House Show Boat, based on the 1920s popular musical Show Boat, offered nostalgia for pre-Depression times.

The greatest hit of the 1930s, however, was a 15-minute serial broadcast six nights a week called *Amos'n'Andy*. The show was written and voiced by Freeman Gosden and Charles Correll, and had a fanatical and devoted public of over 40 million. *Amos'n'Andy* was broadcast in cinemas and at big sporting events to prevent people not attending for fear of missing what happened next. The nation as a whole could discuss the serial in queues, on trains, or with friends in restaurants. In this way, a radio show generated unprecedented public interest and acted as a unifying influence.

*A poster for the 1930s radio show Amos'n'Andy; today, the 'blacking up' by white actors would cause offence, but it was a convention in the inter-war period*

# The radio and politics

From 1933, President Roosevelt made effective use of the medium of radio in his 'fireside chats'. These provided 60 million listeners with a unique contact with their leader. No amount of rallies, meetings or newspaper reports could establish the personal link of the federal government being in one's own home. This was almost a symbol of the change in the nature and role of government brought about by the New Deal. Roosevelt aimed to inspire confidence in the American people. His first broadcast was about the banking crisis, and it was critical in preventing people withdrawing money and closing the banks (see page 65). In this respect, the growth in importance of radio was closely linked to the Depression crisis.

### SOURCE E

I want to talk for a few minutes with the people of the United States about banking – with the comparatively few who understand the mechanics of banking but more particularly with the overwhelming majority who use banks for the making of deposits and the drawing of checks. I want to tell you what has been done in the last few days, why it was done, and what the next steps are going to be. I recognise that the many proclamations from State capitols and from Washington, the legislation, the Treasury regulations, etc., couched for the most part in banking and legal terms, should be explained for the benefit of the average citizen. I owe this in particular because of the fortitude and good temper with which everybody has accepted the inconvenience and hardships of the banking holiday. I know that when you understand what we in Washington have been about I shall continue to have your co-operation as fully as I have had your sympathy and help during the past week.

*Extract from President Roosevelt's*
*'Fireside Chat on Banking', 12 March 1933.*

*Franklin D. Roosevelt gives one of his 'fireside chats' at the radio microphone, 1938*

## The dangers of the new medium

Some commentators were concerned that the power of radio might distort American values and corrupt democracy. In 1936, a popular radio show host – **Father Charles Coughlin**, a Roman Catholic priest (see also page 79) – became increasingly vocal in his condemnation of capitalist greed, Roosevelt's alleged compromises with capitalism and Jewish influences. Coughlin's earlier broadcasts had supported the New Deal, but he now moved towards extremism.

Despite being ordered off the air by the Vatican, Coughlin kept his tirades going; he even gave a Nazi salute in a rally in New York and urged anti-Semitic persecutions in the USA.

**Charles Coughlin (1891–1979)** Coughlin was born in Canada, where he was ordained a priest in 1916. He moved to Michigan and became a pioneer in the use of radio. Initially a supporter of social reform and the New Deal, he was later drawn to the ideals of Nazism. At his peak, he attracted 80,000 letters a week and had an audience of millions.

Roosevelt insisted that his voice should not be imitated on the radio. The dangers were made apparent by a mock news programme made by Orson Welles in 1938, based on H. G. Wells' book *The War of the Worlds*. When Welles announced an invasion from outer space, the sound effects and acting were so convincing that a million listeners believed it; many attempted to flee in panic. The impact was so long lasting that many believed Roosevelt's announcement of the war with Japan after the invasion of Pearl Harbor in 1941 was another Welles-type hoax.

## Activity

Which of the four cultural areas below do you think was most influenced by the Depression? Complete a chart like this to show your assessment.

|  | Summary of how it was influenced by the Depression | Order (1–4) | Explanation |
|---|---|---|---|
| Movies |  |  |  |
| Photography |  |  |  |
| Literature |  |  |  |
| Radio |  |  |  |

Now split the class into four groups. Each group will prepare a presentation on their particular art form, explaining how it was influenced by the Depression.

The Depression affected the arts in the USA through the development of radio, the greater interest of photographers in the people of the nation, and the content of movies, books, plays and paintings. For any other country in the Americas, were there similar developments in the 1930s?

# End of chapter activities

## Paper 3 exam practice

### Question

How far did the Depression affect the cultural life of the USA?
[20 marks]

### Skill focus

Writing a conclusion to your essay

### Examiner's tips

Provided you have carried out all the steps recommended so far, it should be relatively easy to write one or two concluding paragraphs.

For this question, you will need to cover the following possible reasons:

- the direct impact of the Depression on the subject matter of different art forms
- the effect of the New Deal and greater state intervention in cultural life
- the effect on the demand for different types of art from people affected by the Depression
- the indirect effect of the concerns of the Depression years on artists.

With general questions such as this, you should try and avoid too much generalisation and support the points you make with examples from the different arts, such as film, photography and literature. This question requires you to consider a **range** of different reasons/factors, and to support your analysis with **precise** and **specific** supporting knowledge.

Also, such a question, which is asking for an analysis of several reasons, expects you to come to some kind of **judgement** about 'how far'. What other influences were there on the arts in the USA during the Depression years, and how important were the different elements that you are going to write about?

### Common mistakes

Sometimes, candidates simply rehash in their conclusion what they have written earlier – making the examiner read the same thing twice! Generally, concluding paragraphs should be relatively short. The aim should be to come to a judgement/conclusion that is clearly based on what has already been written. If possible, a short but relevant quotation is a good way to round off an argument.

Remember to refer to the simplified Paper 3 markscheme on page 219.

## Sample student conclusion

This is a good conclusion because it briefly pulls together the main threads of the argument (without simply repeating/summarising them), and then also makes a clear judgement. In addition, there is an intelligent final comment that rounds off the whole conclusion – and the core of the essay – in a memorable way.

As the Depression in the USA affected so many people and made many Americans think about their lives and their values, it obviously had a major impact on artistic life. It was not so much the direct effects, though these were important. Films, photographs and novels recorded the sufferings of people in the Depression and some very moving and important cultural developments took place. Films reflected the hardships and brought the plight of many Americans to the notice of their fellow-countrymen and also the government. Bestselling novels reflected upon poverty and the results of economic collapse. The Depression also brought home to Americans how much a part of the world economy they were and how individuals were affected by wider forces. This in turn brought the USA together in awareness of a mass suffering beyond their control. Thus there was a new mass audience for cinema and photographic images and for radio. This in turn stimulated creative artists to offer entertainment us a means of escape or for offering hope, or a commentary on society, leading to a range of cultural forms and not just stories of despair. Some of the trends associated with the art of the Depression had been established beforehand. Cinema-going was well established; there was already a mass audience for radio. Many of the themes in the 1930s, such as physical hardship, had been explored earlier. So Depression culture was not entirely new and did not owe everything to the economic suffering of the 1930s. Also, some changes in art were more a result of innovations that had little to do with the Depression, for example the development of the movies using sound. However, the Depression was too important and too fundamental not to be seen as having a major impact on the culture and art of America, even if this took different forms.

## Activity

In this chapter, the focus is on writing a useful conclusion. Using the information from this chapter, and any other sources of information available to you, write concluding paragraphs for at least *two* of the following Paper 3 practice questions. Remember: to do this, you will need to do full plans for the questions you choose.

## Paper 3 practice questions

1   To what extent was cinema the art form that most reflected the impact of the Depression on American culture?

2   To what extent was the effect of the Depression on the visual arts in the USA greater than its effect on other art forms?

3   Assess the importance of government support for culture and the arts in any country in the Americas between 1930 and 1940.

4   To what extent did the Depression give rise to 'protest art' in any country in the Americas?

5   To what extent did artists and writers show more interest in political and social protest than in purely artistic development in the Depression era? (You may confine your answer to any *one* country in the Americas.)

# 8 Exam practice

## Introduction

You have now completed your study of the main events and developments in the Great Depression and the Americas 1929–39. You have also had the chance to examine the various historical debates and differing historical interpretations that surround some of these developments.

In the earlier chapters, you encountered examples of Paper 3-type essay questions, with examiner's tips. You have also had some basic practice in answering such questions. In this chapter, these tips and skills will be developed in more depth. Longer examples of possible student answers are provided. These are accompanied by examiner's comments that should increase your understanding of what examiners are looking for when they mark your essays. Following each question and answer, you will find tasks to give you further practice in the skills needed to gain the higher marks in this exam.

## IB History Paper 3 exam questions and skills

Those of you following Route 2, HL Option 5 – *Aspects of the History of the Americas* – will have studied in depth **three** of the 12 sections available for this HL Option. *The Great Depression and the Americas 1929–39* is one of those sections. For Paper 3, two questions are set from each of the 12 sections, giving 24 questions in total; and you have to answer **three** of these.

Each question has a specific markscheme. However the 'generic' markscheme in the *IB History Guide* gives you a good general idea of what examiners are looking for in order to be able to put answers into the higher bands. In particular, you will need to acquire reasonably precise historical knowledge so that you can address issues such as cause and effect, and change and continuity. You will need this knowledge in order to explain historical developments in a clear, coherent, well-supported and relevant way. You will also need to understand relevant historical debates and interpretations, and be able to refer to these and critically evaluate them.

## Essay planning

Make sure you read each question **carefully**, noting all the important key or 'command' words. You might find it useful to highlight them on your question paper. You can then produce a rough plan (for example, a spider diagram) of **each** of the three essays you intend to attempt, **before** you start to write your answers. That way, you will soon know whether you have enough own knowledge to answer them adequately. Next, refer back to the wording of each question. This will help you see whether or not you are responding to **all** its various demands/aspects. In addition, if you run short of time towards the end of your exam, you will at least be able to write some brief condensed sentences to show the key issues/points and arguments you would have presented. It is thus far better to do the planning at the **start** of the exam; that is, **before** you panic, should you suddenly realise you haven't time to finish your last essay.

## Relevance to the question

Remember, too, to keep your answers relevant and focused on the question. Don't go outside the dates mentioned in the question, or write answers on subjects not identified in that question. Also, don't just describe the events or developments. Sometimes students just focus on one key word, date or individual, and then write down everything they know about it. Instead, select your own knowledge carefully, and pin the relevant information to the key features raised by the question. Finally, if the question asks for 'causes/reasons' and 'results', 'continuity and change', 'successes and failures', or 'nature and development', make sure you deal with **all** the parts of the question. Otherwise, you will limit yourself to half marks at best.

## Examiner's tips

For Paper 3 answers, examiners are looking for well-structured arguments that:

- are consistently relevant/linked to the question
- offer clear/precise analysis
- are supported by accurate, precise and relevant own knowledge
- offer a balanced judgement
- refer to different historical debates/interpretations or to relevant historians and, where relevant, offer some critical evaluation of these.

## Simplified markscheme

| Band | | Marks |
|---|---|---|
| 1 | **Consistently analytical/explanatory** in approach, with very explicit focus on all demands of the question. **Understanding and evaluation of different historical interpretations**; good synthesis of **plentiful and precise own knowledge** with different interpretations/approaches. **Argument is clear, well-supported and well-structured** throughout. | 17–20 |
| 2 | **Clear/explicit focus** on all the demands of the question, with **consistently relevant analysis/explanation**. Very **detailed own knowledge**. Argument in the main is **well-structured and supported**. Some **awareness of different historical interpretations**, and **some attempts at evaluation.** | 14–16 |
| 3 | **Some relevant analysis/argument**, mainly linked to the question, with **relevant and precise supporting own knowledge. Reasonable structure, with some explanation** and **some awareness of different historical views** – but not all aspects of the question addressed. | 11–13 |
| 4 | Mainly **narrative in approach**, with **reasonable accurate knowledge**; but **limited focus**, and **no real analysis/ explanation. Some structure**, but **links to the question are mainly unclear/implicit.** | 8–10 |
| 5 | **Limited relevant knowledge**, with a **few unsupported comments/assertions. Not well-structured**; and **not linked effectively to the question**, which is not really understood. | 0–7 |

# Student answers

The following extracts from student answers have brief examiner's comments in the margins, and a longer overall comment at the end. Those parts of student answers that are particularly strong and well focused (such as demonstrations of precise and relevant own knowledge, or examination of historical interpretations) will be *highlighted in blue*. Errors/confusions/irrelevance/loss of focus will be *highlighted in white*. In this way, students should find it easier to follow why marks were awarded or withheld.

# Question 1

How far were the Republican governments of the 1920s responsible for the Great Depression in the USA?
[20 marks]

## Skills

- Factual knowledge and understanding
- Structured, analytical and **balanced** argument
- Awareness/understanding/evaluation of historical interpretations
- Clear and balanced judgement

## Examiner's tip

Look carefully at the wording of this question, which asks you to consider **how far** governments were to blame. This is different from explaining *why* they were important and requires you to weigh them against other factors. So, when you start to think about the different causes, you should remember to compare them with the key factor in the question. Don't just explain the role of governments.

## Student answer

The Depression in the USA came about partly as a result of the failure of US governments to regulate the stock market and because laissez-faire policies had left the economy vulnerable to a downturn. However, it would be unfair to blame governments entirely for the Depression. There were long-term weaknesses in the economy and worldwide factors that were not in the control of governments. The depressed state of agriculture and the fall in prices in primary products was a problem experienced by many other countries in the Americas. Also, the disruption of world trade as a result of the First World War could not be blamed on the Republican governments.

### Examiner's comment

This is a clear and well-focused introduction, showing accurate knowledge of the topic and a good understanding of several of the general factors contributing to the Great Depression. The answer now needs to develop a judgement about the importance of each of these factors.

The Republican governments of Harding, Coolidge and Hoover all believed in the freedom of business to make money and the rights of individual Americans to pursue wealth. The boom of the 1920s seemed to indicate that these policies were working. Some sectors of the US economy enjoyed considerable prosperity and more and more people bought and sold shares. It seemed that American capitalism was working and more were participating in it. However, the growth of the stock market was not sufficiently regulated. There was a failure to prevent companies being floated on the stock market with very little to back them up. Traders sold shares 'on the margin' to make fast profits and there was a dangerous rise in share prices that was not related to any real expansion of the US economy. The Florida Land Boom encouraged a lot of speculation, and instead of insisting on regulation, the governments stood by and did little. Thus when the bottom fell out of the share market in 1929, the results were catastrophic. Many investors lost money, banks that lent money too readily began to fail; businesses and banks collapsed and this had a knock-on effect on spending, causing the start of the Great Depression. Confidence in business fell, people stopped buying and investing, and production and trade began to fall. Unemployment began to rise. The government was slow to react, but the main fault was in allowing bad business practices to develop and in not regulating the stock market.

There was a considerable panic in October 1929 when fears for the continued growth of the economy caused people to sell shares. As shares were sold, the prices fell and the confidence in the stock market began to collapse. The value of investment holdings fell sharply and the panic spread so fast that there was nothing that banks and brokers could do. Investors lost millions of dollars and some made the mistake of trying to reverse the trend by buying more. The so-called Wall Street Crash of October 1929 was widely reported and caused other countries to experience financial crises.

## Examiner's comment

Although there is some accurate own knowledge, this is mostly descriptive material, and so is not explicitly linked to the demands of the question. The reader is left to judge the importance of all this in terms of the causes of the Great Depression, and it becomes an account of what happened.

**Examiner's comment**

This paragraph shows awareness of an aspect of historical debate, although these different interpretations are merely mentioned, with no attempt to evaluate them. However, the overriding point is that all this information is largely irrelevant – and so will not score any marks. The candidate is thus wasting time, when they should be writing about the role of the governments, not answering a question about the nature of the Crash.

Some historians see the stock market crash as being the key element in the Depression but others point to the long-term weaknesses of the US economy. Conservative commentators such as Friedman see the crash as essentially just another turn in the business cycle and not necessarily a disaster, and see the policies of the Federal Reserve Bank as being misguided. Left-wing historians such as Galbraith see the Crash as indicative of the inherent problems of capitalism in the USA in the 1920s, and view inequalities of wealth as an important factor.

Certainly, the failure of effective government regulation of the stock market and the failure to control investment by the banks could be seen as a major cause. Commentators had been warning of the dangers since the late 1920s, but the prevailing view was that 'the business of America is business' and regulation would inhibit growth. However, there were other factors that made the crisis worse. One was overproduction in older industries such as engineering and consumer goods such as motor cars. This had been encouraged by new mass production methods, such as those introduced by Henry Ford, and by new selling techniques such as hire purchase. There was the belief that US industries could go on producing and selling, and the prosperity of the northern industrial areas was endless.

**Examiner's comment**

Again, there is accurate own knowledge in this paragraph – but this is not what the question requires. While the opening sentence shows the correct focus, the candidate goes on to produce more narrative that is not linked directly to the question – was this overproduction anything to do with government or not; does it challenge the view that governments were to blame?

Another factor that brought about Depression was the poor state of the agricultural sector. The cultivation of more land during the First World War to meet growing demand for wheat had brought profits and encouraged farmers to invest. However, when demand fell away after the war, farmers were left with falling prices. They had incurred debts that could not be met with income, and on top of that many farmers were hit by adverse weather conditions and droughts. Many agricultural regions sank into poverty and suffered from debt repayments and foreclosures. The spending power of farmers was reduced, and this made problems of overproduction of industrial and consumer goods worse.

[There then follow several more paragraphs giving detailed and accurate accounts of different elements including tariffs and inequalities of income distribution.]

Thus, many factors brought about the Great Depression. Government policies, the failure to regulate the markets and banks, the tariffs that reduced foreign trade and the limited help given to the agricultural system, together with low taxes that helped fuel unwise investments, played a part. The lack of regulation helped to stimulate overproduction as businesses used cheap credit to encourage spending on consumer goods and made heavy investment in mass production, which caused a glut on the domestic markets that could not be remedied by the sales of goods overseas, due to restrictive trade policies. The depression in the agricultural heartland of the USA contributed to misdistribution of income, which did not provide a firm enough basis for consumer demand.

### Examiner's comment

There is some relevant focus on the demands of the question – and some relevant discussion of the relative importance of different elements.

*Thus, governments only made an existing situation worse and their policies and decisions cannot be blamed for the Depression. There had been long-term changes since the growth of a world economy in the later 19th century, as well as changes brought by the First World War.*

### Examiner's comment

This brief conclusion makes a valid judgement. Unfortunately, this is not a supported judgement and comes rather suddenly as an assertion – there has not been much consideration of late 19th century changes or the First World War, and there is not a sustained analysis of the relative importance of different factors.

## Overall examiner's comments

There is plentiful and accurate own knowledge – unfortunately, it is **mostly irrelevant**. While there are some hints of analysis, it is mostly descriptive. The bulk of the answer is thus not really focused on the demands of the question. However, there are brief sections that **are** relevant, so the answer is thus probably good enough to be awarded a mark in Band 4 – 10 marks. What was needed was an answer that focused more on explaining how different factors link with government and compared them with the main factor in the question

## Activity

Look again at the simplified markscheme, and the student answer above. Now try to draw up a plan focused on the demands of the question. Then try to write several paragraphs that will be good enough to get into Band 1, and so obtain the full 20 marks. As well as making sure you address **all** aspects of the question, try to integrate into your answer some references **and** evaluation of relevant historians/historical interpretations.

# Question 2

Compare and contrast the attempts to deal with the impact of the Depression in *any two* countries in the Americas, 1929–39.
[20 marks]

## Skills

- Factual knowledge and understanding
- Structured, analytical and **balanced** argument
- Awareness/understanding/evaluation of historical interpretations

## Examiner's tip

Look carefully at the wording of this question, which asks you to compare and contrast two regions. Questions like this show how important it is to study **all** the bullet points in the sections you study. If you only select a few of the named individuals for detailed study, you could seriously limit your options in the exam. To answer questions such as this in the most effective way, it is best to structure your answer so that the comparisons/contrasts are brought out **explicitly**. In other words, draw up a rough plan with headings for 'comparisons' and 'contrasts' – then jot down where aspects of their policies were similar under 'comparisons'; and where/how they were different under 'contrasts'. Remember: don't just **describe** what their policies were: what's needed is explicit focus on similarities **and** differences.

## Student answer

*Although Mexico and Brazil were countries with very different economies, governments and societies, they were both deeply affected by the Depression and adopted radical policies to deal with its effects. They both expanded the role of government and both broke away from past policies to deal with the Depression. To show this I shall look at the experience of Brazil and then look at what happened in Mexico.*

### Examiner's comment

This introduction starts in a generally promising way. However, the final sentence in this paragraph is **very** worrying. This is because such an approach will almost certainly result in a **narrative** of the two sets of policies with, at best, only some kind of **implicit** comparison/contrast. As has been seen in previous answers, a narrative account, without clear focus on the demands of the question, is unlikely to get beyond Band 4 – 10 marks.

The principal architect of policies to deal with the Depression in Brazil was Vargas. He saw the need to control production of its principal cash crops and also to diversify the economic activity of the country.

From the time that Brazil became a Republic in 1889 to 1930 when the effects of the Depression were felt, the states of São Paulo and Minas Gerais dominated the country. The main product was coffee, though Minas was also famous for its milk production. The country was ruled by oligarchies and the coffee industry was very important. However, the Crash in the USA produced a major crisis when the price of coffee fell dramatically from 1929 to 1930. There had already been a great deal of unrest in the 1920s, but in 1930 a military coup installed a politician from the Rio Grande region as head of state and Vargas tried to deal with the problems caused by the limited products of the economy.

## Examiner's comment

This paragraph contains a lot of very precise information, and is clearly the result of solid revision. However, it is mainly background material – **there is little on his actual policies.**

Vargas was president and dictator of Brazil for 18 years and tried to modernise the country by bringing in a range of social, economic and political changes. He instituted many reforms in the 1930s once he had overcome the opposition of São Paolo. He was influenced by European fascism and set up the Estado Novo movement. He was critical of big business and corporations and his measures to help his people caused him to be known as 'The father of the poor'. He encouraged economic diversity and import substitution industrialisation (ISI) to avoid the dependence on coffee. He also encouraged more migration to the towns and the development of new service industries such as tourism – Rio became a major tourist attraction. He welcomed foreign investment and, at the end of the 1930s, he planned a major new steelworks. Vargas responded to the Depression by restricting the amount of coffee produced, a policy that he inherited, but also by trying to break Brazil's semi-colonial dependence on coffee and diversifying the economy both into new heavy industries and also by tourism. He brought in direct measures of social reform to help industrial workers and urban dwellers, but did less for those who lived and worked on the land.

## Examiner's comment

Again, there is a lot of accurate own knowledge – this time, some of it **is** relevant, as it deals with Vargas's reforms and the situation that he inherited. However, so far, this answer seems to be turning into a descriptive account of what Vargas did. There has, as yet, been no attempt to address the **key** issue of similarities/differences. This is the danger with such a 'one by one' approach to questions like this.

From 1930, Vargas gave priority to the stimulation of Brazil's economy, which was suffering from low prices for its products and rising unemployment. He saw the importance of working with organised labour and protected workers by enforcing better conditions and a minimum wage while trying to promote industrial growth. Politically, he was anxious to identify his regime with the people, particularly the urban workers. Impressed by the corporate state ideas in contemporary Italy, he introduced after 1937 the Estado Novo to promote unity between the different industrial classes. Initiatives such as cheap restaurants and drives for education were aimed at getting popular support, but in practice the regime tended to support the existing élites – strikes were forbidden and unlike Mexico there was no sustained programme of land reform.

## Examiner's comment

Again, there is plenty of accurate own knowledge and explanation, some of which supports the policies Vargas followed. Yet, as in the previous paragraphs, few comparisons/contrasts with Mexico have been made. The brief reference to land reform is not developed. The contrast with the regime of Cárdenas, which the candidate has necessitated by his choice of countries, is not made.

[There then follow several paragraphs describing the way that Vargas's regime reacted to the Depression. However, there is very little on Mexico.]

Cárdenas in Mexico was faced with the similar problem of falling prices, but Mexico had not been so dependent on the one crop – coffee – as Brazil, and there was a very different political tradition – that of ongoing revolution – with previous attempts at land reform.

## Examiner's comment

This is a good conclusion – brief and to the point. However, it is not a supported judgement or conclusion, as there is nothing about Mexico's policies in the body of the essay. The only real reference to him comes here in the conclusion.

## Overall examiner's comments

Though there is precise and accurate own knowledge, the essay is basically about Vargas and Brazil. If the candidate had written about Mexico in the same way, then the answer would have been awarded Band 4 – 10 marks – even though it hasn't really addressed the demands of the question.

However, because it almost **only** deals with Vargas, it can only be awarded Band 5 – which would be 7 marks at most. To reach Band 3 and higher, the answer would need some **explicit and well-structured treatment of comparisons and contrasts, with consistent analysis of both similarities and differences**.

## Activity

Look again at the simplified markscheme, and the student answer above. Now try to draw up a plan, with a structure focused on the demands of the question. Then try to write your own answer, making sure you consistently make comparisons and contrasts – so that the answer can get into Band 1 and obtain the full 20 marks.

# Question 3

How successful was the New Deal?
[20 marks]

## Skills

- Factual knowledge and understanding
- Structured, analytical and **balanced** argument
- Awareness/understanding/evaluation of historical interpretations

## Examiner's tip

Look carefully at the wording of this question, which asks the degree of success to be assessed. This may involve considering different sorts of success – the different aims of relief, recovery and reform. The word 'successful' has to be broken down. And remember – don't just describe what happened: what's needed is explicit analysis and explanation, with precise supporting own knowledge.

# Student answer

There has been much debate about the actual aims of the New Deal, and in any assessment of its success it must be judged against what appear to be Roosevelt's aims. It is clear that in the short term there were two main aims: the first was to restore confidence in the American people and the second was to save capitalism and therefore save the democratic basis of US society and prevent the emergence of similar totalitarian systems that developed in the USSR and Germany. At the same time, it can also be argued that Roosevelt had three broader aims: recovery for the economy, relief for those who had lost their jobs and reform of economic relationships. However, he had no intention of creating a new society by transforming the traditional way of American life, and those who have criticised him for doing so are not judging him against his aims. On the surface it would appear that he was successful as he won three consecutive electoral terms and in 1936 won all but two states (Maine and Vermont), achieving a landslide victory.

## Examiner's comment

This is a clear and well-focused introduction, showing a good appreciation of all the demands of the question, and indicating that an analytical approach is likely to be followed. The introduction clearly sets out a range of criteria the candidate is going to use to assess the success of the New Deal, and it will be important for the candidate to keep referring back to them throughout the essay if it is to be a coherent argument. The candidate places the New Deal in context, and in the final suggestion gives a brief comment about the likely direction of their argument, with brief supporting evidence for the point being made. The candidate also makes it clear that the New Deal did not aim to transform US society and therefore this aspect will not be discussed in the answer. However, if the candidate was looking to achieve the very top marks, there could have been some link between the debate about the aims and actual historians. This is a good start and a clear point of view is established.

There can be little doubt that Roosevelt saved the capitalist system and restored confidence in the American people. Within the first 100 days, the banking system on which it was based was saved, as banks were closed for four days, their finances investigated and some 5000 that were secure were allowed to reopen. As a result, the number of bank failures declined and it went a long way to help him achieve his aim of restoring confidence – rather than withdrawing money, over $1 billion was reinvested in banks, which allowed them to make loans and help the economy. Much of the legislation of the first 100 days helped to restore confidence; this was seen with the Banking Act, which protected the ordinary saver from losing their savings. The sheer volume of legislation with the AAA, FCA, CCC, FERA, TVA and NRA all helped to convince people that the government was concerned and, unlike Hoover, was taking action. However, alongside this, Roosevelt also helped to restore confidence through both his inaugural speech, where he told the American people that 'the only thing we have to fear is fear itself', and his weekly fireside broadcasts, where he outlined his policies to the American people. Such an approach was essential, as the winter of 1933 witnessed an increase in bank failures, with Detroit's banks collapsing and many states, such as Kentucky and California, closing theirs. Not only was the banking system saved, but big business, the upholder of capitalism, was also helped through the NRA, which attempted to establish national economic planning and established a series of codes to control production, prices and trading practices. This was vital, as big businesses were the largest employers.

## Examiner's comment

There is some accurate supporting own knowledge, explicitly linked to the question's issue of unity, and this is a well-focused section. The opening sentence links back to both the criteria and the question, offering a clear view on two of the issues raised in the introduction – saving capitalism and restoring confidence. The argument is supported by reference to some of the legislation, but the candidate avoids going into too much detail, as this is a very large topic and the candidate could spend too long dealing with this early period. The candidate also supports the argument that these policies were essential with reference to specific cities and states.

*Despite restoring confidence and saving capitalism, it is much more debatable as to whether the New Deal brought about an economic recovery. One critic argued that the New Deal was the biggest fraud perpetrated on the American people and there is some justification in this view. In simple terms, unemployment fell, but was still at 16 million in 1936 and rose again during the recession of 1937–38 to go back over 19 million. It was only with the advent of the Second World War that the problem was solved. Even many of those who were employed through schemes such as the PWA or WPA were often engaged in meaningless jobs, which disappeared when government funding ended in 1937–38. Yet, it could also be argued that in the best years unemployment had fallen by half. Perhaps the growing concern to balance the budget was the main reason for this limited achievement, as not enough money was spent on employment schemes. However, for the farming community that was already in a weak position before the Depression, the New Deal did bring benefits, but once again only for some. Farm prices recovered as the government paid farmers, through the AAA, not to produce goods. The number of evictions was also reduced through the Farm Credit Act and later the Farm Security Administration. However, it was only with the 1937 Farm Credit Act that loans were made available to tenant farmers and they, along with sharecroppers, did less well than the big farmers. Moreover, the Tennessee Valley, through the TVA, not only recovered but became more prosperous, as the average income of the region rose by 200 per cent between 1929 and 1949. However, attempts to introduce similar plans in seven other regions failed.*

### Examiner's comment

Again, this is a well-focused paragraph. Once again, the opening sentence is very strong – it introduces an idea that is linked back to both the question and the introduction. The argument is supported by reference to statistics, although there is some debate about the actual numbers of unemployed. However, the argument is balanced, weighing up the reduction against the solving of the problem. The answer also considers recovery from a range of perspectives, not just unemployment, but the farmers and regional development, showing that the candidate has knowledge of a range of issues. Yet, once again, the end of the paragraph is weaker, and there is no overall judgement reached as to whether the New Deal brought about economic recovery. This could be developed, as could the use of historians to support or challenge the line of argument pursued. So far, there is reasonable supporting own knowledge with some good detail.

The introduction of federal relief was a success in itself, as before the Depression the unemployed relied on the states, local authorities and charities, who were unable to cope with the scale of the crisis. Schemes such as the CCC provided work for 18–25-year-olds for six months and gave them work experience, even if the pay was low, while the CWA spent over $1 billion on short-term projects to help people through the winter of 1933–34. However, perhaps the greatest success was the PWA, which financed some 34,000 projects costing a total of $6 billion. Relief for those out of work continued throughout the 1930s, as the Second New Deal brought in the WPA, later known as the Works Project Administration, which employed some 8.5 million people, and the Social Security Act, which created guaranteed retirement payments and set up federal insurance for the unemployed. Therefore, throughout the period, those unable to find work were supported through schemes and benefits, a system unthinkable under Hoover.

## Examiner's comment

Again, this is a clear and directly relevant paragraph. Although the opening sentence relates to one of the criteria in the introduction, the sentence needs to be fully developed to state that the federal government took on responsibility. The paragraph would benefit from greater analysis of some of the measures, such as the CCC or CWA – were they a success? Much of the argument that these and other measures were a success is implied, and the candidate would need to develop the analysis in this paragraph to reach the top level.

Although the First New Deal did not aim to bring about long-term reform, the Second New Deal brought some changes to US society. The Second New Deal was successful in improving industrial relations and helping to bring an end to the violent conflict that accompanied many strikes. The National Labor Relations Act helped to peacefully resolve disputes and strengthened the position of unions against employers. These improvements for workers were reinforced by the Fair Labor Standards Act, which brought about a shorter working week and a minimum hourly wage. Even industrial giants such as GM and Ford recognised unions.

*Meanwhile, workers were also protected through insurance and pensions brought in by the Social Security Act. As a result, the state took on new responsibilities and the role of government was transformed. Not all the New Deal was a success, and the Supreme Court declared many measures unconstitutional, but Roosevelt tackled many of the problems through the Second New Deal. There was opposition from those who thought the measures did not go far enough and from those who thought they went too far, but the New Deal did save capitalism and restore confidence and, as Roosevelt said, 'everyone seems against it except the electorate' – who obviously considered it a success.*

### Examiner's comment

The conclusion is thoughtful and well focused, and ends a convincing and analytical argument.

## Overall examiner's comments

This is a good, well-focused and analytical answer, with some precise and accurate own knowledge to support the points made. The answer is thus certainly good enough to be awarded a mark in Band 2. To get into Band 1, the candidate needed to provide some reference to historians' views/historical interpretations, and some critical evaluation of these interpretations.

## Activity

Look again at the simplified markscheme, and the student answer above. Now try to write your own answer to the question, and attempt to make it good enough to get into Band 1 and so obtain the full 20 marks. In particular, make sure you are aware of the main historical debates about this topic – and incorporate some critical evaluation of them in your answer.

CITY AND ISLINGTON
SIXTH FORM COLLEGE
283-309 GOSWELL ROAD
LONDON EC1V 7LA
TEL 020 7520 0652

# Further reading

Badger, A. J. 1989. *The New Deal: The Depression Years, 1933–40*. Basingstoke, UK. Palgrave Macmillan.

Bazant, J. 1977. *A Concise History of Mexico: From Hidalgo to Cárdenas, 1805–1940*. Cambridge, UK. Cambridge University Press.

Bothwell, R. 2006. *The Penguin History of Canada*. London, UK. Penguin.

Bothwell, R., Drummond, I. M., & English, J. 1990. *Canada, 1900–1945*. Toronto, Canada. University of Toronto Press.

Brogan, H. 1985. *The Longman History of the United States of America*. Harlow, UK. Longman.

Bulmer-Thomas, V. 2003. *The Economic History of Latin America since Independence* (2nd edition). Cambridge, UK. Cambridge University Press.

Clements, P. 2008. *Access to History: Prosperity, Depression and the New Deal: The USA 1890–1954* (4th edition). London, UK. Hodder Education.

Creighton, D. 1970. *Canada's First Century*. London, UK. Macmillan.

Dittmer, J. 1994. *Local People: The Struggle for Civil Rights in Mississippi*. Chicago, USA. University of Illinois Press.

Eldridge, D. 2008. *American Culture in the 1930s*. Edinburgh, UK. Edinburgh University Press.

Goodman, D. 2011. *Radio's Civic Ambition: American broadcasting and democracy in the 1930s*. New York, USA. Oxford University Press.

Kennedy, D. M. 1999. *Freedom from Fear*. New York, USA. Oxford University Press, Inc.

Leuchtenburg, W. 1963. *Franklin D. Roosevelt and the New Deal, 1932–40*. New York, USA. Harper and Row.

Leuchtenburg, W. 1995. *The FDR Years: On Roosevelt and His Legacy*. New York, USA. Columbia University Press.

Levine, R. M. 1998. *Father of the Poor? Vargas and his Era*. Cambridge, UK. Cambridge University Press.

McNaught, K. 1973. *The Pelican History of Canada*. London, UK. Penguin Books.

Parrish, M. J. 1994. *Anxious Decades: America in Prosperity and Depression, 1920–1941*. New York, USA. W. W. Norton & Company.

Rowbotham, S. 1987. *A Century of Women: The History of Women in Britain and the United States in the Twentieth Century*. London, UK. Penguin.

Skidmore, T. E. 2007. *Politics in Brazil 1930–1964: An experiment in democracy*. New York, USA. Oxford University Press.

Ross, S. 1997. *Causes and Consequences of the Great Depression*. London, UK. Evans Brothers Ltd.

Ward, B. and Badger, T. (eds.) 1996. *The Making of Martin Luther King and the Civil Rights Movement*. New York, USA. New York University Press.

Zinn, H. (ed) 1966. *New Deal Thought*. Indiana, USA. Hackett Publishing Company.

# Further information

Sources and quotations in this book have been taken from the following publications.

Angelou, M. 1969. *I Know Why the Caged Bird Sings*. New York, USA. Random House.

Bothwell, R., Drummond, I. M., & English, J. 1990. *Canada, 1900–1945*. Toronto, Canada. University of Toronto Press.

Boyer, P. et al. 1995. *The Enduring Vision: A History of the American People, Volume 11: Since 1865* (5th edition). Boston, USA. Houghton Mifflin.

Brogan, H. 1985. *The Longman History of the United States of America*. Harlow, UK. Longman.

Clements, P. 2008. *Access to History: Prosperity, Depression and the New Deal: The USA 1890–1954* (4th edition). London, UK. Hodder Education.

Dickstein, M. 2009. *Dancing In the Dark*. New York, USA. Norton.

Johnson, N. 1940. 'The Grapes of Wrath', screenplay based on the novel *The Grapes of Wrath* by John Steinbeck (accessed at: www.dailyscript.com/scripts/grapes_of_wrath.html).

Katz, W. L. 1967. *Eyewitness: The Negro in American History*. New York, USA. Pitman Publishing.

Kennedy, D. M. 1999. *Freedom from Fear*. New York, USA. Oxford University Press, Inc.

Knight, A. 1998. *Oxford History of the Twentieth Century*. Oxford, UK. Oxford University Press.

Levine, R. M. 1999. *The History of Brazil*. Westport, USA. Greenwood Press.

Lower, A. R. M. 1946. *Colony to Nation: A History of Canada*. Toronto, Canada. Longmans, Green & Company.

McCoy, D. 1972. *Coming of Age*. London, UK. Penguin Books.

McNaught, K. 1973. *The Pelican History of Canada*. London, UK. Penguin Books.

Meier, A. & Rudwick, E. 1976. *From Plantation to Ghetto*. New York, USA. Hill and Wang.

Pedro, A. & McGee, J. 2002. 'The Great Depression in Canada and the United States: A Neoclassical Perspective.' *Review of Economic Dynamics*, Elsevier for the Society for Economic Dynamics, vol. 5(1), January.

Peppino, R. E. 1973. *Brazil: The Land and People*. Oxford, UK. Oxford University Press.

Perkins, F. 1946. *The Roosevelt I Knew*. New York, USA. The Viking Press.

Raeburn, J. 2006. *A Staggering Revolution: A Cultural History of Thirties Photography*. Urbana & Chicago, USA. University of Illinois Press.

Ringel, F. J. (ed.) 1932. *America as Americans See It*. New York, USA. Literary Guild.

Schneider, R. 1996. *Brazil*. Nashville, USA. Westview Press.

Smalley, R. 1990. *Depression and the New Deal*. Harlow, UK. Longman.

Statistics Canada (www.statcan.gc.ca)

Steinbeck, J. 1939. *The Grapes of Wrath*. New York, USA. The Viking Press.

Thorp, R. (ed.) 1984. *Latin America in the 1930s: The Role of the Periphery in World Crisis*. London and Basingstoke, UK. Macmillan in association with St. Antony's College, Oxford.

US Department of Commerce, Bureau of the Census. 1976. *Historical Statistics of the United States: Colonial Times to 1970*. Washington D.C., USA. USGPO.

Wandall, L. 1935. 'A Negro in the CCC' in *Crisis 42*. New Deal Network.

Wright, R. 1946. *Black Boy*. London, UK. Victor Gollancz.

# Index

# Acknowledgements

The volume editor and publishers acknowledge the following sources of copyright material and are grateful for the permissions granted. While every effort has been made, it has not always been possible to trace all copyright holders. If any omissions are brought to our notice we will be happy to include the appropriate acknowledgement on reprinting.

# Picture credits

Cover akg-images; p. 21 © Moviestore Collection Ltd/Alamy; p. 24 © National Geographic Society/Corbis; p.27 Mary Evans/Classic Stock/ H. Lefebvre; p. 33 Getty Images; p. 38 © Underwood & Underwood/Corbis; p. 41 Getty Images; p. 43 © ullstein bild/TopFoto; p. 54 © World History Archive/Alamy; p. 55 © Bettmann/Corbis; p. 56 Peter Newark American Pictures; p. 69 © Corbis; p. 72 © Underwood & Underwood/Corbis; p. 78 The Granger Collection/TopFoto; p. 83 The Granger Collection/TopFoto; p. 85 Library of Congress; p. 105 © Minnesota Historical Society/Corbis; p. 106 The Granger Collection, New York; p. 108 Canada. Dept. of National Defence/Library and Archives Canada/PA-036089; p.115 Archives of Manitoba/Arch Dale; p. 126 Getty Images; p. 136 © Bettmann/Corbis; p. 137 Gamma-Keystone via Getty Images; p. 140 Time & Life Pictures/ Getty Images; p. 144 Getty Images; p. 147 © Interfoto/Alamy; p. 154 © Bettmann/Corbis; p. 156 MCT via Getty Images; p. 163 The Granger Collection/TopFoto; p. 165 Stapleton Historical Collection/HIP/TopFoto; p. 167 © 2004 Topham Picturepoint; p. 172 © Photos 12/Alamy; p. 174 © GL Archive/Alamy; p. 181 © Mary Evans Picture Library/Alamy; p. 187 © 1999 Topham Picturepoint; p. 195 Library of Congress; p. 196 Mary Evans/Library of Congress; p. 197 Library of Congress; p. 200 Time & Life Pictures/Getty Images; p. 206 © Hulton-Deutsch Collection/Corbis; p. 208 Getty Images; p. 209 The Granger Collection, New York; p. 211 Getty Images; p. 212 The Granger Collection/TopFoto.

Produced for Cambridge University Press by
White-Thomson Publishing
+44 (0)843 208 7460
www.wtpub.co.uk

Series editor: Allan Todd
Development editor: Chris McNab
Reviewer: Nigel Haworth
Editor: Caroline Low
Designer: Clare Nicholas
Picture researcher: Alice Harman
Illustrator: Stefan Chabluk